GREECE

Text by
BRUNO D'AGOSTINO

Foreword by
GIORGIO SEFERIS

MONUMENTS OF CIVILIZATION
GREECE

THE READER'S DIGEST ASSOCIATION LIMITED, LONDON

For permission to reprint translated excerpts from the ancient Greek texts, we gratefully acknowledge the following:

Diodorus Siculus, translated by C.H. Oldfather. Vol. III, Book IV. (1st edition, 1939; 1961 reprinting.)

Apollodorus, The Library, translated by Sir James George Frazer. Book I, IX; Book III, XIV. (1st edition, 1921; 1967 reprinting.)

Theocritus, "The Women at the Adonis Festival," from The Greek Bucolic Poets, translated by J.M. Edmonds. Copyright © 1912.

All the above reprinted by permission of the publishers, Harvard University Press (Cambridge, Mass.) and The Loeb Classical Library.

Chapters 6, 7, 20, 21, and 28 from "Atheniensum Respublica," translated by Sir Frederic G. Kenyon from The Oxford Translation of Aristotle, edited by W.D. Ross, Volume X (1921). Copyright © The Clarendon Press, Oxford.

Sophocles, "The Women of Trachis," from The Complete Greek Tragedies, edited by David Grene and Richmond Lattimore, translation of Michael Jameson. Copyright © 1957 The University of Chicago Press.

Euripides, "Ion," from The Complete Greek Tragedies, edited by David Grene and Richmond Lattimore, translation of Ronald Frederick Willetts. Copyright © 1958 by the University of Chicago Press.

The Odes of Pindar, translated by Richmond Lattimore. Copyright © 1947 The University of Chicago Press. And by kind permission of the translator.

Some Odes of Pindar, translated by Richmond Lattimore. Copyright © 1942 by New Directions Publishing Corporation. Reprinted by permission of New Directions Publishing Corporation.

Published by

THE READER'S DIGEST ASSOCIATION LIMITED
25 Berkeley Square London W1X 6AB

London New York Montreal Sydney Cape Town

by arrangement with Cassell & Co Ltd.,
an imprint of
Cassell Ltd.,
35 Red Lion Square, London WC1R 4SG
and at Sydney, Auckland, Toronto, Johannesburg
and an affiliate of The Macmillan Company Inc., New York

First published in Great Britain 1974
1st edition, 3rd impression 1979
Reprinted 1980
Printed and bound in Italy by Mondadori, Verona

Editorial Director
GIULIANA NANNICINI
American Editorial Supervisor
JOHN BOWMAN

Frontispiece:
Segesta: The temple as seen from the southeast.

CONTENTS

FOREWORD

Recently, in a boring waiting room, I happened to pick up a popular magazine in which I came across a full-page advertisement showing the western side of the Parthenon. In the corner of the page there was a sort of abstract vision of two young tourists leaning against the drum of a column that served as a table on which rested two full glasses. The ad proclaimed: "The more you know about ancient architecture, the more you like the Acropolis." The purpose of this little drama was to sell liquor.

I am no great admirer of the "touristocracy" that is tarnishing our age, and when I think of a work that comments most aptly on our attitude toward ancient monumental relics — those "connecting links between the ancients and the men of today" — I think at once of the above episode. It shows, in fact, how distant is the present, which we absorb with all the pores of our bodily substance, from that remote past. "The more you know about ancient architecture . . ." I am not at all sure whether those young people's enjoyment of the Acropolis would be enhanced if we suddenly poured certain slightly specialized but by now well-known architectural details into their heads.

For example, the fact that the Parthenon has not, strictly speaking, even one straight line: if we extended the apparently straight base horizontal of this temple for a mile or so from the existent foundation, it would look like a pyramid. Such fine points, imperceptible to us, were ascertained by men of the present day only after careful measurements, while the same points were visible to the inner eye in that ancient epoch. Thus I am quite afraid that the advertisement that caught my attention indicates in reality only a sort of awe of our technocratic age that drives men on to the accumulation of facts and details, more or less disconnected, about everything. And I wonder if I am not perhaps much more moved by the men of other epochs whose uncertain knowledge of facts would drive us mad but whose feelings were certainly nearer that equilibrium I so long to see sometimes in those around me.

One of those earlier men who comes to mind is an uneducated Greek of the last century, Makrighiannis, who participated in the struggles to liberate Greece from the Ottoman Turks. The few letters Makrighiannis knew he learned at the age of thirty-five in order to write his memoirs, which are quite famous today in Greece. At one point, he speaks, as he tells us, to some soldiers who, at the end of the Greek Revolution, were trying to sell two ancient statues to "Europeans." "Even if they give you ten thousand talents, don't let these things go out of our country: we have fought for them." The words of Makrighiannis are not the rhetorical exhibition of an erudite person. They were uttered by a man who appreciated the importance of language and was well acquainted with pain and grief, as his entire life demonstrated.

The second such "earlier man" is a Muslim traveler of the seventeenth century, educated according to his tradition (he was born in Constantinople), and who echoed — I do not know to what exact degree — what he heard in his various travels. His name is Evlià Tselembí. He visited Greece around 1667 and wrote a sort of guidebook, and this is what he says about Athens: "The city of Athens was lovely and attractive, with tall buildings and glorious habitations, and in this rich city we find all the curious and singular masterpieces that exist on the face of the earth. There are hundreds and thousands of art works sculptured out of crude white marble, singular representations of diverse beings, and statues in the style of the Franks that make those who view them ecstatic. The mind is fascinated, the body faints, the eyes become moist and are delighted."

Now, Evlià Tselembí could not have known much about antiquity. Behind what he writes lie contaminations of Biblical tales with legends from ancient works, all of which is more like the fables of the *Thousand and One Nights* than that little we learn of ancient Greece in the introductory courses of our schools. And yet, however ignorant he may seem to us today, I cannot imagine this man capable of such freakishness as to make lime out of the marble of an ancient statue. And although he speaks about the "style of the Franks" with regard to the statues, he would never have thought — as did a recent contemporary of ours — that the shielded warriors on an architectural frieze were turtles! Indeed, although the scientific level of both the Greek and the Turk may seem to be on a par with that of an infant, they displayed a veneration and feeling for these ancient objects that it would be difficult to find in the hyperscientific epoch of mechanical automation in which we live.

Then, too, we must not forget that one-sided knowledge of ancient architecture might lead us (as I have noticed) to reconstruct an ideal, perhaps hypothetical, form of the original monument: in effect, a rose-colored version of the past. But the present-day reality of the ancient masterpieces is quite another matter. They have been kneaded by the passing of time, "with the events that change with time, which does not yield, and that turn their feet toward good and evil alike" (as it is put in the *Erotokritos*). It is these changeable events that have produced incessant ruin and allowed the Parthenon to become a powder magazine while placing Morosini's cannons on the opposite hill, or led the puritan "philanthropy" (as his apologists call it) of Lord Elgin to remove exposed portions of the temple in order to "protect," in the gloom of a sunless museum, all the pieces he was able to take to England.

Finally, these changing events provide us with glimpses that would be most upsetting if they were to take on the form of dogma. I will limit myself to this one example: "The spiritual gulf between the ancient and the modern worlds is broader than is generally realized. . . . With intensive study the divergence seems even deeper and of wider extent, so that I have heard one of the greatest living authorities on the literature (and on the architecture) startle an audience of classicists by affirming, without qualification, that the Greek mind is very alien to us." This is A. W. Lawrence speaking in his book, *Greek Architecture*. It is one opinion among many.

I think that the whole subject of our attitude toward ancient Greece should be considered from two points of view. And it is really a question of two species, not just of two qualities. One is the man who speaks this language, Greek, naturally; the other is the species of the "alloglot." And here I want to emphasize that I am not at all thinking of all those scholars who, with admirable competence and moving devotion, have given so much of themselves to the investigation of the ancient world. I am thinking, rather, of those who see a world of the past that is already dead, a corpse. It is easy to transport a corpse, whereas it is difficult to transform the living; they suffer, and it is difficult to uproot them in order to transplant them. Our Greek language, for example, should be regarded as the breath of living men, not as the lifebelt of grammarians.

Ancient Greek architecture has been defined as corporeal or sculptural. And, indeed, the modern eye can sometimes distinguish certain features that support this concept, as for example, the entasis, as the ancients called the slight swelling they gave to the middle sections of columns so they should not seem to bend under the weight they bear.

Such details have been described by the specialists. What I wish to point out is that the temple of the ancient Greeks, or more precisely the naos was, in the last analysis, no more than the enclosure of the idol, the statue of a god — Athena on the Acropolis, Poseidon at Sounion, Apollo at Bassae, and other gods in other temples. (It was the "hut" of one of them that was assimilated and absorbed by Christianity.)

It seems that the naos was not a much frequented area. The collective cult manifestations took place in the open, around the altar, outside the architectural monument. That is to say, worship took place outside the compact construction held together like a body molded from imperceptible details capable of unconsciously transmitting the sudden and unexpected vitality of definite structures. I think of Ruskin: "One must not say, as occurred during the last discoveries of the subtle curves of the Parthenon, that what cannot be demonstrated without laborious measurements cannot add to the beauty of line of an architecture. The eye is constantly influenced by things it does not discern with clarity. It is no exaggeration to say that the eye is influenced above all by what it distinguishes least of all."

Scholars of these monuments, concentrating on their perfection, have too often considered them apart from their environment and have regarded them with absolute indifference toward the surrounding countryside. The artistic result of such structures — or so some claim — is such that they can support whatever setting they happen to be in, and it is mere romanticism to say that they must be integrated into the picturesqueness of a panorama.

I must confess that I am not particularly attracted by such sweet feelings as those manifested, let us say, by Goethe in his *Journey to Italy:* "It was an inestimable pleasure to hear that talented lady pour forth her feelings with the tender notes of the piano and at the same time look out the window at the most extraordinary countryside in the world." Goethe was here speaking of the Colosseum, where even the dust is full of great existences of dead ones, as another illustrious romantic traveler remarked. All this is a product of an epoch and brings to mind the tragic irony in Basho's haiku: "Farce of fate/a cricket sings/inside the helmet."

What I want to stress is that such romantic inclinations are quite far from my thought — far from my feeling that these ancient temples of Greece, Magna Graecia, and Ionia are in some way rooted, sown into the countryside. And once these "huts" of the immortals were demolished, the gods without a roof returned to where they came from; they spread out into the countryside once again and now threaten us with fear or with magic, everywhere. "All is full of gods," Thales said. At times one needs myths.

As far as the rational consideration of this architecture allows us to imagine the possibility of transferring, piece by piece, the relics of these edifices to distant lands, I am afraid that we would be doing no more than transferring piles of ruins. It would take too much time to explain the reason for this. The simplest answer would be, "Because the gods do not will it," whatever that means. Unless we prefer to wait until we have stripped ourselves of everything, until there is nothing left but to grow numb in the interplanetary frost.

In other words, I believe that we need faith in these ancient signs rooted within their countrysides: faith that they have a soul. Then the worshiper (and I now dare to call him that) can speak with them, not in tumultuous masses of multicolored touristic madness but, if I am allowed to say so, *alone*, looking at his soul, mirroring it in the soul of those marbles together with their root-soil. It may be that I am a heretic, but it is impossible for me to separate the Temple of Apollo at Delphi from the Phaedriades Rocks or the mountainous crest of Khirpis. Fortunately our Greek earth is hard; its greenery does not irritate; its features are rocks, mountains, and sea. And what light it has!

We must not forget, moreover, that all this transpired originally in a world that was, as far as I know, the most articulate in antiquity. Luckily for us, a good deal of its written language has crossed over the river of time and has reached us. Has it been transmitted to us intact? I would not dare say so. To limit myself to one grave omission, let us look at the drama. Here, too, time has left its marks, its wounds, and not only in the edifices. I am thinking of ancient tragedy, which is the highest expression. At times I have had the impression that ancient tragedy, as we know and perform it, is nothing more than the bones of a fish we have never seen alive in the water. Rhythms, prosody, lyrical passages, choruses, music, and the extremely difficult problems of translation, together with the articulation of the language: in short, everything that we from time to time try to adapt to the so-called spirit of the age, everything that the beat of the Dionysian rite unifies in one single body and penetrates, all that once filled ancient theaters, audiences, and actors — all that, I fear, eludes us. For myself, the most beautiful moments in ancient tragedy (aside from reading the texts) have been experienced in completely empty theaters: as when once I spent a whole week at the theater of Epidaurus after it was liberated from its festival audience.

As for the temples, if an intimate friend wanted to approach them with the help of the ancient texts as a guide, I would dare to advise him to familiarize himself with those texts that lead him there through oblique paths and not by means of direct descriptions. Not, therefore, with the beginning of Euripides' *Ion*, which speaks of dawn in the Delphic countryside, but with the verses, let us say, of Homer, or others able to shake his very soul, if his soul were open to and fit for passions of this kind. I should prefer such an overture, such an introduction. And if the intimate friend asked me to be more concrete, I would tell him that while writing these words, I was thinking of Homer's verse on the fifty serf-women in the palace of Alcinous: "Some weaving their webs or twisting their yarn as they sat all aflutter like aspen leaves on a tall tree" (*Odyssey*, V, 105). That is how far removed my mind was.

One spring morning in Athens, after being away for years, I looked up from the street to see a section of the southwestern corner of the Parthenon: the capitals of a few columns and the pillaged pediment; a little lower the ancient wall called the "wall of Cimon"; and lower yet, the bare rock, dazzling in the light, with prickly pears and agave plants. That afternoon, looking at the Caryatids on the Erechtheum, I realized that their entasis (in the strict architectural sense) was noticeable in the chest and the stiff legs. Two moments that have stuck in my memory, and which inexplicably return to the surface every now and then.

Giorgio Seferis

INTRODUCTION

"Time is a deceiver that hovers over men and diverts the course of their lives; but with freedom, men have some remedy even for this." These verses by Pindar reveal in a single stroke the fundamental theme of Hellenic culture, which unites the quite varied experiences that occurred in the many regions of the Greek world between the eighth and fourth centuries B.C., from the time of Homer and Hesiod to Alexander the Great.

We must start by accepting that the ancient Greeks did not realize political unity autonomously. That was achieved only when imposed from without, first by the Macedonian hegemony and later, in a more thorough manner, by the Roman conquest. In effect, the attainment of political unity coincided with the loss of autonomy. The concept of freedom as the independence of all Greeks emerges only at intervals, in crucial moments such as the struggle against the Persians. Otherwise the sentiment of cultural and religious unity lived above all in the athletic contests and rituals that periodically gathered together all the Greeks, under the banner of a sacred truce, in the great Panhellenic sanctuaries.

Thus, on the political level, freedom belonged to the *polis* — what we have come to know as the city-state. Modern culture harks back continually to the great Athenian experiences, which realized to an ever-growing extent the participation of all citizens in public life (although as we shall soon see, the word "citizens" had a very strict and limited meaning). Democracy, that form of government for which "power is exercised not in the interest of the few but in the interest of the many," was a discovery of Pericles' Athens. It was a reflection of a profound humanism that, although setting man at the center of the universe, did not seek to isolate him in his individuality but considered him a necessary and integral part of the social group. Even beyond Aristotle's definition of man as a political animal, we may listen to the eloquent words of the great fifth-century historian, Thucydides: "Since only among us, he who is not interested in politics at all is not considered a peaceful person but rather a useless one."

The experience of Athenian democracy has been fundamental for civilization and has become the obligatory reference point for anyone animated by the desire for equality among men. Athenian democracy has, in other words, taken on a symbolic value. And this has been an ambiguous fate, because we have ended up looking less closely at the dynamics of the social, economic, and political forces, at the sheer toil of thought, that determined the development of that particular experience, as well as of all human experiences that have related to it. We have lost, at least on the level of common consciousness, its specificity, so to speak. Fifth-century Athens, abstracted by history, moved into a timeless dimension, has ended up being obscured and flattened like some cheap reproduction of a great painting.

Athenian democracy, given the economic and social structures in which it evolved, achieved the maximum of liberty, involving all the citizens in the running of the *polis*. But this was a difficult conquest, and one that came about through the slow maturation of the class consciousness of the lower classes and the conflict between these people and the great noble families, who had obtained their power (at least in the beginning) from their ownership of the best land. However, the clever policies of the upper classes succeeded in containing the drive of the citizenry, channeling their claims and unrest in the least dangerous and most innocuous direction: service in the navy, public works, and the struggles for power with other Greek states. At the same time, the fragmentary nature of Greek politics remained an insurmountable obstacle for the growth of a proletariat that could set itself more progressive tasks for the realization of a more complete system of social justice.

We have been speaking of the "citizens," and we must never forget that political rights were limited to those free men born in Athens of Athenian parents. Below these were the slaves, considered little more than instruments of production. But despite everything attained, even among the free men the concrete possibilities of participation in political life were never uniform: the humble Attic farmer took part only rarely in the meetings of the popular assembly, the *ecclesia*, where the urban proletariat sat. On the other hand, these latter could make their wishes known only in that assembly, whereas other people took the political initiative: and it was these other people who ran the life of the polis. As proof of this, we need only refer to what Thucydides wrote in his portrait of Pericles: "He held the reins of the multitudes in a frank and open manner, and never let himself be guided by them, but rather it was he who led them." Free speech and the equality of all with respect to the law were two fundamental victories, but they were not enough to guarantee complete social justice or even equality in the enjoyment of political rights. Clarifying the intrinsic limits of the Athenian experience — especially its laborious emergence through the dialectic of antagonistic forces — means regaining the concreteness and specificity of such historical facts, extracting them from myth.

Thus the monuments of Pericles' Athens, in their sublime forms, remain silent for those who neglect the motives behind their construction and the meanings they had for their contemporaries. To the public for whom they were built, these monuments communicated a complex message, interwoven with political, religious, and ideological implications that, in turn, contributed to determining the appearance of the architectural work. Most important of all was the need for the monument itself to become a part of the discourse, of the *logos* that united all the citizens of the polis, with a well-defined role of its own, expressing the subtle connections between the noble traditions and their heroes. Finally, too, the world of the gods reflected in a particular light the ethnic world and the social structure as well as the current history of the city-state. For example, how could it be possible to understand the labor behind Phidias' art — recreated so vividly by the ingenious interpretations of various scholars — or the structure of the Erechtheum and the Propylaea, without taking into account the labor of the city of Pericles during the Peloponnesian War, the tragedies of Sophocles and Euripides, the pungent comedies of Aristophanes, and the thought of the Sophists and Socrates?

In our attempts to extract the monuments from a static ideal set outside time, it may be that in the pages that follow we have approached the ancient experience with too much spirit of participation, with a spirit not freed from the passions of the present — almost as if we were weighing Pericles' Athens against our own concerns and values. This, too, would be a serious mistake, no less so than those of past interpretations. But perhaps it is useful at times to break up for a moment the usual picture that emerges from erudite research, in our search for a more relevant and possibly more serene way of understanding the ancient world. Above all, today, as we think of the Athens of Pericles, perhaps it would be most opportune and realistic to place special emphasis on how Athenian democracy had succeeded in achieving, through the participation of its citizens in the life of the polis, the miracle of a civilization in which everybody felt himself at the same time both spectator and creator. We might begin by meditating painfully on the words of Pericles' speech: "We enjoy, in fact, a constitution that has nothing to envy in the laws of neighboring states."

THE ANCIENT AEGEAN WORLD

BLACK SEA

EPIDAMNUS

ILLYRIA

THRACE

PANGAEUS

MARONEA

BYZANTIUM

PELLA

POLLONIA

MACEDONIA

AMPHIPOLIS

SEA OF
MARMARA

THASOS

SAMOTHRACE

PIDNA

KHALKIDHIKI

OLYNTHUS

IMBROS

DARDANELLES

PHRYGIA

MT.
OLYMPUS

POTIDAEA

LEMNOS

TROY

EPIRUS

THESSALY

LARISA

AEGEAN

LESBOS

THERMI

CORFU

PHARSALUS

SKYROS

PERGAMUM

LEUKAS

ACARNANIA

EUBOEA

SEA

CUMA
PHOCAEA

LYDIA

AETOLIA

PHOCIS

DELPHI

CHALCIS
ERETRIA

CHIOS

IZMIR
CLAZOMENOS

SARDIS

ITHACA

BOEOTIA

THEBES

ERETRIA

IONIA

MAEANDER RIVER

ACHAEA

ELEUSIS

MARATHON

EPHESUS

ELIS

SICYON

MEGARA

ATTICA

ANDROS

SAMOS

PRIENE

ZAKYNTHOS

ELIS
PISA

CORINTH

ATHENS

TENOS

ICARIA

CARIA

OLYMPIA

ARCADIA

MYCENAE

AEGINA

SOUNION

MILETUS
DIDYMA

PELOPONNESOS

ARGOS

EPIDAUROS

ARGOLID

MYKONOS

HALICARNASSUS

BASSAE

LACONIA

MESSENE

DELOS

NAXOS

KOS

MESSENIA

SPARTA

PAROS

CNIDOS

LYCIA

PYLOS

SYPHNOS

AMORGOS

MELOS

THERA

RHODES

CYTHERA

KARPATHOS

CRETE

KASOS

KYDONIA

KNOSSOS

MALLIA

GORTYNA

PHAESTOS

THE AEGEAN WORLD TO 1000 B.C.

1. Knossos: The south propylaeum of the palace, its lower part hidden by the wall of the corridor of the procession. This gives a good impression of how Sir Arthur Evans selectively restored the palace, using much of the original stone but replacing all the wooden elements with concrete. The frescoes depicting a procession of cupbearers are copies of the restored originals, now in the museum of Iraklion.

Achievements of the Minoans

There was a day when the classic Greek civilization associated with Athens was spoken of as a miracle, as though it sprang full-grown from the soil of Attica like Athena from the brow of Zeus. But once we accept that Greece was always very much a part of the continuum of Aegean culture — and this is increasingly clearer with each new discovery — it becomes more necessary, more sensible, and indeed more stimulating to search for the origins of Greek civilization. That then opens up an almost unlimited search, but we may fairly (if somewhat arbitrarily) begin with Crete, which by about 2000 B.C. had already attained a relatively high cultural level. Yet this island was not particularly blessed with primary resources; although forests furnished abundant supplies of timber, the land was for the most part hilly or mountainous, mainly supporting grazing or the cultivation of olives and grapes. There were, to be sure, some coastal plains as well as the large Messara Plain that stretched along the south-central region. But in the easternmost part of the island, which seems to have been the earliest region to be settled, the terrain was so rocky that fishing must have been the principal means of subsistence.

If Crete's agricultural resources were no better than those in the rest of the Aegean, the island nonetheless enjoyed a privileged geographical position at the center of the routes used by mariners and merchants on their voyages throughout the eastern Mediterranean. Crete lay halfway between the centers of Greece and Egypt; from the southern coast, it was an easy matter to reach the Nile Delta, either by a direct course or by skirting the Libyan coast; from the northern coast, a series of islands provided safe harbors all the way to the Greek mainland. To the east, it was also easy to reach Cyprus, rich in metals, and the Levant coast, rich in many products. In this favorable position, Cretans had early adapted to become a commercial-craftsmen people, and in the centuries after 2000 B.C. their ships and goods were an influential presence in the eastern Mediterranean.

Agriculture still provided the basic sustenance of Cretan society, and it is no coincidence that the three main centers that grew up — Knossos, Phaestos, Mallia — dominated plains suitable for the cultivation of grains. These centers were also within easy reach of the sea, and each had a port at its disposal, although only Mallia was situated directly on the coast. Each of the three centers was probably somewhat autonomous, but Knossos evidently became at least "first among equals." It was the ruler of Knossos who, through myth and legend, entered the Greek world as Minos, who has in turn given his name to the people and civilization that flourished on Crete from about 2600 to 1100 B.C. From 2000 B.C., the principal administrative, political, economic, and religious functions seem to have become centralized in the man who ruled from Knossos, and he most likely controlled such sectors of Cretan life as sea-trade, metal-working, and the arts and crafts in general. To administer this society, Minos availed himself of a class of functionaries, again undoubtedly organized so as to be responsible to himself.

The tangible expression of this centralized power — not unlike that of the Egyptian Pharaoh and other Near Eastern potentates — was the palace-complex. It is misleading to think of them as palaces in the modern sense, both because of the variety of activities that took place and because of the way they grew architecturally. The Minoan palaces are no longer regarded as merely random agglomerations, as they once appeared; but the patterns and organization that are now recognized still leave them seeming more like organisms than structures. They are laid out on multilevel terraces that fit the natural contours and surroundings; at the heart is the spacious courtyard, while entranceways and windows always connect with the outer environment. The Minoan kings, furthermore, were able to rule without engaging in military operations, so that the palaces lack fortification walls. Likewise, although the Minoan palaces

make their own impression, they do not seek to impose their power through an abstract monumentality, as do, say, so many Egyptian structures. Yet we need not pretend that the gap between the king's entourage and the mass of people must not have been unbridgeable. The precious metals, stones, and works of art that stand today as the image of the Minoan world were royal prerogatives; the luxury of the palace life only indirectly reflects the economic realities of the majority of Minoans. So, too, within the social organization, roles and functions were immutably established: the palaces may delight us, but they should not deceive us.

The most complex and richest of the Minoan palace-centers was the one at Knossos, associated with King Minos. The palace actually resulted from a series of reconstructions and elaborations that occurred over some five hundred years, but its present aspect basically reflects the last period, when the Minoans were under the influence, if not the outright dominance, of Mycenaeans from the Greek mainland. Many elements of this last phase of Knossos have been preserved by the work of its great excavator, Sir Arthur Evans. But it should be noted that, quite aside from

2. **Knossos: The original throne in the palace's throne room is made of gypsum; the fresco of the griffins is a modern reconstruction of fragments found in the room. It is now thought that the room dates from sometime after 1500 B.C., when the palace was evidently controlled by Mycenaeans.**

3. Knossos: The bastion with its second-story colonnade, and the just-visible fresco of the bull, was erected in the last phase of the palace to flank the ramp that leads to the central court. In the foreground are some of the pillars in the Pillar Hall just inside the north propylon. The red-painted cement columns were originally trees, placed topside down.

THE CATALOGUE OF THE GREEK SHIPS SETTING FORTH FOR TROY

Tell me now, ye Muses that dwell in the mansions of Olympus—seeing that ye are goddesses and are at hand and know all things, but we hear only a rumor and know not anything —who were the captains of the Danaans and their lords. But the common sort could I not number nor name, nay, not if ten tongues were mine and ten mouths, and a voice unwearied, and my heart of bronze within me, did not the Muses of Olympus, daughters of aegis-bearing Zeus, put into my mind all that came to Ilios. So will I tell the captains of the ships and all the ships in order. . . .

And the Abantes breathing fury, they that possessed Euboea and Chalcis and Eretria and Histiaia rich in vines, and Kerinthos by the sea and the steep fortress of Dios, and they that possessed Karystos, and they that dwelt in Styra, all these again were led of Elephenor of the stock of Ares, even the son of Chalodon, and captain of the proud Abantes. And with him followed the fleet Abantes with hair flowing behind, spearmen eager with ashen shafts outstretched to tear the corslets on the breasts of the foes. And with him forty black ships followed.

And they that possessed the goodly citadel of Athens, the domain of Erechtheus the high-hearted, whom erst Athena daughter of Zeus fostered when Earth, the grain-giver, brought him to birth—and she gave him a resting place in Athens in her own rich sanctuary; and there the sons of the Athenians worship him with bulls and rams as the years turn in their courses—these again were led of Menestheus son of Peteos. And there was no man upon the face of earth that was like him for the marshaling of horsemen and warriors that bear the shield. Only Nestor rivaled him, for he was the elder by birth. And with him fifty black ships followed.

And Aias led twelve ships from Salamis, and brought them and set them where the battalions of the Athenians stood.

And they that possessed Argos and Tiryns of the great walls, Hermione and Asine that enfold the deep gulf, Troizen and Eionai and Epidauros full of vines, and the youths of the Achaeans that possessed Aegina and Mases, these were led of Diomedes of the loud warcry and Sthenelos, dear son of famous Kapaneus. And the third with them came Euryalos, a god-like warrior, the son of king Mekisteus son of Talaos. But Diomedes of the loud war cry was lord over all. And with them eighty black ships followed.

And of them that possessed the established fortress of Mycenae and wealthy Corinth and established Kleonai, and dwelt in Orneiai and lovely Eritrea and Sicyon, wherein Adrestos was king at the first; and of them that possessed Hyperesie and steep Gonoessa and Pellene, and dwelt about Aigion and through all the coastland and about broad Helike, of them did lord Agamemnon son of Atreus lead an hundred ships. With him followed most and goodliest folk by far; and in their midst himself was clad in flashing bronze, all glorious, and was pre-eminent amid all warriors, because he was goodliest and led folk far greatest in number.

And of them that possessed Lacedaimon lying low amid the rifted hills, and Pharis and Sparta and Messene, the haunt of doves, and dwelt in Bryseiai and lovely Augeiai, and of them too that possessed Amyklai and the sea-

the long-standing disagreement over the propriety of actually reconstructing major segments (rooms, stairways, etc.), there is a more current debate over just how much of the Knossos we see today was actually the work of the Minoans in their prime, and how much was the work of the Minoans when they were under the Mycenaeans.

The details of this debate, however, need not concern us, for we are interested in finding early forms of later Greek architecture. Consider the South Propylaeum, for instance (Figure 1), with its columns and other structures, its distribution of space, its proportions and rhythms. Without in any way suggesting that these were models for the later Greeks (who, after all, never even saw the Minoan structures), they convey at least a feeling for architecture that anticipates later Greek forms more, say, than they look to Near Eastern forms. So, too, the northern entrance, with its propylon, its hall with two rows of pillars, its ramp, its columned and frescoed gallery (Figure 3) — here again there prevails the Minoans' love of openness, variety, and dynamism which, if contrary to pure classic architecture, nevertheless conveys some of the same feeling.

Finally, of course, the analogies with later Greek architecture cannot be pushed too far. There is nothing quite comparable to the great courtyard that dominates the very heart of the Minoan palace. Nor were later Greek structures asked to perform so many different functions as these Minoan palace-complexes. The west wing of Knossos, for instance, as well as its many ceremonial and religious rooms, also contains a vast series of storerooms; while the east wing, along with the royal residential chambers, also houses workshops for artisans and palace functionaries. And if we could focus on individual rooms, we would see other differences: the throne room, for example (Figure 2), is directly accessible from the great courtyard through a small open anteroom, suggesting a closeness to life. Yet directly opposite the throne is a small sunken chamber, assumed to have been a lustral basin that, when filled with water, was used for purification rites — reminding us of the remoteness of these Minoans. Nevertheless, throughout the palace at Knossos, we are struck by the recurring motifs that express a recognizable humanity: an arrangement of the parts and the whole that respects the natural setting, the vivid colors and elastic contours of the decorative elements, and through it all the accommodations to ensure light and air.

And Knossos was by no means alone in constructing with such elements. There were the two other major palaces, at Mallia and Phaestos, plus many secondary palaces and villas. Several ambitious structures are found in the immediate neighborhood of Knossos, the famed summer palace at Ayia Triadha near Phaestos, and the palace at Zakro, only discovered during the 1960s. The palace at Phaestos is especially impressive (Figure 4) with its great courtyard, its grand staircase and propylaeum, its theatrical area — all monumental, yet all floating; all solid stone, yet all creating a stupendous scenographic effect. At the less regal and more commercial sites, such as Gournia or Palaikastro in the eastern part of Crete, the habitations take on a different but no less natural aspect, set as they are against rocky prominences. These are essentially towns, but the small palace sitting on the top of the hill at Gournia does repeat the plan of the large palaces, albeit reduced to the minimum essentials. Around this palace — and the governor's mansion might be a truer label — the houses press together in compact blocks separated by narrow, irregular streets. These small roadways follow the contours of the slope, surmounting the steepest points with steps. Gournia provides the typical aspect of the Aegean and Mediterranean to this day, with the front of the houses facing the sea, like an impenetrable shield facing possible aggressors, yet also like a lighthouse reflecting the light of safety and welcome.

The architecture must remain our point of departure, but we should not forget that the same people who built these various structures filled them with appropriate objects, whether works of high artistry or of the plainest utility. This becomes particularly clear even if we simply mention the pottery which, from the early neolithic times to the late period of Minoan culture, the Cretans seem to have taken a special pride in making. The pottery attained an especially refined level during the time when the palaces were also at their peak, with eggshell-thin ceramics, fantastic polychrome designs, and pigments that still hold their vivacity after thousands of years. Such advanced artistry and technology presupposes a large market and highly specialized production, both requiring large numbers of persons. Pottery must have been a profitable enterprise, and the extensive distribution of some of the fine wares suggests that, even outside the immediate palace circles, Minoans had an eye for a well-turned pot and a bit of extra money to buy it.

In any case, although Knossos seems to have asserted its dominion over a large part of Crete, it seems to have fallen under the dominion of Mycenaeans from the mainland shortly after 1500 B.C.; to the extent these Mycenaeans controlled Knossos, they probably controlled Crete. At Knossos, the palace bureaucracy adapted the old Cretan script to the Greek language of the new overlords; the syllabic system known today as Linear B thus came to be used to write down on clay tablets the detailed accounts of the palace's economic and administrative activities. Linear B

coast fortress of Helos, and that possessed Laas and dwelt about Oitylos, of these was the king's brother leader, even Menelaus of the loud warcry, leader of sixty ships, and these were arrayed apart. And himself marched among them confident in his zeal, urging his men to battle: and his heart most of all was set to take vengeance for his strivings and groans for Helen's sake.

And of them that dwelt in Pylos and lovely Arene and Thryon the fording-place of Alpheios, and in established Aipy, and were inhabitants of Kyparisseis and Amphigeneia and Pteleos and Helos and Dorion—where the Muses met Thamyris the Thracian, and made an end of his singing, as he was faring from Oichalia, from Eurytos the Oichalian; for he averred with boasting that he would conquer, even did the Muses themselves sing against him, the daughters of aegis-bearing Zeus; but they in their anger maimed him, moreover they took from him the high gift of song and made him to forget his harping — of all these was knightly Nestor of Gerenia leader, and with him sailed ninety hollow ships. . . .

And Odysseus led the great-hearted Kephallenians, them that possessed Ithaca and Neriton with quivering leafage, and dwelt in Krokyleia and rugged Aigilips, and them that possessed Zakynthos and that dwelt in Samos, and possessed the mainland and dwelt in the parts over against the isles. Them did Odysseus lead, the peer of Zeus in counsel, and with him followed twelve ships with vermilion prow.

HOMER: *Iliad* (II: 484–493, 536–602, 631–637)

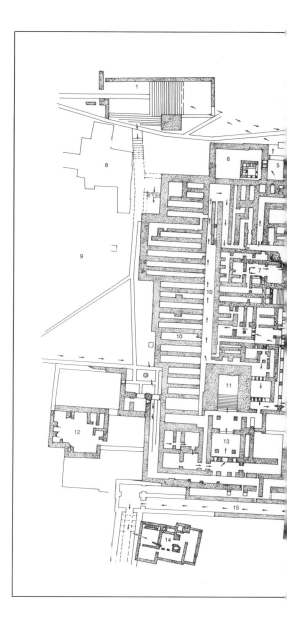

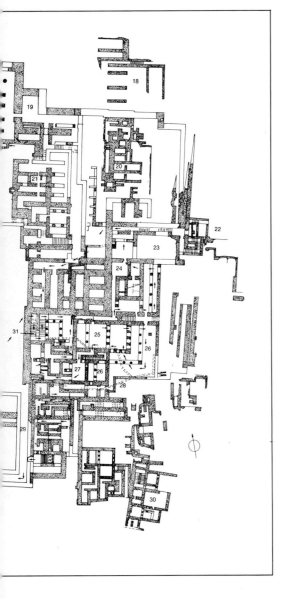

was also used at several of the Greek mainland centers of the Mycenaeans, and this fact plus several other factors suggests that the Mycenaean hegemony over Knossos and Crete was based mainly on economic-administrative practices rather than military prowess.

Then, around 1400 B.C., the great Cretan palace-centers were seriously destroyed; the exact circumstances are not known, but certainly an earthquake was involved and it may well have been related to the great explosion of the volcanic island of Thera, due north of Crete. Life continued on Crete, however, if at a reduced economic level; the phenomenon of Crete's decline is now thought to have been far more gradual than Sir Arthur Evans and his early followers believed. The large settlements that had formed around the palaces continued to live off the work opportunities created by the Mycenaeans. Trade activities had become the Mycenaeans' prerogative; Minoan civilization was going under. The parasitical character of the large settlements became more obvious compared to the countryside that alone produced subsistence goods, and by 1200 B.C. the urban centers were falling apart. Within another century, the population was spreading out across the island in more numerous, if less ambitious, communities. By 1100 B.C., the distinctive core of Minoan Crete had ceased to generate.

Attainments of the Mycenaeans

The people we have been calling Mycenaeans were most likely the people whom later Greeks called Achaeans; from the Linear B tablets, we now know that they spoke a language that is the direct ancestor of classic Greek. Assuming all these links to hold, then the Achaean-Mycenaean people were part of the wave of peoples who spoke languages belonging to the Indo-European family. Around 2500 B.C., they began to appear in the basin of the Danube, Macedonia, and Anatolia (where some developed what came to be known as the Hittite civilization). These Indo-Europeans, as they may be called, were a cattle-raising, warrior-caste people who acquired the agricultural arts from the neolithic peoples living in the areas where they settled. By about 1900 B.C. (if not earlier), the beginning of the Middle Helladic Period as this phase of the Bronze Age in Greece is known, some of these Indo-Europeans made a relatively violent appearance in central Greece and in the Peloponnesos, while another group set off through Thrace. About 1800 B.C., this latter people conquered Troy, the ancient settlement on the left bank of the Dardanelles that controlled the trade routes between Europe and Asia. The cultural aspect of this city changed radically at this point, and there appeared the types of ceramics typical of the Middle Helladic culture. This inaugurated the so-called Troy VI phase (1800–1300 B.C.) — that is to say, the sixth of the main layers, one set upon the other, which make up the great Hissarlik hill that has supplied modern archaeologists with so much evidence of the life of the Trojans through the ages.

Meantime, those Indo-Europeans who went into central Greece and the Peloponnesos — and whom we may call Achaeans in this early stage — developed upon contact with the indigenous population a social organization quite different from the Minoans'. The Achaeans brought with them a tribal organization, which we can vaguely reconstruct on the basis of available evidence and by analogies with better-known models. The tribe is a form of organization that ultimately maintains an aristocratic society but which is originally based on the genus, or what the Romans called the *gens:* a large group of persons who considered themselves descendants of a common founder of a family, be he human or divine. The structure of the gens does not correspond to that of the family as we know it. The gens had a different and much more inclusive extension; furthermore, the family is based on descent along paternal lines, while the gens was probably formed in a period and setting in which descent was established along maternal lines. Various gens then formed a larger structure, the phratry in ancient Greek terms (and what we might think

of as a clan), a mother gens they all considered themselves derived from. Finally, many related phratries formed the tribe.

Originally the tribe had an egalitarian organization; it was run by a council that included the chiefs of the various peoples, and these chiefs in turn elected a tribal chieftain. The tribes could also form a federation and, in turn, designate a federal chieftain. By the time the Achaeans had settled down and developed the various cities of Greece — including Mycenae, which has since given its name to this particular phase of Achaean culture — it was this federal organization that gave pattern and order to Mycenaean society. Thus, Mycenae asserted its hegemony over the Argos and Corinth regions; yet individual cities such as Argos and Tiryns seem to have been quite independent: each had its own ruler, palace, and fortified citadel. For certain tasks, however, and especially in case of warfare against foreigners, the authority of the leading sovereign was spontaneously recognized by the various tribal city-states. The power of Agamemnon of Mycenae was of this nature when he led the Achaeans in their Homeric expedition against Troy.

Another aspect of this form of society was that land was not the prop-

4. **Phaestos: From the west court, or so-called theater area (sunken area, lower right), one could proceed up the grand staircase that led through the propylaeum and on to the central court, the large flat area (center background). Phaestos sits on the edge of a high promontory and seems to float and merge with its surrounding landscape.**

20   GREECE

5. **Mycenae: Grave Circle A, discovered by Schliemann in 1876 with its gold-laden burials. Originally outside the acropolis proper, this grave circle was enclosed by the great citadel wall erected about 1350 B.C., at which time, too, the double row of sandstone slabs was added, indicating that the area was still venerated.**

Following page:
6. **Mycenae: Gate of the Lions. The sculptured triangular slab, which rests on the monolithic lintel, conceals a hollow space that lightens the load. The heads of the lions were carved separately; they have never been found. The two lions (actually lionesses) in their heraldic pose represent a motif going far back in time and carried on to our own day.**

erty of individuals but was divided among the tribes, which then assigned the exploitation of the land over to its member gens. The ruler of each tribe, in return for his services, had the right to a reserved part of the best arable land, as well as a privileged portion of any war booty. This resulted, sooner or later, in concentrations of great wealth in the chieftains' families, as evidenced today by the finds in various Mycenaean tombs. In the early dynasties of Mycenae itself, the kings were buried in shaft graves enclosed by a circular wall of stone slabs. The first set of such tombs, situated outside the later citadel, form the so-called Circle B, which is dated to the 1600s. Circle A (Figure 5) is the one that eventually came to be enclosed within the citadel near the Lions' Gate. It dates from the 1500s and the tombs were marked by stone funerary steles, some of which had carved decorations. In both grave circles, the funerary furnishings included valuable artifacts such as gold and silver cups, swords and daggers, and precious personal ornaments; some skeletons had gold masks on their faces and these seem to have reproduced the individual's features. Today, the Mycenaean grave finds impress us less for their intrinsic value and more because of their handsome artistry.

But there is no escaping the fact that the people who could afford such extravagance must have been wealthy. Later, the Mycenaean monarchs preferred to be buried in domed, or *tholos*, tombs, characterized by an access road (*dromos*) and by a burial chamber covered by a dome constructed with corbeled stones. The monumental architecture of these tombs conveys the image of strong political power; their continued use over many decades by members of the same families suggests inherited royalty; and the economic power implied by such expensive tombs and burials also suggests considerable differences that had appeared within Mycenaean society. Heinrich Schliemann, the man who first excavated Troy and Mycenae, tried to connect the shaft graves and tholos tombs with the famous Homeric characters, Agamemnon, Atreus, and Clytemnestra, but all these tombs were actually built long before the Trojan War of Homer. Furthermore, the Agamemnon of the *Iliad* was far from the ancient tribal chief who derived his authority from the consent of other members; he was a sovereign surrounded by his court of nobles. Yet even the Homeric Agamemnon could call upon the ancient loyalties of the Achaean tribes when he summoned them to war against the outsiders.

Well before that episode, however, a change seems to have occurred in Mycenaean life. By about 1350 B.C., various Mycenaean centers, including Mycenae and Tiryns, began to build walls and gates: palaces were becoming forts. The acropolis of Mycenae was enclosed in a huge wall in which there were two gates defended by jutting bastions; these latter left the invaders vulnerable from their right, unprotected by their shields. The northwest gate at Mycenae is the famed Lions' Gate (Figure 6), with its gigantic monolithic lintel surmounted by a triangular slab of local limestone. On this slab, which affords both visual and architectural relief to the otherwise massive structure, two heraldic lions are sculptured on opposite sides of a downward-tapering column. It was at this time, too, that the royal palace was constructed on the acropolis at Mycenae. New as it was, however, it incorporated the *megaron*, or great hall, that was such a distinctive feature at sites in Greece and Anatolia of a thousand years earlier. The Achaean-Mycenaeans seem to have made the megaron their own. Another example, roughly contemporaneous with the one at Mycenae, is found at the palace at Pylos (Figure 7), said to have been the palace of Homer's King Nestor, in the bay closed off by the islet of Sfacteria on the southwestern coast of the Peloponnesos. The typical megaron is approached from a courtyard and includes a small porch, an anteroom, and the inner room. This inner room, at Mycenae and at Pylos, had a circular fireplace in the center; at Mycenae the roof was supported by four columns, which may have demarcated a skylight or an opening in the roof used as a craft for the hearth.

After the establishment of Mycenaean hegemony in Crete, Mycenaeans replaced the Minoans as a maritime-commercial presence, not only in the Aegean but further afield. Mycenaean settlements flourished in Rhodes, Kos, and Miletus, while the Mycenaeans' influence was felt in Egypt, Syria, Troy, southern Italy, and Sicily. Yet by 1300 B.C., the Mycenaeans began to give way in the face of Phoenician and Cypriot competition. A series of disasters then rocked the Aegean world. About 1300 B.C., Troy VI was destroyed by an earthquake; it hastily rebuilt and kept up its dealings with the Mycenaeans, but soon the city was under siege. Proof of this has been found in the huge vases set into the floors of houses within the walls — reserves of foodstuffs. About 1260 B.C., a violent fire and destruction like that sung of by Homer in the *Iliad* marked the end of the life of Troy VIIA.

About this time, too, Thermi on the island of Lesbos, Mycenaean settlements on Sicily, and the cities of the Hittite empire were destroyed. And on the Greek mainland, a number of the major Mycenaean palace-forts were destroyed; Mycenae recovered somewhat, but by 1100 B.C. it was totally destroyed. It is assumed that the attackers responsible for the destruction of the Mycenaean centers on the mainland were the Dorians, another group of Greek-speaking people who had long lived to the north of Greece. But without knowing exactly who was responsible, or precisely when it began it can be said that Greece entered into a "dark age."

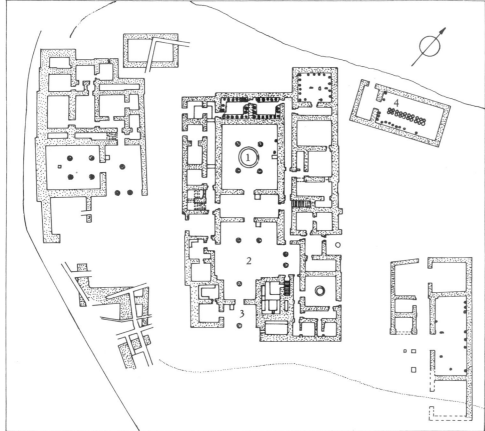

7. Pylos: The palace of Nestor, some remains of which we see here, was distinguished from the great Mycenaean strongholds such as Mycenae and Tiryns by a number of features: its location on an exposed, unprotected site; the absence of defensive walls; a general blending with its environment. However, specific elements such as the megaron mark it as typically Mycenaean.

Pylos: Plan of the Palace of Nestor
1 Megaron
2 Courtyard
3 Propylaeum
4 Storehouses

GREECE FROM HESIOD TO THUCYDIDES

The Crisis in Tribal Society

The Dorians, new lords of Greece, had a tribal organization similar to that of the Achaeans. But by the time the Dorians settled into their new homes, the Mycenaean civilization had already declined too far for these newcomers to reverse events. The inhabitants of Greece — both conquered and conquerors — tended to remain within their own borders, resigning their activist role in the Aegean.

So it was that in the first centuries after 1000 B.C. the economy of Greece was reduced mainly to agriculture. But it was not long before a profound crisis began to corrode the very foundations of this peasant tribal society. The portions of land assigned to the single gens, long worked in common by members of the social units founded on the family relationships, became insufficient for the increasing population. At the same time, the aristocratic elements, by means of political power, had assured themselves of the best land. With this economic advantage, a minority of wealthy and powerful families gained possession of other people's land, often by granting credit to the poor farmers until the latter became so indebted as virtually to be serfs.

Those farmers who no longer could or would live off the land on these terms were forced to look for other means of subsistence. Increasingly they found new opportunities in commerce, both in the trade that provided the mother country with the food and raw materials lacking and also in the small luxury-item trade that had developed in the eastern Mediterranean, particularly under the Phoenicians. The new economic activities gradually separated groups of persons from the rural areas of Greece, giving birth, as Heichelheim has put it, to "the city in the economic sense; that is to say, settlements in which a large proportion of the inhabitants were able to live without undertaking agricultural activity or any other type of work related to primary production."

The emergence of differences in wealth was incompatible with the traditional tribal organization that was basically egalitarian and based on common property, mutual solidarity, and exchange of reciprocal gifts. Meanwhile, the rural crisis was forcing more and more farmers to become city-dwellers in order to find other means of living. This situation was particularly advanced at Corinth, where the isthmus had always served as an obligatory passageway for some of the principal routes of the Greek world. And there, during the eighth century B.C., members of the Bacchidae gens — whose name derived from Bacchis, their claimed progenitor — were driven to engaging in trading activities. In 747 B.C., moreover, the kings of Corinth were replaced by annual magistrates, the Pyrtanes, who also belonged to the Bacchidae gens. The Pyrtanes took an active part in trade, becoming among other things the promoters of that colonization of lands to the west that was one of the crucial mainsprings for the economic development of the Greek world.

But the more precocious the trading activities, the more they stimulated the sense of alienation from the country and the land; the ex-farmers, now become sailors, minor traders, or artisans, were more conscious of their role in society and of the attendant problems. They tended to return to the land, reinvesting in it their meager incomes; their animosity toward the great aristocratic landowners merged with that of those who had remained in the country under miserable conditions. And precisely because Corinth was in a more advanced economic situation than the rest of Greece, the social tension reached a critical point there before anywhere else. We thus witness the emergence of the first of the many Greek tyrants, who were to establish their powers not upon hereditary right or traditional prestige but on their ability to interpret the

Enfolded, on the tender meadow grass
And bedded flowers of spring: and when from
 her
Perseus the head dissever'd, then upsprang
Chrysaor huge, and Pegasus the steed,
So nam'd, near ocean's fountains born; but he,
Chrysaor, in his hands a falchion held
Of beamy gold: rapt on the winged horse
He left beneath him Earth, mother of flocks,
And soar'd to heaven's immortals: and there
 dwells
In palaces of Zeus, and to the god
Deep-counsel'd, bears the bolt and arrowy
 flame.
Chrysaor with Calliroe blending love,
Nymph of sonorous ocean, sprang to birth
Three-headed Geryon: him did Herakles
Slay spoiling, 'midst his oxen pliant-hoof'd,
On Erythia girdled by the wave:
What time those oxen ample-brow'd he drove
To sacred Tyrinth, the broad ocean-way
Once past; and Orthus, the grim herd-dog,
 stretch'd
Lifeless; and in their murky den beyond
The billows of the long-resounding deep,
The keeper of those herds, Eurytion, slain.

HESIOD: *Theogony* (270–294)

8. Corfu: The pediment of the Temple of Artemis. Between the two large felines (panthers?) is the Gorgon Medusa with her sons, the hero Chrysaor and the horse Pegasus. In the pediment corners (not visible) were scenes from the battle with the Titans and the (Corfu Museum) destruction of Troy.

needs of the populace and then satisfy them.

Corinth had been sending its ships to the coasts of Asia Minor and northern Syria for some time, and the Near Eastern world had already permeated the arts and handicrafts of much of Greece long before 657 B.C. when the tyrant Cypselus, also related to the Bacchidae, took over the reins of power. The model for the tyrant-figure also came from the Near East, as is demonstrated by the traditions concerning Cypselus' childhood and rise to power. Such traditions bear the stamp of truly ancient archetypes that can be traced back to at least as far as the story of the great Mesopotamian sovereign, Sargon of Akkad (2371–2316 B.C.). The same story emerges in traditions concerning Moses, Romulus and Remus, Cyrus the Great, and other "father-founders." The tradition concerning Cypselus clearly shows how, in the minds of the Greeks, there existed two contradictory representations of tyranny. We must realize, too, that much of the information about the perfidy and cruelty of the tyrant springs from the aristocrats' reactions to the drastic reform measures for the good of the populace adopted first by Cypselus and later, at Athens, by Pisistratus.

During the Age of Periander, Cypselus' son and successor, the temporary reconquest of Kerkyra (Corfu) was undertaken. This island was a vital stage in the passage from Greece to the west, and so at the time of the foundation of Syracuse in Sicily (734–733 B.C.), Corinth took it from the Eritrians, who had been among the first to found colonies on the Tyrrhenian Sea. But the relationship between Corinth and Kerkyra-Corfu did not go smoothly, and it was probably Periander who ordered the erection of the Temple of Artemis in order to win the good graces of the islanders who, it seems, had no great sympathy for their Corinthian overlord.

9. Lavrion: The painted clay tablet (a *pinax*) depicts miners at work; typical of such votive offerings, both the subject and the style depart from the aristocratic tradition of ancient art and express more popular concerns. (Berlin Museum)

10. Corinth: The Temple of Apollo, one of the oldest temples extant in Greece. The marked swelling of the columns (entasis) and the bulging form of the echinus on top of the columns are typical of the archaic style in stressing the sculptural values of architectural elements.

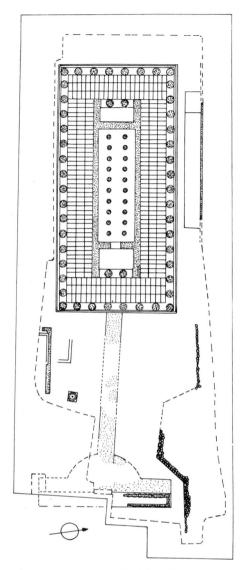

Corfu: Plan of the Temple of Artemis

Along with the Temple of Hera at Olympia, this Temple of Artemis on Corfu is one of the earliest examples of monumental Greek architecture; it is by no means an accident that its construction originated in the will of a tyrant. The old agricultural society was basically egalitarian. Its religious life was still connected with conceptions that were more ancient than the one brought into Greece with the Indo-European language speakers (as will be seen more clearly shortly when we examine the great sanctuaries). Hesiod, for instance, still felt that the gods of Olympus and supreme Zeus were the new generation who had only recently supplanted the worship of the deified expressions of the primordial forces of nature. Monumental architecture, on the other hand, grew up with the advent of strong personal power, such as a tyrant's, which set itself up above any social class, no longer recognizing itself as the expression of even the landed aristocracy. Within the concept of this power there took shape for the first time, although indistinctly, a concept of the state as something above and beyond the gens: an institution that began to consider the members of the ancient tribal society as mere citizens.

The temple at Corfu was a singular edifice that in many aspects seems to foreshadow monumental structures in Ionia. A large peristyle, with eight columns on the short sides and seventeen on the long sides, enclosed a long, narrow sekos, similar to the one in the Temple of Hera at Olympia. The interior of the naos, however, divided into three naves by the two rows of columns, was more clearly articulated than that in the Olympia temple, which was slightly older. In the architecture of this period, the interest seemed to be concentrated on the sculptural-plastic values of the single elements, treated almost as parts complete in themselves.

The roof of the Corfu temple consisted of a multicolored terra-cotta covering, which protected the wooden structures from the weather and at the same time served a decorative function. The pediment already included sculptures — in this instance, the figure of Medusa, one of the Gorgons who in more ancient buildings served as an acroterion on the main beam on top of the roof, was placed in the center of the pediment. Corfu thus represents the prototype of pediment decoration as it would later be developed in Greek architecture. When in the high archaic period, for instance, the Greeks felt the need to paint that neutral surface represented by the tympanum, they resorted to simple decorative motifs taken from the Near Eastern repertoire — as, for example, felines biting their prey. And at Corfu, on either side of Medusa, are two large feline figures. However, a new narrative function had been woven into the fabric of this ancient motif. Medusa is flanked by the winged horse Pegasus and the hero Chrysaor (Figure 8), the children of Medusa (by Poseidon) who arose from her blood when she was decapitated by Perseus. In addition, there were battle episodes in the extreme corners of the pediment. One can thus say that with the Corfu temple, along with monumental architecture, there emerged a new need: the use of architectural surfaces no longer as a neutral area to be decorated but rather as a support for representations that often, as we shall see, define and state the ideological and religious contents that have determined the birth of the monument.

The figures on the Corfu pediment, although sculptured in low relief, are characterized by their precise definition of the contours and by the clear-cut articulation typical of Corinthian art. The large surfaces are rich in plastic modulations, subtle inflections emphasized by well-characterized shadows set in the pivotal points of the composition; yet at first sight the sobriety of the accents serves to underscore the structural rigor that frames the sculpture. From an aesthetic point of view, there are no early forms of art: the Corfu pediment demonstrates this beautifully. The greatness of sculpture was born in Greece during this period, arising from the discovery of anthropocentric dimensions. Without a doubt, a most important contribution to this discovery was the emergence of strong individual personalities such as the tyrants.

One of the principal stimuli of commercial activity that so deeply affected the transformation of archaic society was the search for sources of

Corinth: Plan of the Temple of Apollo

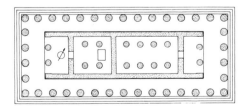

metal-bearing ore. One of the most important areas for the supply of these metals was Armenia; the Greek presence — Corinthian and Euboean — on the coasts of Asia Minor and northern Syria aimed at obtaining metal through Assyrian and Hittite intermediaries. But the crisis that shook the Near East in the first half of the sixth century led to the decline of this trade and the Greeks then went to mining centers closer by, such as Pangaeus in Thrace and Lavrion in Attica. A Corinthian clay tablet (a *pinax*) from the middle of the sixth century (Figure 9), found at Lavrion, is a votive offering of a miner and clearly depicts a mining operation. This painting preserves a small part of the life lived and suffered by those who, in general, do not make history. The protagonist of the little drama, presumably the man who made the offering, is easily recognized in the largest figure, who is occupied in striking the wall of the mine with a pick. With a crude realism (and perhaps a touch of bitterness), the exhaustion of such enervating work is emphasized. While the bearded men carry out the more difficult tasks, the beardless youths

11. Athens: The limestone pediment of the old Temple of Athena Polias on the Acropolis. The vivid polychrome that animates the three-bodied figure was used on almost all Greek sculpture of the early centuries as well as on many of the architectural elements. (Acropolis Museum)

As soon as he was at the head of affairs, Solon liberated the people once and for all, by prohibiting all loans on the security of the debtor's person: and in addition he made laws by which he canceled all debts, public and private. This measure is commonly called the Seisachtheia ("removal of burdens"), since thereby the people had their loads removed from them. . . .

Next Solon drew up a constitution and enacted new laws; and the ordinances of Draco ceased to be used, with the exception of those relating to murder. The laws were inscribed on the wooden stands, and set up in the King's Porch, and all swore to obey them; and the nine Archons made oath upon the stone, declaring that they would dedicate a golden statue if they should transgress any of them. This is the origin of the oath to that effect which they take to the present day. Solon ratified his laws for a hundred years; and the following was the fashion in which he organized the constitution. He divided the population according to property into four classes, just as it had been divided before, namely, Pentacosiomedimni, Knights, Zeugitae, and Thetes. The various magistracies, namely, the nine Archons, the Treasurers, the Commissioners for Public Contracts, the Eleven, and the Exchequer Clerks, he assigned to the Pentacosiomedimni, the Knights, and the Zeugitae, giving offices to each class in proportion to the value of their rateable property. To those who ranked among the Thetes he gave nothing but a place in the Assembly and in the juries. A man had to rank as a Pentacosiomedimnus if he made, from his own land, five hundred measures, whether liquid or solid. Those ranked as Knights who made three hundred measures, or, as some say, those who were able to maintain a horse. In support of the latter definition they adduce the name of the class, which may be supposed to be derived from this fact, and also some votive offerings of early times.

ARISTOTLE: *Atheniensium Respublica*
(VI:1, VII)

load the heavy baskets with the extracted ore and lift them onto the edge of the mine. Another delicate touch is to be seen in the center among the figures — the water container, the sole remedy against the parching thirst provoked by the labor and the dust. Work in the mines was, even in the classical age, something for the slaves, and one of Cypselus' major achievements while serving as tyrant of Corinth was to set certain limits on the possession of slaves.

We know very little about the history of archaic Corinth after the fall of the family of Cypselus (584 B.C.). It appears that a moderate oligarchical regime set itself up, and this government was probably responsible for the construction of the Temple of Apollo at Corinth (Figure 10). In this temple there was established a closer relationship between the sekos and the peristyle. The former is still very long, in the archaic tradition. Within it, the pronaos and the opisthodomos, at opposite ends, both gave access to two distinct sections of the naos. The eastern section was longer and divided into three naves by two rows of columns; the western section was shorter and decorated by four columns. We do not know what this latter room was used for, although possibly it housed the treasury, carrying out one of the important functions of the temple (so well documented by the Temple of Athena Polias in Athens and the Temple of Apollo at Delos). Whatever the function of this unusual chamber was, the complex plan of the Corinth temple anticipated the plan of the Parthenon. The construction reveals the high levels achieved by the architects and workmen in the use of subtle technical devices intended to consolidate the unity of the architectural organism and correct those distortions that the human eye perceives when faced with the neutrality of pure geometric lines. Thus, for example, in order to make sure that the level stylobate does not appear to be slightly concave from a distance, its line was slightly curved at the center. It is impossible today to appreciate the architectural value of this structure. Only seven of the original thirty-eight columns remain, but we can sense that these rather short and monolithic columns must have appeared more slender because of the width of the intercolumniations. Such was the sophistication that a mid-sixth-century Greek city was capable of achieving.

Archaic Athens Under Solon and Pisistratus

At Athens, the social conflict reached a critical point a little later than in Corinth and had a different result, due to the intervention of Solon. In some respects this complex aristocrat — statesman and poet — affected the fate of Athens even more than did Pericles. In Athens, the small landowners were also in heavy debt. The land was no longer free, and those who were not able to meet their debts could be reduced to slavery, or at best could remain serfs, forced to give their creditors a large portion of their meager harvest. There was a strong popular movement that demanded the redistribution of land according to the old tribal custom, somewhat along the lines of what Cypselus had done at Corinth. In this conflict, Solon did not set himself up as a tyrant in the sense of self-assumed interpreter of the popular will and welfare. As an enlightened aristocrat, he firmly believed in the need for concord among Athens' classes, and he acted in the proud conviction of accomplishing a rational work of social justice. He abolished the debts that burdened the land; he gave back freedom to those who had been made slaves because of debts; he favored the return of those who had left their native Athens to escape from debts and slavery. These measures had the effect of displeasing many on both sides; eventually, however, the aristocrats profited from them. The debts were the only link, albeit inhumane, that kept the small farmer tied to the land. Releasing this link, without worrying about remedying the causes of the crisis, meant encouraging the abandonment of the land and the urbanization of a laboring class now deprived of other means of existence. A solution to this problem was sought in the measures that favored handicrafts and the immigration of artisans. The face of the city began to change and the products of Attic pottery workshops were soon reaching the most remote points of the known world. The laborers who were not absorbed by this flourishing handicraft industry made a precarious living as members of the crews of the Greek ships that were crossing the Mediterranean in ever-growing numbers.

However, these measures did not suffice to create steady work possibilities for the urban populace, the part of the citizenry in continual growth. Because of its social position, this segment of the population (the *demos*) could not aspire to public office; its sole form of political expression was the popular assembly, the *ecclesia*. Moreover, the market outlets were greatly limited, and made more so by the fragmentary politics of the Greek world. The economic organization, meanwhile, was too primitive for the surplus profit derived from landholdings to be invested in production activities. Finally, the work of the slaves excluded the urban proletariat from many sectors of productive work. The drama of Athenian society will consist, from this time on, of the need to find a minimum income for this laboring class without encroaching upon the privileges of the aristocrats.

In any case, Athens took on the dimensions of a city. On the Acropolis the first monumental edifices were built, the most important of which was the Temple of Athena Polias (the large foundation of which is still visible today near the Erechtheum). The architect had as a model the Temple of Apollo at Corinth, which must have just been built. He maintained the dimensions of the front part, the division of the naos into two independent sections, and the arrangement into three naves of the eastern section by a double row of columns. Compared to its model, however, the Temple of Athena Polias was built in a more organic manner; it no longer had the extremely elongated form characteristic of early archaic structures. The relationship between the length and width of the stylobate, and consequently between the numbers of front and side columns, was already close to being perfect. As for the complex arrangements within the sekos, with the western section of the naos essentially divided into three rooms, these succeeded because of the coordination between the axes of the walls of the sekos and the corresponding columns of the peristyle, and also because of the reduced depth of the pronaos and the opisthodomos.

The monumental character of this edifice was further enhanced by the rich sculptural and painted decorations. Marble Gorgons set on the top of the roof, served as acroteria; the intimate fusion of anatomical elements in the structure of the face distinguished this Attic Medusa from the Peloponnesian type. The contrast between the two diverse artistic expressions is especially clear when we compare the sculptured figures of the Athenian temple with the central figure of the Corfu temple pediment. The generic motif of the felines biting their prey decorates a pediment in both temples. In the Temple of Athena Polias, however, there appeared beside this motif representations of myths: on the left, Herakles struggling with the Triton; on the right, a monster in the form of a snake, perhaps representing Proteus.

The search for a more forthright relationship with space is also demonstrated in the complicated figures of the Temple of Athena Polias, although they are conditioned by the room available in the corners of the pediments. In the Proteus grouping, the fan-shaped arrangement of the three human torsos — emphasized by the heads looking in different directions — breaks up the one-dimensional quality of the decorative rhythm (Figure 11). The entire dynamics that animates the faces establishes a quite strong, almost domineering, relationship with the onlooker. The whole was brightened by a vivacious polychrome that continued in the upper oblique cornice where birds with unfolded wings, alternating with enormous lotus flowers, were painted. Incidentally, in this ancient edifice, dated between 570–560 B.C., there might already have been on the pronaos a continuous figured frieze, to which are attributed some slabs with large figures of panthers, from an otherwise unknown structure on the Acropolis.

Herakles, the favorite hero of the Greeks because of his profoundly

THE DYING HERAKLES

Many are the toils for these hands, this back,
that I have had, hot and painful even to tell of.
But neither the wife of Zeus nor hateful
    Eurystheus
has ever condemned me to such agony as this
that the false-faced daughter of Oeneus has
    fastened
upon my shoulders, a woven, encircling net
of the Furies, by which I am utterly destroyed.
It clings to my sides, it has eaten away my inmost flesh; it lives with me and empties the
    channels
of my lungs, and already it has drunk up
my fresh blood, and my whole body is
completely killed, conquered by these unspeakable fetters.
Neither the spear of battle nor the army of
the earth-born Giants, nor the violence of
    beasts,
nor Greece, nor any place of barbarous
    tongue, not all
the lands I came to purify could ever do this.
A woman, a female, in no way like a man,
she alone without even a sword has brought
    me down.
O my son, now truly be my true-born son
and do not pay more respect to the name of
    mother.
Bring her from the house with your own hands
    and put
her in my hands, that woman who bore you,
    that I may know
clearly whether it pains you more to see *my*
    body
mutilated or *hers* when it is justly tortured.
Come, my child, dare to do this, Pity me,
for I seem pitiful to many others, crying
and sobbing like a girl, and no one could ever
    say
that he had seen this man act like that before.
Aways without a groan I followed by painful
    course.
Now in my misery I am discovered a
    woman. . . .
Oh, oh, the pain!
That malignant tearing scorches me again,
it shoots through my sides, it *will* have me
    struggle,
it will not let me be—miserable, devouring
    sickness.
O King Hades, receive me!
O flash of Zeus, strike!
Drive against me, O King, hurl down the bolt
of lightning, Father. Now it feeds on me again,
it has sprung out, it blooms. O my hands, my
    hands,
O my back, my chest. O my poor arms, see
what has become of you from what you once
    were. . . .
Now look at me, torn to shreds, my limbs unhinged,
a miserable ruin sacked by invisible disaster, I
who am called the son of the most noble
    mother,
I who claim to be begotten of Zeus in the
    heavens.
But I tell you this, even if I am nothing,
nothing that can even crawl, even so —
only let her come who has done this to me —
these hands will teach her, and she can tell the
    world: alive
I punished the evil, and I punish them in
    death.

SOPHOCLES: *The Women of Trachis*
(1046-1111)

12

12. Athens: A pediment from the archaic temple on the Acropolis representing the apotheosis of Herakles, who is being welcomed to Olympus by Zeus and Hera after his tragic earthly death. (Acropolis Museum)

human experiences, appeared in a marble pediment from another unknown edifice on the Acropolis. After so many dangerous feats and labors, the hero's love for Iole proved fatal; his jealous wife Deianeira sent him the deadly poisoned shirt given to her by the centaur Nessus, whom Herakles had killed. Seized with horrible pains, Herakles set himself on a pyre and asked someone to set it on fire; when only Philoctotes complied, Herakles gave him his bow and arrows, which were later to play such a part in the Trojan War. But Herakles was not consumed by fire; the gods liberated him from his mortal body and he entered Olympus, accompanied by Athena.

This very touching aspect of the myth of Herakles must have been dear to the Athenian populace, which perhaps instinctively put itself in the hero's place. Moreover, this myth emphasized, with Athena's intervention, the relationship between Athens and the Peloponnesos, where Herakles was the national hero. In the important tradition involving the return to the Peloponnesos of the hero's descendants, the Heraklidae, which is thought to have occurred about 1100 B.C., there seems to lie concealed a memory of the appearance of the Dorians. Certainly the

Heraklidae were considered the common progenitors of most of the
people who lived in the eastern Peloponnesos (Sparta, Argos, Corinth,
Sicyon); and certainly too these people were Dorians. Even at the end of
the fifth century B.C., when the Peloponnesian War had seen Athens and
Sparta fighting to the bitter end, the credit due to Athens for having
received the Heraklidae was used by Euripides an an element of political
propaganda.

In the pediment from the unknown structure from the Acropolis (Figure 12), dated to about 570 B.C., the figures were executed in strong
relief, almost completely free-standing full relief. At the center, dominating the group, are Zeus and Hera, both seated, the god in profile and the
goddess in frontal position. Herakles, covered with a lion's skin, advances
toward the divine couple; in the face of the hero, the taut and receding
cheeks, perfectly merged with the facial pattern, produce a compact volume. The leonine head used as a headdress forms a vivid contrast in its
exaggerated decorativeness with the compact structure of the head; the
light that glides down over the subtle lines of the skin collects and then
breaks up in the mane, which is divided into tufts marked by thick groups
of parallel grooves.

The same contrast animates one of the masterpieces of Attic sculpture
of this period, the so-called Rampin Knight (Figure 13): any search for
clearly delineated limbs or planes in the shaping of the torso, so typical of
Peloponnesian taste, would be in vain here. The inflections of the volumes are hidden by the entire corporeal structure; the anatomic markings are barely indicated. The slender bust opens onto the large and
powerful thorax without any break in the flow; in the face, the hollow
cheeks gather in a light shadow from which there emerges the expression
of an intense smile. It is extremely difficult for anyone today who looks at
the body of the knight to imagine the precious play of color that was
intended in the beard, in the hooked curls that come down over the
forehead, and in the little crown placed over the complex hair style. A
subtle torsion animates the figure, and then boldly ends in the neck and
in the head that is slightly turned toward the left. The archaic frontal
position, the echo of an immobile world, fixed in its slow dimensions of
time and space, is broken up in this figure, in which the herald of a new
relationship between man and his world takes concrete shape.

The figure of knights, or horsemen, were frequently found among the
statues dedicated to the gods who populated the Acropolis; a specimen in
barbarian garb, for example, seems to have been dedicated by Miltiades
for the battles he undertook in the Chersonesus. These were votive
statues dedicated by the upper classes: having a horse at one's disposal in
a war was the sign of distinction of the second of Solon's esteemed classes,
the knights, who had an annual income equal to three hundred measures
of grain, oil, and wine. Even more numerous than the statues of knights
were those of young girls (*kourai*) and young men (*kouroi*). A great
number of *kourai* were found near the Erechtheum, obviously having
some relationship with the enclosure of the Temple of Athena Polias.
This tradition continued, in the fifth century, in the figures of the
Caryatids, the female figures that stood in the place of columns in the
Erechtheum portico — the Erechtheum by then having taken the place
of the Temple of Athena Polias.

Solon's intervention did not spare Athens from tyranny, and from 561
until 510 the city was dominated by Pisistratus and his sons, Hipparchus
and Hippias. It is uncertain whether Pisistratus effected the redistribution of the land requested by the rural proletariat during Solon's time.
One point in favor of this hypothesis is that while the important landowners dominated Attica during Solon's time, by the fifth century small
and medium landowners prevailed. Yet known sources contain no mention of any measure of this kind, which would surely have made a great
impact on society.

In many ways, the policies of Pisistratus anticipated those of Pericles, at
least in the general sense that both dealt with the various aspects of social
and economic reality in an organic manner and with a singular breadth
of vision. Pisistratus instituted, like Cypselus, a tax on incomes, using this

14. Aegina: The Temple of Aphaea. This view of the southeastern corner shows how far Greeks had advanced from the archaic style in their search for a more solid unity of volume.

Page 39:
15. Aegina: The figure of armed Athena that occupied the west pediment of the Temple of Aphaea. The Aegina sculptures were restored by the nineteenth-century Danish sculptor, Thorwaldsen and are now in a museum in Munich, Germany. (Glyptothek, Munich)

to finance a vast building program that must have resolved, at least temporarily, the problem of employing the masses. The reconstructed Temple of Athena Polias was now provided with marble pediments; numerous other temples and altars were constructed, and these and other projects were integrated with another aspect of the tyrant's policy. He promoted the rebirth of Homeric religion, and with the introduction of new cults he attempted to consolidate the cultural and religious unity of all the citizens. Seen in this light, the introduction of the cult of Dionysus Melanaigis ("with the black goat's skin"), which we shall examine in more detail later, was an essential development; under Pisistratus' initiative, this cult was linked with a new form of spectacle that he himself promoted: tragic drama. With the representation of the myths and the traditions of the city-state, these dramas contributed to the deepening of cultural unity, causing a more intense participation of all classes in the life of the *polis*.

Among the temples built by Pisistratus was the one dedicated to Olympian Zeus in the sanctuary situated outside the city walls, southwest of the Acropolis. But the peripteral temple erected by Pisistratus was soon replaced (on the initiative of his sons Hipparchus and Hippias) by the foundation of a colossal temple with a dipteral peristyle, inspired by the contemporaneous models at Samos and in Asia Minor. But Hipparchus was killed in 514 B.C., and with the expulsion of Hippias from Athens in 510, the ambitious project remained unfinished. The colossal stylobate was abandoned for more than three centuries (Figure 104), not only because of the aristocrats' hatred for the tyrants but also because the artistic language to which the project aspired was substantially foreign to the sense of proportion and the formal clarity of the classic Attic style.

The Polis and the Struggle Against the Barbarians

The programs of Pisistratus certainly did not resolve the grave problems confronting Attica; nonetheless, with the rise of the tyrants, the power of the landed aristocracy was for some time pushed into the background and the polis began to take on the character of a state. And yet, despite the reforms effected by Solon and Pisistratus, the powerful aristocratic groups continued to form the economic and political backbone of Athenian society. From about the middle of the fifth century, when Pericles assumed power, the real causes of the political struggle lay in the conflict between aristocratic groups; when one prevailed, the other tried to supplant it by gaining the support of the populace. Thus, the pro-democratic attitudes were basically a political expedient, even though from the complicated mesh of this ruthless struggle the people obtained important reforms that allowed the development of an awareness. An example of this can be seen in the rise to power of Cleisthenes, a member of the Alcmaeonidae, and in his important social reforms.

The Alcmaeonidae, sent into exile by Pisistratus, had managed to gain the favor of the Delphic Oracle by taking on the task of constructing the new temple of Apollo at Delphi. The Delphic sanctuary probably played an important role, as Herodotus says, in convincing the Spartans to end the dominion of the Pisistradae, even if strategic considerations also prompted the Spartans' intervention. But when Cleomenes, king of Sparta, had liberated the city, the aristocratic factions played upon the old hatred for the Alcmaeonidae; Cleisthenes was ousted by his rival, Isogoras, who assumed power. And this was all to the good of the populace, for the Alcmaeonidae, having come off second best, were forced to seek popular support at any cost. Cleisthenes thus presented a proposal for more progressive constitutional reforms, and with one stroke obtained the backing of the *ecclesia*.

THE REFORMS OF CLEISTHENES

After the overthrow of the tyranny, the rival leaders in the state were Isogoras son of Tisander, a partisan of the tyrants, and Cleisthenes, who belonged to the family of the Alcmaeonidae. Cleisthenes, being beaten in the political clubs, called in the people by giving the franchise to the masses. Thereupon Isogoras, finding himself left inferior in power, invited Cleomenes, who was united to him by ties of hospitality, to return to Athens, and persuaded him to "drive out the pollution," a plea derived from the fact that the Alcmaeonidae were supposed to be under the curse of pollution. On this Cleisthenes retired from the country, and Cleomenes, entering Attica with a small force, expelled, as polluted, seven hundred Athenian families. Having effected this, he next attempted to dissolve the Council, and to set up Isogoras and three hundred of his partisans as the supreme power in the state. The Council, however, resisted, the populace flocked together, and Cleomenes and Isogoras, with their adherents, took refuge in the Acropolis. Here the people sat down and besieged them for two days; and on the third they agreed to let Cleomenes and all his followers depart, while they summoned Cleisthenes and the other exiles back to Athens. When the people had thus obtained the command of affairs, Cleisthenes was their chief and popular leader. And this was natural; for the Alcmaeonidae were perhaps the chief cause of the expulsion of the tyrants, and for the greater part of their rule were at perpetual war with them. . . .

The people, therefore, had good reason to place confidence in Cleisthenes. Accordingly, now that he was the popular leader, three years after the expulsion of the tyrants, in the archonship of Isogoras, his first step was to distribute the whole population into ten tribes in place of the existing four, with the object of intermixing the members of the different tribes, and so securing that more persons might have a share in the franchise. From this arose the saying "Do not look at the tribes," addressed to those who wished to scrutinize the lists of the old families. Next he made the Council to consist of five hundred members instead of four hundred, each tribe now contributing fifty, whereas formerly each had sent a hundred. The reason why he did not organize the people into twelve tribes was that he might not have to use the existing division into trittyes; for the four tribes had twelve trittyes, so that he would not have achieved his object of redistributing the population in fresh combinations. Further, he divided the country into thirty groups of demes, ten from the districts about the city, ten from the coast, and ten from the interior. These he called trittyes; and he assigned three of them by lot to each tribe, in such a way that each should have one portion in each of these three localities. All who lived in any given deme he declared fellow-demesmen, to the end that the new citizens might not be exposed by the habitual use of family names, but that men might be officially described by the names of their demes; and accordingly it is by the names of their demes that the Athenians speak of one another. He also instituted Demarchs, who had the same duties as the previously existing Naucrari — the demes being made to take the place of the naucraries. He gave names to the demes, some from the localities to which they belonged, some from the persons who founded them, since some of the areas no longer corresponded to localities possessing names. On the other hand he allowed every one to retain his family and clan and religious rites according to ancestral custom. The names given to the tribes were the ten which the Pythia appointed out of the hundred selected national heroes.

ARISTOTLE: *Atheniensium Respublica* (20, 21)

Cleisthenes' reforms, promulgated in 507 B.C., struck a heavy blow at the old social structures that had been the backbone of aristocratic hegemony. The four Ionic tribes, the phratries, which represented the foundation of the nobles' organization, were deprived of all political authority; only their religious prerogatives remained. The four ancient tribes were replaced by ten others of an exclusively territorial nature. Within the tribes, the territorial units were grouped together in such a way as to avoid, at least in theory, the domination of the fief by a particular gens within a tribe. This was especially important, as can be seen if we consider that the tribes elected the magistrates. Naturally, too, a spirit of partiality guided Cleisthenes in his reforms: the Alcmaeonidae, it goes without saying, were certainly not left weakened.

Just as within the city-state the gens relationship was stronger than any other ideology, so in the relationship between individual city-states the feeling of civic solidarity was subordinate to the community of descent — the race, or stock (*syngeneia*). For the Ionians (to which Athenians traced their descent), for the Dorians of Sparta, for the Aeolians — for such basic stocks, the common ancestry took precedence. The antagonism between city-states that did not belong to the same stock was not much different from the conflicts between Greeks and non-Greeks, at least in the early period.

For example, from time immemorial Athens had been struggling against Doric Aegina, the tortoise-shaped island that lay opposite Athens in the Saronic Gulf. Because of its poor soil, this island had become active in trading at an early date; it had been one of the first Greek cities to mint coins (circa 665 B.C.) and its famous *chelonia* (tortoises), so called because of their shape, were accepted in Egypt and even in the Near East. In fact, Egypt was the island's most important market, and Aegina, like other Greek cities, had its own trading port and temple at Naucratis on the Nile Delta. Aegina transported large quantities of silver there, partially in the form of its own coins or of those minted in other centers in northern Greece that had rich sources of this metal; in exchange, Aegina bought grains that Egypt had in abundance. A large part of the island's wealth derived from the redistribution of Egyptian grains to the cities of central Greece. Aegina, a natural ally of Sparta because of its Dorian stock and for reasons of expediency, represented to Athens a rather awesome rival exactly in those sectors of production that the Athenians had tentatively begun to engage in since the time of Solon. The period of greatest conflict between the two Saronic Gulf powers began a short time after Cleisthenes' reforms, when the Athenian entrepreneur class began to make its weight felt. When Darius again menaced Athens and Eritrea (an Attic colony on Euboea) with a newly strengthened army and fleet, after the first Persian expedition had failed because of a storm, one of the first to offer hospitality to the Persians was Aegina (491 B.C.).

And while Athens, aided only by the faithful Plataea, defeated Darius' awe-inspiring army at Marathon in 490 B.C., thanks to the heroism and wisdom of Miltiades, Aegina was building the stupendous Temple of Aphaea (Figure 14). Aphaea was an ancient local goddess; as we shall see when we come to the major sanctuaries, goddesses were generally early divinities, and their preeminent function often dated from a time when society was still matriarchal. Toward the middle of the sixth century, an altar and a small chamber had been dedicated to Aphaea; the ancient dedication was found buried in the terrace on which the temple lay. However, we do not know whether the new edifice was dedicated to the same goddess, as is commonly suggested, or was consecrated to Athena, who stands out in the center of the pediments (and who was associated with a temple that Herodotus mentioned as being on the island).

The form of the artificial terrace created for the temple was conditioned by the shape of the hilltop. The monumental entrance (propylon) was situated, as at Sounion later, on a long side of the sacred enclosure, in axis with the ramp that connected the main front of the temple with the altar. After the tiring ascent up the hill, the worshiper would enter through the propylon and face the southeastern side of the edifice. With the strongly angled vision thus imposed, the columns on the long

Yet some statute of the immortals has made
  this seagirt land also
to strangers from all far places
a wonderful column of safety;
may time, uprolling falter
never in accomplishment of that end.

Since Aiakos it was under stewardship of a
  Dorian people.
That hero Leto's son and Poseidon, wide-
  ranging of mind
in purpose to put a wreath of towers on Ilion,
  called to their aid
for the wall whose doom had been written,
how in the upsurge of war,
in the battle to storm the citadel,
smoke of destruction must blaze its end.

And at its first establishment three pale snakes
writhed aloft that rampart. Two, collapsing
overborne, gave up their lives.
One reared up with a cry.
Apollo, pondering the portent before him,
  spoke:
"Hero, Pergamos shall be taken where your
  hands have wrought.
So speaks to me this vision sent
by Kronos' deep-thundering son, even Zeus.

Nor without help of your children after you; it
  shall be broken
in the first and fourth generation."

                        PINDAR: *Olympia 8* (25–26)

*Aegina: Plan of the sacred enclosure and the Temple
of Aphaea*
  1 *Eastern peribolus*
  2 *Fifth-century altar*
  3 *Priests' habitations*
  4 *Portico*
  5 *Sixth-century altar*
  6 *Foundation*
  7 *Sixth-century propylaea*
  8 *Foundation*
  9 *Cistern*
 10 *Seventh-century altar*
 11 *Access ramp*
 12 *Fifth-century propylaea*
 13 *Seventh-century peribolus*
 14 *Terrace wall*
 15 *Archaic circular construction*

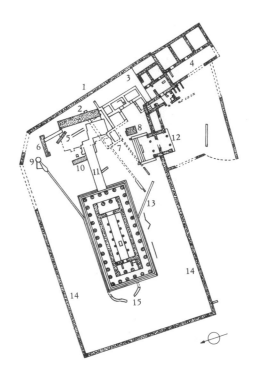

16. Aegina: This figure of a fallen warrior occupied the left corner of the east (the more recent) pediment of the Temple of Aphaea. Although the sculptures represented episodes from the Trojan War, they were understood to symbolize the Greek's struggles with the Persians. (Glyptothek, Munich)

sides, slightly closer to one another, made the edifice seem longer than it actually was, with only twelve columns on the side. Proceeding from the propylon toward the temple, one reached the ramp that led to the altar, seeing more and more of the main, or eastern, end, with its clearly articulated structure. The accentuated tapering of the upper third of the slender columns made the narrow entablature even lighter; the columns were set at quite some distance from one another, and the prevalence of space over height in the peristyle emphasized the difference in quality between the peristyle and the closed-off walls of the sekos. The plan of the edifice is based on elementary designs, and there was nothing accidental in its structure, as is demonstrated, for example, by the perfect cadence of the joints in the various stones of the stylobate. The architectural organism was no longer merely the sum of the elements set near one another. It lived in the space that surrounded it, and itself determined its own space, even if the contrasts between space and volume, between the supporting and the horizontal elements, tended to balance off themselves. The end result was a kind of agitated stasis.

Once through the long pronaos, which clearly marked off the principal end from the western end, one entered the naos. Divided into three naves with two rows of Doric columns in two succeeding ranks, this room's design revealed the search for interior space that still remained unrelated to the exterior space of the temple. From an architectural point of view, the temple can be compared to late archaic edifices, such as the Temple of Ceres at Paestum, Italy, or the one dedicated to Herakles at Agrigento, Sicily; both have, for example, the same rather slender type of columns. At Aegina, though, the style of the sculptured decorations leads us to set the date for the temple at about the time of the battle of Marathon.

Marathon did not help to end the strife between the gens within Athens itself; it was said that the Alcmaeonidae had betrayed Athens right after the battle by signaling to the Persians to attack the undefended city. Miltiades himself was sent into exile because of the accusations made by Xanthippus, the father of Pericles and a member of the Buzyges and Alcmaeon families. When Xerxes, Darius' successor, planned a new expedition against Greece, the Delphic Oracle also acted in the Persians' favor by advising the Greek cities not to intervene. However, at a meeting in Hellenion in 481 B.C., the Greeks were able for a short time to forget the rivalry that existed among them. So it was that at the naval battle of Salamis (480 B.C.), the people of Aegina fought side by side with the Athenians, even occupying the most exposed position. This temporary unity, which ended as soon as the Persian threat was thwarted, did not have any appreciable political consequences, even though it did have a profound effect on the conscience of the Greeks.

Perhaps it was during the struggle with Xerxes that the east pediment of the temple on Aegina was damaged and had to be replaced. In any case, the older sculptured pieces were set up in front of the temple as a commemoration of the events of the time. (So it is that the west pediment is ten years older than the east pediment.) Quite in keeping with the traditions we have described, in which the dominating element was the peculiarity of the gens and the polis, the myths chosen for the pediment decoration exalted the heroes of the Aegina, almost as if to set the glorious history of the island against the one boasted of by its rival, Athens. This intention was more clearly marked in the older pediment; in the more recent one, which followed in the wake of the battle of Salamis, it was more subtle and subdued. Unfortunately we do not know to what extent the new east pediment preserved or altered this theme with regard to the preceding version.

On the west front, there was represented an episode set in Troy, but not one connected with the expedition of all the Greeks with the purpose of bringing back Menelaus' unfaithful wife; rather, it treats the feat of Herakles and Telamon, the son of Aeacus and hero of Aegina, against the Trojan king, Laomedon. Herakles, shooting arrows from a kneeling position, in his splendid armor and his lion's skin headdress, was set near a corner of the relief in order to leave the place of honor, next to Athena, to Aegina's hero, Telamon. Meanwhile, on the east pediment was represented the most famous Trojan episode, the one that united all the Greeks against the Trojans of Priam. However, here too at Athena's side was Ajax, Telamon's son and a hero from Salamis who fought alongside Odysseus in order to conquer Achilles' weapons. And even Achilles was associated with Aegina, for he was the son of Telamon's brother, Peleus.

In this east pediment, the more recent of the two, the rhythmic poses of the figures are distinquished by a stressful torsion. Yet the form of the bodies is softened, colored by a less definable chiaroscuro, which renders the skin more vibrant. Particularly remarkable is the Olympian expression of the glance, which seems to have dimmed under the veil of a sorrowful humanity (Figure 16). In the west pediment, the figures appear to be embossed and highlighted on different planes; this is to be seen not only in the powerful chests but even in the facial planes (Figure 15). The same love for sharp contrasts characterizes the movements and the poses of the slain. The stylistic differences between the two pediments of the Temple of Aphaea do not derive merely from their slight

There is no city so barbarian or backward of
    speech
it knows nothing of the heroic fame of Peleus,
    the blessed son-in-law of the gods,

no city that knows not of Telamonian Aias
and his father. Alkmana's son, on his way by
    ship
to battle loud in bronze at Troy, a trial of
    fighters, took as a fain helper
Telamon with the men of Tiryns, to bring
vengeance upon Laomedon for his deceptions.
He took the city of Pergamum, and in the same
    hero's company smote
the hosts of the Meropes and the oxherd
    mountain-high,
Alkyoneus, encountered in the Phlegraian
    Fields. The hand
of Herakles spared not the deep-voiced

bowstring. First summoning Aiakides
to the venture, he came on the young men at
    their feasting.
Strong Telamon saw him standing in the lion's
    skin, called in invitation
Amphitryoniadas of the heavy spear
to begin the outpouring of nectar, and put in
    his hands
a wine goblet cut in shuddering gold.
Herakles, lifting into the sky his invincible
    arms,
spoke aloud: "If ever before, Zeus my father,
you have been moved to listen kindly to prayer
    of mine,

"now, in divine supplication,
I entreat you, give this man by Eriboia a brave
    son
to be my guest and friend, and a destined man.
Grant him strength unbreakable like this beast
    hide that is wrapped about me,
this skin of a lion that, first of all my labors,
I killed at Nemea long ago.
Let his heart be such also." As he spoke the god
    sent
the lord of birds, a great eagle; and sweet de-
    light troubled his heart within,

and he spoke aloud, as if he had been a seer:
"You shall have the child you ask for, my
    Telamon.
For the bird that showed him forth, call him
    mighty Aias, to be
in the tumult of armies a man of terror."
He spoke, and sat at their table.

PINDAR: *Isthmia 6* (24–56)

chronological differences, but more likely from the diverse temperaments of the two masters who conceived them.

Aegina had a great sculptural tradition; the island was especially famous for its bronze sculptors, and the sculptures of the temple pediments show the effects of this tradition. This may be seen in the very conception of the figures as fully rounded statues, carefully finished even on the side not visible to the onlooker. Many accessory parts were added in metal, such as tufts of hair and elements of armor, which must have made a vivid contrast with the Paros marble, although even this was probably painted. But it cannot be said that these were bronze works translated into marble; it might be said, rather, that the very language of this Peloponnesian style, when pushed to its limits, required a means of working marble similar to the techniques used in working bronze.

Great Sanctuaries: Olympia and Greece

For the ancient Greek tribes, the need to reassert their relationships with other tribes of the same stock was satisfied by periodic gatherings in a common sanctuary. On these occasions, rivalries and wars were held in abeyance by a sacred truce, and each group, and each member of a group, could assemble in a holy site in perfect tranquility. As was natural in a society based on an agricultural economy, the gathering took place when the season allowed a break in the farm work. For example, at Olympia the athletic events were held "at a time when the thistle blooms, and the warm cicada sitting on a tree utters his sharp song, without interruption, from under his wings, in the season of fading summer." This was the period between the harvest and the vintage when even the indefatigable Hesiod could then go on to advise the farmer: "Well, at this point you can find the shade of a rock and some resinated wine."

The religious aspects of these gatherings at sanctuaries was preeminent and served the important purpose of binding the stock to its heritage. But the festivities at the same time represented the occasion for the exchange of the surplus produced by the various groups, at first in the form of reciprocal gifts that one was obliged to make, and then later in the form of buying and selling. In the gift economy, typical of a society in which family ties were still the basis of economic relations, a competitive element was intimately linked with this exchange. Essentially, as anthropologists have pointed out, there is a contest to show who is the richest and most lavish in his generosity: underneath lies the principle of antagonism and rivalry. The meetings between clans and tribes thus provided an occasion to give vent to the competitive impulse in a more idealized situation. This explains the formal pairing, which may at first seem strange to the modern mentality, of athletic events with the great religious centers in ancient Greece. This peculiar character of Greek religious life had its roots in a type of socioeconomic formation in which the family structures, the gens loyalties, and the tribal solidarity were still the determining factors. Even in the classical age, Pindar's odes continued to recall how the national character of the Olympics was emphasized with pride. At the same time, victory meant prestige and social dignity, whether for an ancient tribal chief and his clan or for a man like Hieron, the tyrant of Syracuse celebrated for his victories by Pindar.

The Alphaeus River Valley, green and level, cuts crosswise through the mountainous countryside of Elis in the northwestern Peloponnesos. At the center of the valley, under Mount Kronion, where the Alphaeus and the Kladeos rivers join, there grew up (perhaps starting in the late Bronze Age) an important sanctuary (Figure 17) called Altis by the ancients, but more generally known as Olympia.

It is difficult, at the level of archaeological documentation, to grasp the features of the earliest period of Olympia. The population of Elis — known as Eleans — appears to have been divided into many

Following pages:
17. Olympia: The sanctuary of Altis, in the plain where the Kladeos and Alphaeus rivers flow together; the Alphaeus is in the background, while Mount Kronion is on the left. The two columns rising above the trees (about midpoint, left) belong to the Temple of Hera; the colonnade in the foreground is the Palestra, part of the gymnasium dating to the third century B.C.

groups of diverse origins. It seems that the most ancient people were the Pisaeans who lived on the northern bank of the Alphaeus. Strabo mentions eight cities of the Pisaeans, and the town of Pisa was probably the head of this league of village communities; perhaps the sanctuary that was to become the great Panhellenic shrine was originally the religious center of this small league. Meanwhile, to the north of the Alphaeus lived the Eleans and the Epeians, Dorians from Aetolia; to the south of the river were the Phyllians from Thessaly. This complex ethnic situation was reflected in the characteristics of the cults practiced at Olympia. The most ancient religious element still bears the marks of a matriarchal society; the goddesses prevailed here — Gaea, Hera, Hippodameia. Perhaps with the arrival of the Doric element these goddesses were overshadowed by Zeus, even if at the outset there was only one statue of the god (and that in the Temple of Hera) and one altar dedicated to him.

Originally the most important divinity was Hippodameia ("the horse-tamer"), whose name was reflected in the Hera Hippia venerated at Olympia. Legend said that Hippodameia was loved by her father Oenomaos, Sterope's husband; Oenomaos, king of Pisa, wanted to prevent his daughter from marrying and had established the condition that her suitors would have to defeat him in a chariot race. The suitor had to take his place in a chariot with Hippodameia at his side; and if he did not win the race, he would pay for his boldness with his life. Twelve or thirteen suitors had met this grim fate when Pelops arrived on the scene. The son of Tantalus, Pelops was loved by the sea god Poseidon and had obtained from this god a chariot drawn by two winged horses. With the complicity of Oenomaos' charioteer, Myrtilus, Pelops managed to win the race and thus became Hippodameia's husband. Oenomaos and Myrtilus were both killed, the former because his unfaithful charioteer had replaced the lynchpins of the chariot's wheels with some made of wax. Myrtilus himself died because he expected as his reward for this treachery the right to pass the wedding night with Hippodameia, whom he had secretly loved for some time.

Hippodameia was venerated in the Hippodameion, an almost inaccessible edifice; only once a year was access allowed to the sixteen women who, at every Olympic Games season, wove a new robe for the goddess Hera. Hippodameia was particularly associated with the competition that was to make the sanctuary famous throughout the Greek world — namely, the foot race of the virgins. With the coming of the Dorians, however, Hippodameia and her consort Pelops were cast into relative obscurity by the two great Olympic gods, Hera and Zeus. A legend also grew up that attributed the creation of the Olympic Games to Herakles, the hero so beloved by the Dorians. Herakles was supposed to

18. **Olympia: The Temple of Hera.** Originally this temple had a wooden entablature and columns; the walls, set on a row of vertical stone slabs, were made of bricks. The replacement of the wooden columns by stone ones began about 600 B.C. and was not entirely completed when Pausanias visited the sanctuary in A.D. 176.

PELOPS AND OENOMAOS

Son of Tantalus, against older men I will say
that when your father summoned the gods
to that stateliest feast at beloved Sipylos,
and gave them to eat and received in turn,
then he of the shining trident caught you up,

his heart to desire broken, and with his horses
    and car of gold
carried you up to the house of Zeus and his
    wide honor. . . .
And when at the time of life's blossoming
the first beard came to darken his cheek,
he thought on winning a bride ready at hand,

Hippodameia, the glorious daughter of a king
    of Pisa.
He walked alone in the darkness by the gray
    sea,
invoking the lord of the heavy trident,
and he appeared clear at his feet.
He spoke: "Look you, Poseidon, if you have
    had any joy of my love
and the Kyprian's sweet gifts, block the brazen
    spear
of Oenomaos, and give me the fleeter chariot
by Elis' river, and clothe me about in strength.
Thirteen suitors he has killed now, and ever
puts aside the marriage of his daughter.

The great danger never descends upon a man
    without strength;
but if we are destined to die, why should one sit
to no purpose in darkness and find a nameless
    old age
without any part of glory his own? So my way
lies this hazard; yours to accomplish the end."
He spoke, with words not wide of the mark.
The god, increasing his fame, gave him
a golden chariot and horses never weary with
    wings.

Breaking the strength of Oenomaos, he took
    the maiden and brought her to bed.
She bore him six sons, lords of the people, blazing in valor.
Now he lies at the Alpheus
crossing, mixed with the mighty dead.

PINDAR: *Olympia 1* (36–42, 67–101)

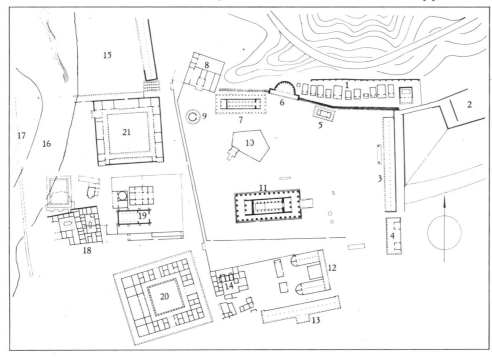

Olympia: Plan of the sanctuary of Altis and surrounding structures
  1 *Terrace of the treasuries*
  2 *Stadium*
  3 *Echo Portico*
  4 *Southeast edifice (Hellanodikeion)*
  5 *Metroon*
  6 *Exhedra Herodes Atticus*
  7 *Temple of Hera*
  8 *Prytaneum*
  9 *Philippeion*
 10 *Pelopion*
 11 *Temple of Zeus*
 12 *Bouleuterion*
 13 *South portico*
 14 *South baths*
 15 *Gymnasium*
 16 *Kladeos River*
 17 *Ancient boundary wall*
 18 *Roman hospitium*
 19 *Phidias' workshop*
 20 *Leonidaion*
 21 *Palestra*

have planted the sacred olive tree, brought back from the land of the Hyperboreans at the extreme north of the earth; leaves from this tree were then used to crown the winners of the various events. Because of the influence of the great center of the Zeus cult — the sanctuary at Dodona in Epirus — Zeus now uttered oracles at Olympia as well, although this aspect of the cult never attained primary importance.

When the first known list of winners was made, from 776 B.C. on, the sanctuary at Altis, although in the hands of the Pisaeans, proved to be the meeting place of the Dorian peoples. Soon there were winners from Corinth, Megara, and Sicyon; from 716 to 580 B.C., the Spartans prevailed. About 580 B.C., the Eleans are thought to have won a decisive victory over the Pisaeans. Certainly, by 471 B.C. the people of the city of Elis, with the help of Sparta, took over control of the sanctuary from Pisa. The once leading city of Pisa was destroyed, and Elis, taking its cue from Sparta, established a constitutional oligarchy that controlled Olympia. The sanctuary by this time had assumed Panhellenic dimensions and — allowing for that particularism that distinguished the policy of the various city-states represented — together with the other sacred sites all over the ancient Greek world, provided the tangible signs of the unity of race and culture that linked the Hellenes.

Among the peoples that dedicated little temples used to house the votive gifts, structures known as treasuries (*thesauroi*), the cities of Peloponnesian extraction were definitely in the majority. Leading these were Megara, Sicyon, and the colonies of the western Peloponnesian cities: Byzantium, Epidamnus, Selinos. Then followed the Achaean colonies in Magna Graecia, or southern Italy: Metaponto and Sybaris; and finally the Sicilian colonies, Syracuse and Gela. Yet despite its great prestige, Olympia never played a political and diplomatic role comparable to that of Delphi. It became rich from those tyrants who intended to use the benevolence of the gods to legitimize their personal power in the eyes of the Greeks. The case of Cypselus, the tyrant of Corinth, was typical: according to one tradition, he had vowed before rising to power that he would consecrate to Zeus the patrimony of the Corinthians. The legend was surely believed by the aristocrats, who would have preferred a tyrant less devout and more indulgent with their interests. And yet Cypselus was truly lavish when it came to the sanctuary at Olympia, where he dedicated a gold statue and the celebrated gold and ivory ark, famous as a masterpiece of archaic Greek art.

The most ancient phase of the sanctuary may be viewed by tracing the history of the Temple of Hera (Figure 18). The elongated foundation consisted of only two steps; the widely spaced columns presuppose a wooden entablature, even if it had a Doric frieze composed of triglyphs and metopes. Differing from one another in diameter, structure, and profile, these columns were erected over a range of time that started about 600 B.C. — the date of the foundation of the temple — and continued into the Hellenistic age. This is made evident by an examination of the capitals, some of which had a large, swelling echinus, as was typical of the high archaic period; others had a profile that grew more rigid and "steeper" with the approach of the Hellenistic age. The older capitals had an astragal, or small molding, of hanging bronze leaves such as was found at Corfu and Paestum (although by this time the astragal was engraved onto the capital). Originally the peristyle was made of wooden columns, and these were replaced by stone columns as decay made a change inevitable. (Pausanias, visiting Olympia in the second century A.D., managed to see the last of these wooden columns in the opisthodomos of the temple.) In this tenacious desire for conservation there was perhaps a residue of that primitive religiosity that could identify the wooden column with the ancient cult image of the god. For example, it has been suggested that the column that Pausanas recognized as the last remains of the house of Oenomaos, held together by metal strips and protected by a canopy, might have represented the ancient image of Zeus. However, perhaps the preservation of the primitive structures was due only to the veneration of this most ancient and sacred place of worship. Such conservation extends to the other parts of the temple; thus the upper part of the

19. Olympia: Head of Hera, double-life-size and made of a local limestone. This cult statue of the goddess on her throne, with her head wrapped in a band over a crown of leaves, was beside one of Zeus wearing a helmet. The sculpture dates from the time when the temple was being built, around 600 B.C. (Olympia Museum)

Page 50:
20. Olympia: A Centaur seizes a Lapith, from the west pediment of the Temple of Zeus. The dramatic intensity of the figure does not affect the composure of the face, but is expressed entirely through the composition, as by the inclination of the head in relation to the rectangle formed by the arms. (Olympia Museum)

naos was made of crude bricks, set upon a base of vertical stone slabs. The naos had two rows of columns, alternately made up of free elements and of supports connected to the walls by means of small transverse walls. The roof was covered with architectural terra-cotta pieces that, with their vivid polychrome paint, marked the only decorative note in the whole edifice.

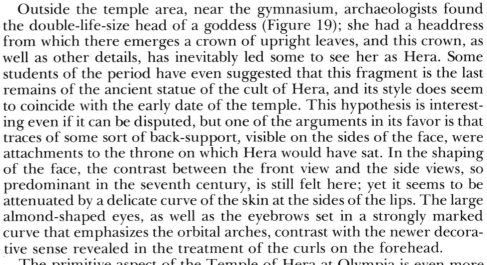

20

Outside the temple area, near the gymnasium, archaeologists found the double-life-size head of a goddess (Figure 19); she had a headdress from which there emerges a crown of upright leaves, and this crown, as well as other details, has inevitably led some to see her as Hera. Some students of the period have even suggested that this fragment is the last remains of the ancient statue of the cult of Hera, and its style does seem to coincide with the early date of the temple. This hypothesis is interesting even if it can be disputed, but one of the arguments in its favor is that traces of some sort of back-support, visible on the sides of the face, were attachments to the throne on which Hera would have sat. In the shaping of the face, the contrast between the front view and the side views, so predominant in the seventh century, is still felt here; yet it seems to be attenuated by a delicate curve of the skin at the sides of the lips. The large almond-shaped eyes, as well as the eyebrows set in a strongly marked curve that emphasizes the orbital arches, contrast with the newer decorative sense revealed in the treatment of the curls on the forehead.

The primitive aspect of the Temple of Hera at Olympia is even more surprising if we consider that it was almost contemporaneous with the Temple of Artemis at Corfu, in which the Doric stone architecture had already achieved a high level of elaboration. On the other hand, until the time of the construction of the Temple of Zeus, Olympia did not have a monumental character. In the sixth century, besides the Temple of Hera, the sanctuary included the pentagonal enclosure of the Pelopion (claimed as the tomb of Pelops), the Hippodameion, the altar of Zeus (not all of which have yet been positively identified), several treasuries, the stadium, and the administrative buildings.

In the sixth century, the stadium consisted merely of a track with earthen slopes for the spectators. At that time it was a part of the sanctuary area (that is, it was west of its final location) and the finish line was situated near the altar of Zeus. The trophies, especially the weapons from war booty, which were dedicated to the gods, were displayed on the earth steps of the stadium. This explains the abundance of finds during the recent excavations there, and in particular the great number of helmets. Among those deserving special mention are ones dedicated by Hieron of Syracuse, following the victory over the Etruscans at Cumae in 474 B.C. Adjacent to the ancient enclosure wall, but just outside it, were the Prytaneum and the Bouleuterion, used to house the functionaries who administered the sanctuary. The Prytaneum also contained the altar of Hestia, from which they obtained the sacred fire for the altars; here, too, the distinguished quests and the winners of the contests were received.

During the archaic period, Olympia had its own administration, independent from that of the cities that had hegemony over the sanctuary. This situation began to change at the time of the Persian Wars. After the battle of Plataea (479 B.C.), certain citizens of the city of Elis overthrew the oligarchical government, establishing an Athens-type democracy. Themistocles was no stranger to the development of these events; he wanted to take part in the first Olympic Games after the war, and was received by the Eleans with greater enthusiasm than that reserved for the winning athletes. For a moment, the struggle against the Persians seemed to have given political consistency to the Panhellenic ideal. In this outburst of enthusiasm, Olympia was the perfect symbol of recovered unity. Yet this sentiment proved to be full of contradictions and of brief duration; it never really permeated the consciousness of the Greeks, even though the experiences of the Persian Wars profoundly affected their outlook on the world. Still, one tangible sign of that complex of forces that contained the thrust of future Greek history was erected a few decades later at Olympia: the Temple of Zeus.

Olympia's Masterwork: The Temple of Zeus

When the Eleans decided to build the temple for Mount Olympus' sovereign god — until then housed at Olympia in the temple of his wife,

HERAKLES FOUNDS THE SANCTUARY OF ALTIS

But, without striving, few have won joy of victory
to be a light upon their lifetime for all deeds accomplished.
The rights of Zeus are urgent with me to sing that pride of
contests that Herakles by the primeval grave of Pelops

founded sixfold for his labors
when he had slain Poseidon's son,
the perfect fighter, Kteatos,

and slain Eurytos, in will to extract from Augeas
unwilling the mighty price of his lackey-service.
Lurking in ambush under Kleonai, Herakles smote them by the wayside,
since aforetime they had shattered
his following, the men of Tiryns,
as they lay in the deep places of Elis,

these Moliones in their high pride. The king of the Epeians,
treacherous to his very guest-friends, not long thereafter saw his own rich city under stark fire
and the stroke of iron settling into the deep pit of destruction.
No man can fend aside
the onset of stronger men.
Augeas also, at the last, in his fool's counsel
was taken and dragged to the edge of steep death, nor escaped it.

But the strong son of Zeus at Pisa,
gathering together his host and all their spoil,
ordained the grove sacred to his father, and fixed the Altis about in a clean place;
and a level floor circle-wise.
he dedicated to the banquet place,
doing honor to the Alpheus crossing

with the twelve gods who are lords; he named the hill of Kronos. Before this,
under sway of Oinomaos, nameless it had been sunk under deep snow; and at this festival birth
the Fates were attendant, with him
who alone makes apparent
truth and that which things are,

Time. Who in his sweep forward has made plain
the way of the battle gift
and the division Herakles made of his war-spoil, the sacrifice, how he established
with his first Olympiad the five-year festival
and with prizes for games won.

PINDAR: *Olympia 10* (22–59)

Hera — they were celebrating several important events. First and foremost was the foundation of the Confederation of Elis, which took place about 471 B.C., from the union of the little communities of Elis. They were also observing the establishment of democracy, which had seen Elis move away temporarily from its alliance with Sparta in order to draw nearer to Athens, the city-state that still appeared to be the model of democracy. Finally, Elis had reaffirmed its supremacy over the surrounding region, destroying some cities of Triphylia. Gradually of course, the city transferred the administration of the Olympia sanctuary to within its own walls, and this proved to be good business. We need only mention that in 312 B.C. the treasury of the sanctuary at Olympia had reached the sum of fifty silver talents, a large sum in those days.

The Temple of Zeus, erected between 468 and 457 B.C. by the architect Libon of Elis, was one of the largest in Greece, and its powerful colonnade on its high stylobate must have dominated the plain of the Altis. The design codifies in almost canonic form the pattern that will later become part of the classical Doric temple, establishing a close relationship between the axes of the columns and those of the sekos walls, all the while keeping the proportions of the plan and of the upper portions within a single and simple form. In this sense, the temple ends a period of experimentation and elaboration. Only one characteristic remains from the archaic period: the slightly larger diameter of the columns on the shorter ends of the edifice. The interior of the naos was divided by two rows of columns in double series, as was also done at Aegina and Corinth. Unfortunately, the state of this monument today does not allow us to make a stylistic reading; only the surviving sculpture can afford us an image of its beauty.

In the east and west pediments there were, respectively, twenty-one and twenty-two fully rounded statues. In the east pediment, the race between Oenomaos and Pelops was represented, but the recollection of this basic myth in the tradition of Olympia did not aim simply at the exaltation of the local heroes and traditions. Indeed, it should be noted that the sculptures did not reproduce the course of the actual race but the moment that immediately preceded it: the pact made in the presence of Zeus, custodian of vows and oaths. Thus, what these pediment sculptures were intended to exalt was the inviolability of the sacred pact (the *ekecheiria*) of the Greek people. This was the crucial moment of all sacred contests such as those at Olympia; and the heralds sent to the most remote parts of the Greek world to announce the sacred truce for the next Olympic Games, summoned under this sign each city-state and each Greek to this unique and grandiose Panhellenic occasion. And the ancient pact, which had its roots in the most remote tribal tradition, appeared after Salamis to be fraught with totally new meanings.

In the west pediment, the theme of *hybris*, that violent and arrogant pride that the arrows of Apollo guarded against, was a terrible warning to anyone who dared to violate the sacred, if unwritten, laws that regulated the behavior of the good man toward other men and the gods. At the wedding of Pirithous, the Thessalian hero and king of the Lapiths, and his bride Hippodameia (not, however, the Olympic Hippodameia), the Lapiths were enjoying the wedding feast when they were brutally attacked by the Centaurs. These creatures who were half-human, half-horse, were finally unable to conceal their wild nature behind a human face. The Centaurs tried to take the Lapith women away, including Pirithous' bride, but their *hybris* was finally crushed with the aid of Apollo.

We are naturally tempted to note in this west pediment — with its theme of the opposition between civilization and barbarity — the exaltation in a mythical key of the conflict between the Greeks and the Persians, the burning memory of which was still freshly imprinted on the Greek mind. But we must also realize that the choice of subject may well have focused on the Centaurs of Thessaly for yet another purpose; in fact, in the battle at the side of his friend Pirithous appears Theseus, the most famous of Attic heroes and author of the union that established the city-state of Athens. And the figure of Theseus in the framework of the new relations between Elis and Athens (and especially if Themistocles

22. **Olympia: A Lapith woman being abducted by the Centaur Eurytion. Although the expression of emotion of the Olympia pediment groups was essentially based on the composition of each group, they were related by a rhythm that rose to an intense crescendo resolved by the central figure of Apollo. (Olympia Museum)**

HERAKLES AND THE OLIVE OF THE HYPERBOREANS

The wreaths bound over my hair are an influence
to this duty formed in the hands of God,
to mix the lyre's intricate voice, the clamor of flutes, and the set of the words
for Ainesidamos' son the right way; and Pisa bids me speak. From her,
driven of God, songs speed to a man,

over whose locks and brows an upright judge of the Hellenes,
an Aitolian, fulfilling the ordinances of Herakles
anciently founded, has cast
the pale glory of the olive that long ago,
from the shadowy springs of Ister,
Amphitryon's son brought back, to be
the loveliest memorial of the games at Olympia.

By reason he persuaded the Hyperboreans, Apollo's people.
In sincerity of heart he asked, for the grove of Zeus
open to all, that growth to shadow men always and crown their valor.

Before this in his time, when his father's altars were hallowed, at mid-month,
it had cast back the full orb of evening,
riding in gold. He established the sacred test of the fifth-year games
under the magic hanging hills of Alphaeus river.
But the lawn in the valley of Kronian Pelops had blossomed not to the beauty of trees.
He thought the garden, naked of these, must endure the sun's sharp rays.
Then it was the urge took him to journey
to Istrian country. There Leto's daughter, the runner with horses,
received him when he came from Arcadia's ridges and winding gullies,
when, at Eurystheus' command,
the doom of his father had driven him
to bring the doe with the golden horns
that once Taygeta had written in fee
to be sacred to Artemis Orthosia.

On that errand he saw the land at the back of the cold north wind,
and he stood amazed at the trees.
A sweet longing came upon him to plant them at the twelve-lap running place
of horses. Now he visits in graciousness that festival, with the god-like
twins, the children of deep-girdled Leda.

He came to Olympos and left those heroes guidance of the magnificent games,
man's might and the chariot's speed handled.

PINDAR: *Olympia 3* (6–38)

took part in the union of Elis, as has been suggested) must have been full of significance for these ancient Greeks.

Over the entrance to the pronaos and the opisthodomos there were two groups of sculptured metopes, six in each group, all representing the labors of Herakles. As mentioned earlier, according to Doric tradition this hero had been the founder of the contests and certainly merited this place inside the temple. The acroteria were made of bronze; the corner ones consisted of gilded basins on tripods — the ancient world's prize for winners of athletic events. On opposite peaks of the roof were two statues of Nike, holding out the Olympic crown as a promise to the athletes who had come from every part of the Greek world to participate in the Olympic Games. Historic sources do not give us the name of the sculptor who conceived and executed the pediment and metope sculptures at this Temple of Zeus. Paeonios of Mende (in Thrace) is known to have done the statues of Nike for the acroteria, and Pausanias claimed that Paeonios also did the east pediment, while the west pediment sculptures were the

23. Olympia: A metope from the Temple of Zeus representing Herakles taming the Cretan bull. There were two sets of metopes, six in each set, all depicting the cycle of Herakles' twelve labours, as this hero was considered the founder of the Olympic contests. (Olympia Museum)

work of the Athenian Alkamenes; neither attribution has been sustained by modern scholars. The Master of Olympia, whoever he was, was perhaps the greatest Greek sculptor.

When we examine the sculptures themselves, the first thing we may note is that the compact surfaces, devoid of definition, and the essence of the gestures, concede nothing to insistent anatomical analysis (Figure 20). The articulation of the volumes grows out of the interior dynamics of the figures, out of the inexorable linking of these dynamics in the composition. And perhaps exactly this intimate need that links the expression to the form and is intolerant of any unresolved residue, perhaps this was the newest and most unusual element, if the Master of Olympia was Peloponnesian, as is probable. This was the bond that brought his experience close to that of his most worthy heir, Phidias, the master of the Parthenon. On comparison, the analogies between the oldest part of the Parthenon sculptures, the metopes, and the pediments in the Temple of Zeus (Figure 21), are surprisingly apt. And it is only natural to think that the relationship between Phidias and the Panhellenic sanctuary goes back to before the time when, as an exile from Athens, this artist went to Elis to give shape to the Temple of Zeus. One can conclude that the invitation made to Phidias was motivated not only by his great fame but also by the memory of his apprenticeship in the sanctuary under the Master of Olympia. One need only note that in the pediments in the Temple of Zeus, the drapery — generally so essential — curls up in places into bundles of complex folds that capture the shadows or open up into sudden breaks, both devices that occur frequently in the Parthenon sculptures.

In the east pediment of the Temple of Zeus (and it should be admitted that there is some disagreement over the reconstruction of this pediment) the figures, caught in the moment preceding the action, appear concentrated on themselves. The repressed tension is slightly betrayed by the nervous turning of the head, while the glances evince the nature of the secret meaning that brings them together. The central group includes, at the sides of the dominant figure of Zeus, the two couples of the myth: Oenomaos and his wife, Sterope, and Hippodameia and her suitor, Pelops. The five standing figures are set within the frame determined by the two chariots standing ready for the race. The horses of the chariot interrupt the juxtaposition of vertical elements, linking the central group with the figures kneeling, sitting, or lying in the corners of the pediment.

The solemn, static, albeit precarious, nature of the east pediment contrasts with the continuous dynamics that spins off from the middle group of the west pediment, and ends by pervading the entire sculpture. At the sides of the pivotal figure, the imperious Apollo with his arm out-

24. Olympia: The stadium seen from the northwest. What we view today is the third phase of the stadium, with the track moved quite some distance from its original location; it dates from shortly after the middle of the fourth century B.C. The long, slender row of limestone blocks marks the finish line; the distance from this to the starting line is 210 yards.

24

25. Olympia: The Leonidaion, with the Ionic capitals of the colonnade resting on the bases of the columns. The edifice, dedicated and planned by Leonidas of Naxos, son of Leotas, measured 264 feet by 242 feet.

stretched, Theseus and Pirithous are arranged in a wedge-shape, which produces the effect of a subtle torsion. The figures of the two heroes, unfortunately lost for the most part, must have assimilated the lesson derived from the group of Tyrannicides. If we leave aside the figures in the corners, each half of the pediment is articulated in three related groups, the middle one of which is made up of two figures and the remaining ones of three. In each group, the complex crossing of the limbs determines the central pivot points of the composition (Figure 22); and yet the precise linking up of the gestures and of the axes between the various groups melds the ensemble into one dynamic flow. The opposing tensions that arise from the two halves of the pediment are relieved in the center by Apollo's awesome gesture.

Among the twelve metopes representing the labors of Herakles, the one representing the Cretan bull is stylistically closest to the west pediment. Legend had it that this powerful animal had risen out of the waves and that Minos, who had promised to sacrifice to Poseidon whatever emerged from the sea, did not have the courage to kill the beautiful bull. Instead, Minos substituted another bull for the sacrifice, which so enraged Poseidon that he made the original bull go mad. Herakles was ordered by Eurystheus to capture the bull alive. The rolling mass of the bull makes a strong diagonal that dominates the composition (Figure 23). Upon this mass there stands out the body of the hero, which creates an opposite diagonal; he is stretching every muscle in the effort to drag the wild beast with the rope that passes through its nostrils. In this supreme tension, the body of the hero is twisted into an antagonistic structure, consisting of the head turned to the rear, the back arched, and the legs

26. Olympia: The Palestra, a large court surrounded by a Doric colonnade, dating from the third century B.C. On all four sides within the colonnade were small rooms used for athletic exercises, dressing rooms, baths, or reading rooms.

(which have not survived) bent in the direction of the movement. The compact mass of the animal contrasted with the spasm of Herakles' body, with the rhythm of its anatomical structure on which the light remains and breaks up into fragments. The unresolved tension and the same compositional pattern will reappear, in a less exaggerated key, in some of the Parthenon's metopes with the battle of the Centaurs. A new world was born at Olympia, and its newly discovered values and language are intact in these pediment sculptures.

When the exiled Phidias arrived at the sanctuary, he had to rearrange the naos in order to install what the ancient world considered his masterpiece: the colossal gold and ivory statue of Zeus. In this case, too, the model came from Athens, where the same artist had recently finished the gold and ivory statue of Athena Parthenos. The insertion of this colossus in the Temple of Zeus upset the interior space of the naos, and Strabo observed that if Zeus were to stand he would break through the ceiling with his head. Phidias had not been able to overcome the limits set by the existing structures, despite the fact that his workshop (which has also been discovered) reproduced exactly the dimensions of the naos so that the work could be done with the precise knowledge of the conditions of light, setting, and available space. The colossal statue, like the Athena Parthenos, also served as the support for heavy decorative sculpture, which at Olympia extended over onto the surfaces of the throne. On some parts, for example, the Amazon battle of Herakles was represented; this included twenty-nine figures, among which Theseus once again appeared. Herakles, after having fought with Telamon against the Trojan king Laomedon, went with Telamon and Theseus to do battle with the Amazons, the tribe of warrior women said to live at the mouth of the Thermodon River. Herakles' assigned labor was to take away Queen Hippolyte's girdle in order to satisfy the desire of Admete, Eurystheus' daughter, to possess it. Hippolyte agreed to give her girdle to Herakles, but Hera interfered, causing strife and discord because of her old grudge against Herakles; the hero was thus forced to kill the Amazon queen in order to accomplish the labor imposed on him by Eurystheus.

In the fifth century, architectural activity at Olympia was limited basically to the construction of the Temple of Zeus. But the accommodations and popularity of the sanctuary were improved with the building of the western baths and the pool. However, it was in the fourth century that the sanctuary grove began to take on a truly monumental character as a whole. The great Echo Portico was erected, dividing the sacred zone from the stadium (Figure 24), which was moved to the east; to the south of the Bouleuterion, another portico was erected with its colonnaded front lying opposite the sanctuary and blocking its view of the outside. To the west of that portico, near one of the entranceways of the enclosure, the Leonidaion (Figure 25) was built between 330 and 320 B.C.; this edifice took its name from its architect and donor, Leonidas of Naxos. It is a vast, square edifice, surrounded by an arcade with Ionian columns. A wide entranceway, decorated with two rows of Doric columns, led to the interior, composed of four sets of rooms placed around the peristyle of the interior atrium. The Leonidaion was basically a hostelry, used to house important guests and the embassies of the various city-states.

Within the enclosure of the great Panhellenic sanctuary a place was also found for the Philippeion, a small circular structure dedicated by Philip of Macedonia in 338 B.C. to mark his victory over the rest of the Greeks at Chaeronea (although the structure probably was finished by his son, Alexander the Great). The unity of the Hellenes was by that time a reality, but it had been the Macedonian dynasty that had realized it, by force; later it would be maintained by the domination of the Romans. This, however, did not necessarily signify any decadence at the sanctuary of Olympia, which in the third century B.C. became even richer by the addition of a large Palestra (Figure 26) and a gymnasium. Then, after a period of decline, it once again enjoyed its former splendor, if only for a brief period, in the epoch of imperial Rome. Thus did Olympia survive the world that had given birth to it; the games continued until the last Olympics in A.D. 393.

27. Delphi: The sanctuary on the slopes of Mount Parnassos is surmounted by the Phaedriades Rocks and looks out over the Pleistos Gorge. In the distant background, one can glimpse a bit of the sea where the port of Delphi, Khirra, was situated. Clearly visible on the terraces that descend from the Phaedriades Rocks are (highest level) the stadium, the theater, and then the Temple of Apollo.

29

28. Delphi: The theater and the Temple of Apollo seen from the east. The Portico of Attalus lies behind the temple, outside the sacred enclosure. The sites of the most ancient cults were concentrated in the area between the theater and the treasury of the Athenians (seen at left, just below the temple).

29. Delphi: The theater and the Temple of Apollo, viewed from the west and looking down toward the Castalian spring. The rough, mountainous panorama seems to remove this site from the rest of the world and even today evokes the frightening myth about the battle between Apollo and the Python.

GREECE FROM HESIOD TO THUCYDIDES   63

Delphi and the World Beyond

Since classical times, Delphi has been associated in most people's minds with the god Apollo; but by the time Apollo arrived "under snow-capped Parnassos, on the slope facing Zephyrus," Delphi had long taken on a sacred character. On the slope dominated by the Phaedriades Rocks that reflect the sunlight (Figure 27), for instance, a Mycenaean-age cult had a center in the very place where the sanctuary of Athena Pronaia would later rise in the seventh century B.C. Under her temple there, archaeologists found two hundred Mycenaean votive figurines; among these, a goddess with her arms extended is particularly suggestive.

The place where the sanctuary of Apollo stood (Figure 28) was also originally inhabited by a goddess, Gaea — Mother Earth and mother of so many gods. Her sanctuary, south of the Temple of Apollo, dominated a spring that issued from the fissure in the cliff. According to a belief widespread in Mediterranean religion. Gaea appeared here as the goddess-serpent, just as in Minoan Crete a Mother Earth was venerated as the goddess of serpents. The memory of this cult, replaced later by the Apollo cult, survived in the myth narrated in the *Homeric Hymn to Apollo*, a work that goes back to well before 600 B.C. A female dragon — in some sources called the daughter of Gaea — lived in Delphi by a spring. Hera

Hera said; and from the etherial synod broke,
Then smote the earth, and thus indignant spoke —
"O hear me, earth! and heaven's supreme domain!
And hear, ye powers in Tartarus who reign!
Hear, hear me all — and far from Zeus, alone,
O let my womb a potent offspring own:
And in his frame superior strength inspire,
As far as Zeus excell'd his hoary sire,"
She said, and struck — beneath her mighty hand,
From its foundations shook the solid land.
Hera with joy the happy omen bless'd,
And deem'd fulfill'd the wishes of her breast.
A long revolving year she pass'd alone,
Far from the Thunderer's genial bed and throne,

30. **Delphi: Metope from the Sicyonian treasury, representing Castor, Pollux, and Idas with the oxen of Idas and Lynceus. The metope was originally quite long, occupying the entire space between one column and the next — that is, with no triglyph dividing the metopes. (Delphi Museum)**

30

Brooding in silence o'er her deep designs,
Or drinking incense from her votaries'
    shrines —
But when the days and nights fulfill'd appear,
And the swift hours complete the circling year,
A hideous monster to her vows was given,
Unlike to all that breathed in earth or heaven.
Of size immense the vast Typhaon spread,
A dragon fell, of all mankind the dread.
Her awful hands on earth, malignant, place
The dire destroyer of the human race.
Onward he pass'd, dispensing Fate around,
Till the avenger's mighty arm he found:
Immortal Apollo, from his silver bow
Launch'd the keen shaft that laid the monster
    low;
Writhing in death he rolls, while hideous cries
And roars tremendous shake the vaulted skies,
Till pouring forth his life in crimson tide,
Exulting Apollo speaks with conscious pride
— "On earth's maternal bosom here remain,
Once the dire terror of her filial train,
Living no more the pious race to awe,
Who to my shrines the frequent victim draw.
Typhoeus' might, and dark Chimaera's power,
Were weak to avert the inevitable hour;
Here sable earth and Hyperion's ray
Shall bid the putrifying corse decay." Thus
    with triumphant voice the god exclaim'd!
The baleful serpent hence was Pytho named:
And hence the bards, to Apollo's praise who
    sing,
Hail him, in votive verse, the Pythian king.
Then found he that the nymph, whose cares
    preside
O'er fair Delphusa's silver-flowing tide,
Had with fallacious words deceived his breast,
And wrathful thus the goddess he address'd
— "No more thy arts my purpose shall
    elude,
No more these pleasant seats and crystal flood,
Sacred to thee alone, shall honor claim;
Lo, I partake the pleasure and the fame!"
    Thus spoke the god; and from the
    mountain's side
Hurl'd a vast rock across the hidden tide,
While near the gliding stream a choral train
Tend, mid embowering shades, his sacred
    fane;
And while Delphusa's waves are veil'd in
    shame,
Hail, great Apollo, by Delphusius' name!

Hymn to Pythian Apollo (277–309, 355–374)

DELPHI AT THE RISING OF THE SUN

Look, now the sun's burning chariot comes
Casting his light on the earth.
Banned by his flame, the stars flee
To the awful darkness of space.
The untrodden peaks of Parnassos,
Kindling to flame, receive for mankind
The disk of the day.
    The smoke of unwatered myrrh drifts
To the top of the temple.
The Delphian priestess sits on the
Sacred tripod chanting to the Greeks
Echoes of Apollo's voice.
You Delphians, attendants of Phoebus,
Go down to Castalia's silvery eddies:
When you have bathed in its holy dews,
Return to the temple.

EURIPIDES: *Ion* (82–97)

Page 66:
31. Delphi: This figure of a warrior is from
the frieze along the east, or back end, of the
treasury of Syphnos; the warrior may represent Aeneas helping Hector in his duel with
Menelaus, as narrated in the *Iliad*. (Delphi
Museum)

entrusted her with the upbringing of her son Python, identified in the
Homeric Hymn with Typhon, or Typhoeus, a fierce, cruel being unlike
either men or gods. Apollo eventually killed him with his arrows and let
the black Gaea (the earth, that is) and the shining Hyperion (the sun)
make the body rot *(pythein):* hence the name given to the god, Pythian
Apollo, as well as to the monster. In the dragoness it is easy to recognize
Gaea, the mother of all, where everything is hidden and from whom
nothing can be hidden and who was therefore an oracular divinity. She
was the expression of a matriarchal society, one that existed prior to the
Achaean and Dorian invasions. Apollo killed her to rule the place, yet the
serpent remained a symbol closely connected with the Delphic oracle.
Hence the need to create, alongside the ancient dragoness who was the
god's enemy, another monstrous being who no longer had any female
associations. In the *Homeric Hymn*, Typhon-Typhoeus has a somewhat
confused and vague role; other sources eliminate the dragoness and
speak of only Python, the son of Gaea. But in any case, the passage of
power from Gaea to Apollo marked the triumph of a patriarchal concept,
probably imported from the Dorians, over the matriarchal organization
typical of the earlier stages of Mediterranean civilization.

Homer mentioned a temple of Apollo at Delphi, but tradition tells us
that it was made of perishable materials. But by the second half of the
seventh century, the oracle had already reached a noteworthy level of
political power, and its fame was spreading all over the Greek world. An
echo of this was evoked by the words that the author of the *Homeric Hymn*
attributed to Apollo: "Here I have decided to build a lovely temple that
shall be an oracle for the men who will always bring me great sacrifices;
those who possess the rich Peloponnesos and those in Europe and in the
islands in every part of the sea will come to me to question the oracle."

As we have seen earlier, Corinth, located on the crossroads of important land and sea routes, showed an early interest in trade. Within the
framework of relations with the Greek colonies to the west — specifically
those in southern Italy and Sicily — control of the sanctuary at Delphi
was an important weapon. In fact the oracle of Apollo played a decisive
role in the coordination of the colonial movement. At the beginning of
the colonizing period — say, about 750 B.C. — the West represented for
most Greeks an almost unknown world. But in the sanctuary at Delphi
the experiences of the Corinthian and Euboean sailors were deposited,
accumulated during the course of the earliest voyages made for the purpose of trading with the indigenous populations and acquiring the metals
that came from such places as Etruria, the central region of Italy. In this
way, the oracle was able to coordinate the colonial movement, telling the
adventurers going to the West where to found their new cities. Ancient
sources hand down the text of the oracles given to the founders of
Rhegium, Croton, and Tarentum, and even if we may doubt the reliabil-
ity of these texts, they still are a precious indication of the role played by
the sanctuary of Delphi in that period.

On an ideological level, the support of the sanctuary of Apollo at
Delphi was essential in order to legitimize a position of power not yet
consolidated. This aspect is clearly seen in certain moments of Greek
history. For example, Cypselus, son of Labda (a Bacchidae) and Eetion,
and tyrant of Corinth from 657 B.C. on, consolidated his power by nar-
rating two oracles of Apollo. One had purportedly been handed down to
Labda: in this, he was designated the restorer of justice in the city; the
other oracle pronounced the impending defeat of the Bacchidae. In any
case, it was Cypselus who erected the oldest of the treasuries in the
sanctuary at Delphi, which during his rule began to change from a simple
oracular site into an important architectural complex. Thus in the
polygonal sacred enclosure built at the end of the eighth century B.C.,
the first Temple of Apollo was constructed between 680 and 640 B.C.,
the work of two legendary architects, Trophonius and Agamedes.

The decisive turn in the life of the sanctuary was determined by the
first so-called Sacred War (595–586 B.C.), when the Delphi region became part of the federation of the twelve tribes of northeastern Greece,
administered by the Amphictionic League and extending over a vast

The other division took guides, and proceeded towards the temple of Delphi, keeping Mount Parnassos on their right hand. They too laid waste such parts of Phocis as they passed through, burning the city of the Panopeans, together with those of the Daulians and of the Aeolidae. This body had been detached from the rest of the army, and made to march in this direction, for the purpose of plundering the Delphian temple and conveying to King (Xerxes the riches which were there laid up. For) Xerxes, as I am informed, was better acquainted with what there was worthy of note at Delphi, than even with what he had left in his own house; so many of those about him were continually describing the treasures — more especially the offerings made by Croesus the son of Alyattes.

Now when the Delphians heard what danger they were in, great fear fell on them. In their terror they consulted the oracle concerning the holy treasures, and inquired if they should bury them in the ground, or carry them away to some other country. The god, in reply, bade them leave the treasures untouched — "He was able," he said, "without help to protect his own." So the Delphians, when they received this answer, began to think about saving themselves. And first of all they sent their women and children across the gulf into Achaea; after which the greater number of them climbed up into the tops of Parnassos, and placed their goods for safety in the Corycian cave; while some effected their escape to Amphissa in Locris. In this way all the Delphians quitted the city, except sixty men, and the Prophet.

When the barbarian assailants drew near and were in sight of the place, the Prophet, who was named Aceratus, beheld, in front of the temple, a portion of the sacred armor, which it was not lawful for any mortal hand to touch, lying upon the ground, removed from the inner shrine where it was wont to hang. Then went he and told the prodigy to the Delphians who had remained behind. Meanwhile the enemy pressed forward briskly, and had reached the shrine of Athena Pronaia, when they were overtaken by other prodigies still more wonderful than the first. Truly it was marvel enough, when war-like harness was seen lying outside the temple, removed there by no power but its own; what followed, however, exceeded in strangeness all prodigies that had ever before been seen. The barbarians had just reached in their advance the chapel of Athena Pronaia, when a storm of thunder burst suddenly over their heads — at the same time two crags split off from Mount Parnassos, and rolled down upon them with a loud noise, crushing vast numbers beneath their weight — while from the temple of Athena there went up the war cry and the shout of victory.

All these things together struck terror into the barbarians, who forthwith turned and fled. The Delphians, seeing this, came down from their hiding places, and smote them with a great slaughter, from which such as escaped fled straight into Boeotia. These men, on their return, declared, as I am told, that besides the marvels mentioned above, they witnessed also other supernatural sights. Two armed warriors, they said, of a stature more than human, pursued after their flying ranks, pressing them close and slaying them.

These men, the Delphians maintain, were two Heroes belonging to the place — by name Phylacus and Autonous — each of whom has a sacred precinct near the temple; one, that of Phylacus, hard by the road which runs above the temple of Pronaia; the other, that of Autonous, near the Castalian spring, at the foot of the peak called Hyampeia. The blocks of stone which fell from Parnassos might still be seen in my day; they lay in the precinct of Pronaia, where they stopped, after rolling through the host of the barbarians. Thus was this body of men forced to retire from the temple.

HERODOTUS: *History* (VII: 35–39)

territory from Thessaly to Phocis (the Delphi region) and to Boeotia. In 595 B.C., the Amphictionic League intervened, with the help of Athens and Sicyon, in order to defend Delphi from the ambitious designs of the city of Krissa, which was near the sanctuary and could control the approaches from the northeast and — with its seaport — from the coast. In commemoration of the victory, the Amphictionic League instituted the first Pythian Games, modeled after those at Olympia. Delphi, however, did not become the capital of the League; this honor remained with Anthela, near Thermopylae, and its sanctuary of Demeter.

After the Sacred War, the treasuries at Delphi multiplied rapidly; at least fifteen such edifices were built between 586 and 548 B.C., and some of them were genuine masterpieces of stone architecture. The dedicating cities were scattered all over the Greek world from Asia to the West, among the most famous being Sicyon, Megara, Athens, Cnidos, Clazomenos, Syphnos, and Massalia (Marseilles). The first Sicyonian treasury was built about 580 B.C., probably by the tyrant Cleisthenes of Sicyon, the maternal grandfather of the Athenian statesman of that name. A few years before, Cleisthenes of Sicyon had sanctioned the friendship with the Athenian gens of the Alcmaeonidae by means of the marriage between his daughter Agariste to Megacles. Athens and Sicyon had been the only city-states — at least of those having no direct interest in the matter — that had intervened in favor of Delphi in the recently ended Sacred War. Thus the construction of the treasury was the tangible sign of the bind that connected the tyrant Cleisthenes and his gens, the Orthagoradae, to Apollo at Delphi.

The architectural remains that were utilized in the foundation of the later Sicyonian treasury, built about 500 B.C., are usually attributed to the first Sicyonian treasury (or, by some scholars, to a treasury of Syracuse). The newer edifice was a prostyle tetrastyle, with four columns on the front and two on the sides. The frieze was unusual, with triglyphs only on the axis of the columns while those in the center of the intercolumniations were lacking. The metopes, therefore, were in an elongated form, and were without a doubt the most important elements in the monument. The metope sculptures represent, among other things, myths that were unusual subjects for such important art of the time.

At least two of the reliefs dealt with myths crucial to the Aeolian race: the one with Phrixis and Helle who flew on the ram with the golden fleece toward Colchis on the Black Sea; the other with the Argonauts, led by Jason, who set off for that distant land in order to bring the golden fleece back to Pelias, the king of Iolkos. Pelias was the half-brother of Aeson, the father of Jason, and both of them belonged to Phrixis' stock. Pelias was the son of the princess of Tyro by Poseidon, whereas Aeson was her son by Cretheus. Jason had been brought up by the wise centaur Chiron in his grotto overlooking the city of Iolkos. When he was twenty, Jason went down to Iolkos to demand the throne that Pelias had usurped from Aeson. Pelias had been warned to beware of a man who would arrive wearing only one sandal, as this man would kill him. And Jason did indeed arrive on the scene with only one sandal; he had lost the other while crossing a river with Hera. Alarmed, Pelias decided to get rid of the hero by urging him to bring back the golden fleece of the ram that had taken Phrixis over to Colchis. Heroes from all over Greece — Herakles, the Dioscuri, Orpheus, and others — took part in the expedition, which set sail on the *Argo* ("the swift") for Colchis, at the far end of the Black Sea. After many vicissitudes, the ship reached its destination, but two obstacles still lay between the Argonauts and the golden fleece: the terrible dragon that watched over it, and the tests and traps devised by King Aeetes. However, his daughter Medea, who had fallen in love with Jason, helped him with her magical powers. Jason was thus able to return with both the golden fleece and Medea to Iolkos. There Medea the enchantress avenged her husband's wrongs by persuading Pelias' daughters to cut the king to pieces, with the promise that in this way she would be able to rejuvenate him. This story in the metopes of the Sicyonian treasury was an evocative allusion to the decisive role played by the Delphic Oracle in the first adventures of Greek ships bound for unknown destinations. The golden fleece that the Argonauts went to gain on the edge of the

Caucasus certainly symbolized the memory of the first voyages through the Dardanelles in search of metals in Asia. The Oracle of Apollo played a crucial part in this affair: Pelias had heard of his impending death at the hands of one of the descendants of Aeolus from the Delphic Oracle, "uttered near the *omphalos* that marks the center of the mother earth covered with woods," as Pindar described the site. And the Argonauts' journey itself was also suggested to them by a Delphic Oracle.

The conception of the metope with the Argonauts was particularly bold. In the center, between the Dioscuri (Castor and Pollux) on horseback, lies the hull of the *Argo;* on it are Orpheus and another singer playing the lyre. Unfortunately, this relief is not in very good condition. But we can appreciate the high stylistic level of the other metope (Figure 30), with the Dioscuri stealing the cattle from Lynceus and Idas. The background is taken up by the cattle arranged in groups; their hooves, slightly staggered, are arranged as a repetition of the contour line, in a thick tong-like motif that emphasizes the direction of their movement. Some of the animals, one for each group, turn their heads toward the outside; the result is a strong projection that creates a relationship with the human figures who, in high relief, emerge in the foreground over the bodies of the animals. These human figures are really frontal *kouroi* set in profile. The heavy masses of the buttock muscles and the powerful forearms would probably have appeared to be more refined and subtle in a totally frontal view, and yet the edge of the cloak, which breaks irregularly over the torsos, defines, along with the outline of the front leg, the meeting between two diverging planes in a spiral rhythm, thus lending a dominant sense of volume to the figures. The decisive, and yet never geometric, correspondence of the pairs of javelins, which cut obliquely through the background, serves as a dynamic element, as does the repeated hooves of the animals.

The quality of these sculptures is so high that they have few rivals in contemporaneous sculpture. In every detail, and exactly where the temptation of symmetry was the greatest, there is a rejection of any pattern or formula; put another way, the rigid structure of archaic symmetry is brought to the limit of its expressive capacity by a rigorous creative imagination. These reliefs are made of Sicyonian limestone, and probably were made by a Sicyonian master; on the other hand, the style is Peloponnesian, with its love for the clear definition of volumes and surfaces.

The original Temple of Apollo at Delphi was destroyed in 548 B.C. by a fire; this greatly affected the affairs of the sanctuary. The new temple was begun soon after the disaster and was finished only twenty years later; in the meantime, new treasuries were being built, and the sanctuary grew richer and richer. Even before the fire, Croesus (560–546 B.C.), the Lydian king famous for his wealth, had dedicated a crater of gold in the treasury of Clazomenos. This edifice, like the one built by Massalia, was in the Aeolian style; like the Ionian treasury, it had ornate figures at the base and on the top of the walls, but the columns had leaf capitals.

The treasury built at Syphnos, an island in the Cyclades rich in gold and silver, dates to about 530 B.C. Built entirely of Parian marble, it must have appeared more like sculpture than architecture. Engraved figures decorated the walls; the entablature and the columns, as in the older Ionian treasury of Cnidos (circa 560 B.C.), were replaced by two statues of maidens. On the top of the cornice (or *geison*) and on the *sima* (or gutter) were relief friezes with lotus flowers and palm leaves. In addition, the edifice supported a variety of other sculptures. On the east pediment, in completely full-relief figures, the struggle between Apollo and Herakles for the Delphic tripod was represented. This tripod, from which the Pythoness uttered the oracles, had been stolen by Herakles, when he had arrived at the sanctuary sick and bloody, in order to get Apollo to tell him how he might be cured. The quarrel was resolved by Zeus: Apollo took possession of the tripod once again, and Herakles got the advice he sought. A continuous relief frieze ran along the top of the walls and on the front of the treasury. In the front (which faced west, an exception to most Greek temples) there was a scene of uncertain meaning — perhaps the judgment of Paris. Along the eastern end was an episode from the Trojan cycle: the duel between Hector and Menelaus,

THE DIOSCURI

Since Kastor came to Pamphaes' entertainment
and Polydeukes his brother, it is no marvel
that to be good athletes runs in their blood. The lords
of Sparta and the wide dancing lawns dispose
the ordinances of games in their beauty, with
   Herakles and with Hermes beside them.
They care for men that are righteous. Indeed,
   the race of the gods fails not their friends.

They with life changing to and fro dwell one
   day beside their father beloved,
Zeus, and the day that follows under the secret
   places of the earth in the hollows of
   Therapne.
The destiny they fulfil is the same; such
was the choice of Polydeukes rather than be
   god indeed
and dwell in the sky, when Kastor fell in the
   fighting,
whom Idas, angered over some driving of cattle, stabbed with the bronze spearhead.

Lynkeus, staring from Taygetos, saw them hiding
in an oak tree, for beyond all mortals else his
   eye
was sharpest. And in ravening speed of their
   feet
they came down and devised at once a monstrous act,
and terribly did these sons of Aphareus suffer
   at the hands of Zeus; for straightway
Leda's son, Polydeukes, came pursuing, and
   they stood at bay by their father's tomb.

Ripping aloft the dedication of death, the
   smoothed gravestone,
they cast it at Polydeukes' chest, but availed not
   to shatter
nor drive him back. He, leaping with quick
   spear,
buried the bronze in Lynkeus' side,
and Zeus on Idas crashed the flame of the
   smoking thunderbolt.
These two burned, forlorn. Men find strife bitter when they undertake those who are
   stronger.

With speed Tyndareus' son ran back to his
   mighty brother,
and found him not dead, drawing yet some
   shuddering breath of life.
In grief, letting fall hot tears,
he cried aloud: "Kronion, my father, what release
shall there be from sorrow? Grant death also to
   me with this man, my lord.
Bereft of his friends a man's honor is gone.
   Few mortals are steadfast in distress

aided respectively by Aeneas and Meriones, over the body of Euphorbos (Figure 31).

Along the north side was the most beautiful scene in the entire cycle on this treasury: the battle between the Titans and the gods (Figure 32). This theme occupied an important place in Greek religion because the triumph of the gods over the Titans marked the consolidation of the Olympic pantheon and of Zeus' power. In the Syphnos treasury frieze, quite aside from the religious significance, we might also recognize an allusion to the Sacred War that had established Delphi. The Titans here are not represented as powerful and wild supernatural beings but as soldiers, in Greek armor and with Corinthian helmets. On the south side, between chariots and knights, there was represented the abduction of the Leucippides by Castor and Pollux. The divine twins, sons of Leda by Zeus and Tyndareus and brothers of Helen and Clytemnestra, took on the name of Dioscuri ("sons of Zeus") from their divine father and Tyndaraea after their earthly father, Tyndareus, king of Sparta. They abducted from the sacred enclosure of Aphrodite, Phoebe and Hilaeira, daughters of Tyndareus' half-brother Leucippus, who had been promised in marriage to another pair of divine twins, Idas and Lynceus.

In considering this sculpture from the treasury of Syphnos, we are prompted to exclaim: how different island art was from that of the Peloponnesos! The latter seemed all intent on the architectural construction of the figures, while the former was concerned with light and color values. In the Aeneas figure from the eastern frieze (Figure 31), the body, with its slim waist, expands into the ample form of the torso and hips; the structure of the nude body is obscured by the more formal mass, and even the emergence of the muscles does not express the interior dynamics but serves as a pretext for the reflection of light. In the Syphnos frieze, the background does not act as the boundary of the volume of the figures but contributes its own quality to the total expres-

"to endure hardship." He spoke, and Zeus came near
and answered: "You are my son; but thereafter her lord, a hero,
embracing your mother, shed seed that is mortal:
this man. Behold: of these two things I give you choice
entire; if you would escape death and age that all men hate,
to dwell beside me on Olympus with Athena and Ares of the black spear,

"that right is yours. But if all your endeavor is for
your twin, and you would have in all things shares alike,
half the time you may breathe under the earth,
half the time in the golden houses of the sky."
He spoke, and no twofold counsel divided the hero's heart,
but he set free from darkness the eyes of Kastor of the brazen belt, and his voice thereafter.

PINDAR: *Nemea 10* (51-90)

33. **Delphi: This metope from the treasury of the Athenians represents Theseus fighting an Amazon. The style prevalent in these metope sculptures has led them to be compared to the red-figured Attic pottery made at the end of the sixth century B.C. (Delphi Museum)**

34. **Delphi: The treasury of the Athenians. Built after Cleisthenes took over power in Athens, it is — like the Temple of Apollo — a tangible sign of the Alcmaeonidae's devotion to this god. (It was reconstructed in its present form in 1904–6.)**

sion. Background and relief, although homogeneous in the compactness of the surfaces, contrast in such a way as to enrich the composition with chromatic effects.

As with the Parthenon of a later period, the sculptured relief on the short sides of the Syphnos treasury is composed of figures arranged on one plane only; on the long sides the planes were multiple so that the interweaving and superimposition of the forms became more complicated and stressed the contrasts of light. The taste for narrative, that joy of telling tales so deeply rooted in the Greek-Eastern world and which would find its highest literary expression in the work of Herodotus, here found a way to unfold in this world interwoven with figures.

Sacred Sites at Delphi

The reconstruction of the Temple of Apollo, after the fire of 548 B.C., was begun with local limestone and was finished in Parian marble by the Alcmaeonidae in exile from Athens. This powerful Athenian gens, wanting to demonstrate their reverence for the Delphic Oracle, gained the support of the god against the Athenian tyrant Pisistratus. The work on the temple was completed by Cleisthenes, one of the Alcmaeonidae, between 513–505 B.C.; the temple collapsed in an earthquake in 373 B.C., but was rebuilt in the second half of the same century with the same plan (Figure 29). In building the late archaic temple, the Greeks preserved the adyton from the temple of more than a century earlier, the one attributed to Trophonius and Agamedes; this was probably because the Pythoness entered the oracular cavity through this section and it was too special to be tampered with. The plan of the temple was extremely elongated, as was true with earlier archaic temples; this indicates that the project was conceived shortly after the fire of 548 B.C., about the time that the Temple of Apollo was being built at Corinth. In the temple at Delphi, the naos was divided into three naves by the two rows of columns. And within the temple were various famous and ancient cult sites — the *omphalos*, or navel, considered to be the center of the earth, the altar of Poseidon, the tomb of Dionysus — but we can no longer be sure where these were located.

The east pediment of the Temple of Apollo at Delphi was dominated by Apollo's chariot, with the Muses, Delphus, and Hephaistos' children between groups of fighting beasts. (Incidentally, we know of this sculpture only because of Pausanias' description.) The dominant theme of the west pediment was the battle of the Titans and the gods. Other sculptures decorated the metopes and the acroteria, the latter representing statues of Nike and marble sphinxes.

The link between the Alcmaeonidae and the Delphic Oracle remained strong, and the Oracle — ever sensitive to the most powerful presence of the moment — incited the Spartans to help free Athens from the tyranny. When Cleisthenes managed to take power despite the hostile attitude of the Spartans, he wanted to consolidate the old bond between Athens and Delphi. Thus the new Athenian treasury was erected in 507 B.C. (although others claim that it was built after the battle of Marathon). This edifice, a Doric structure of the in antis type (Figure 34), was distinguished by the elegance of its proportions and the wealth of its sculptured decorations. (It is also unique in having on its interior wall, among other inscriptions, a hymn to Apollo with actual musical notations.) On the small pediment, the greatness of Apollo was celebrated in sculptures representing the theft of the tripod or the killing of the monster at Delphi. On the metopes the exploits of Herakles were united with those of the Attic hero Theseus, so that the image of the Athenian aristocratic traditions would shine for all to see. The metope with Theseus and the Amazon (Figure 33) shows how even late-archaic mannerism, which indulges in decorative effects and in an excessive formalism of poses, does not impair the organic nature of the figures in the Attic work but preserves intact the balance between surface and structure.

When the Persian menace was imminent, the Delphic Oracle behaved

35 (a, b). Delphi: The Charioteer, a bronze statue that was part of a gift made by a member of the Deinomenidae, the tyrants of Gela and Syracuse. The figure stood inside a chariot, and thus his exaggerated height was "corrected." Likewise, the chariot and missing arm helped to conceal the contrast between the vertical grooves of the man's gown and the almost calligraphic complexity of the drapery over his bust. The close-up of the head reveals the mixture of realistic details and stylized simplifications that Greek sculpture could contain in a single work. (Delphi Museum)

35a

36

36. Delphi: The tholos in the sanctuary of Athena Pronaia, evidently designed and conceived by Theodorus of Phocaea. The cella was surrounded by an outer circle of twenty Doric columns, while nine Corinthian semicolumns were set against the interior wall.

ambiguously: it foretold a sad fate for the cities trying to decide whether to intervene, and when the Persians actually arrived in Greece, the Oracle even tailored its predictions so as not to offend the potential conquerors. But this did not prevent the sanctuary from accepting later on the votive offerings that celebrated the Greek victories, such as the Marathon trophies or the golden tripod on which were engraved the names of the cities that had participated in the battle of Plataea. In the same period, the Deinomenidae, tyrants of Syracuse, did not miss the opportunity to show off their power in the sanctuary. While the Greeks were defeating the Persians, they too were struggling against "barbarians," and their victory at Himera over Carthage in 480 B.C. not only occurred in the same year as the battle of Salamis but also had the same significance: the defense of Hellenic civilization. But perhaps this aspect of the matter was exploited in order to make people forget that (if Herodotus was telling the truth) Gelon, the tyrant of Syracuse, by making such absurd demands, had practically refused to help the Greeks when the Persian danger was imminent. In 478 B.C., Gelon dedicated at Delphi four tripods and golden Nikes, or statues of the goddess of victory, weighing the equivalent of fifty talents, as a votive offering for his victory at Himera; they were placed near the approach to the Temple of Apollo.

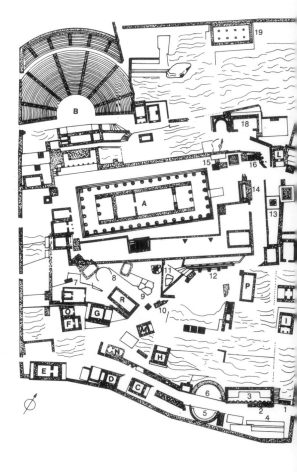

The Syracuse tyrants Gelon and Hieron participated many times in the Pythian Games at Delphi and often were among the winners. After a victory in 486 B.C., the famous group in bronze representing the charioteer (Figure 35a) and his chariot was dedicated. The base of the group bore the dedicatory inscription, but this version was changed (in 478 B.C.) by Polyzelos, Gelon's younger brother. The group as a whole thus must be thought of as dating from 486–478 B.C., although there are varying opinions about technical matters; for example, some scholars have suggested that a base signed by Sotades of Boeotia should be reconnected with the group. Then, too, in attempting to assign the work to some known scholar, some scholars have suggested Pythagoras of Rhegium, the sculptor with the severe style so celebrated by ancient writers. But the comparison between the charioteer's head and certain coins from the Deinomenidae cities of Gela and Syracuse make us think rather of an ancient Sicilian sculptor; actually, certain incongruities found in the Delphi charioteer have been noted in several ancient Sicilian works.

In any case, the charioteer was executed by a great artist who conceived the figure to be viewed principally from one point by utilizing optical corrections, especially in the facial features (Figure 35b). But this plan marks a break from the rigid frontal view inherited from late archaicism: the head is slightly turned toward the right compared to the torso, which in turn is rotated in relation to the lower part of the body. Seen from the point of view prepared by the artist, the figure was in a three-quarter position toward the right, and the slight rotations, no longer noticeable, highlighted the bust and the face. The bodily structure is not obliterated by the thick drapings; in fact it is rendered tangible by the belt that holds the fabric to the waist, by the little cord that runs along the shoulders, and by the soft falling of the folds over the chest and shoulders. The lower part of the body, which to us today seems too long, was partially hidden by the edge of the chariot (only fragments of which have been preserved). The expressiveness of the group was probably increased by the contrast between the rather astonished rigidity of the charioteer and the trembling of the horses (which also have disappeared for the most part).

All the structures and activities we have described so far were rooted in Delphi's Apollonian heritage, but as we have already noted there was a still earlier cult attached to the site, the cult dating back to the Mycenaean age and centered in the sanctuary of Athena Pronaia ("guardian of the temple"), located below the sanctuary of Apollo. A stone temple was built in the third quarter of the seventh century and was replaced by a new temple at the end of the sixth century. The columns of the first edifice clearly demonstrate their derivation from wooden prototypes; they are tall and slim, surmounted by a capital with a flat, wide echinus. The location of the Athena sanctuary, set on the mountain slope, influenced the very life and form of the temple. This late archaic edifice was built

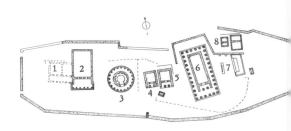

without an opisthodomos and with only twelve columns on its long sides in order to adapt it to the available space. In 480 B.C. it was destroyed by an avalanche of rock from the overhanging cliffs. The new temple, erected in the fourth century B.C., was set more to the west in order to avoid this danger in the future.

Within the sanctuary bounds, besides a treasury of the Aeolians and another Athenian treasury, there was a tholos, or round temple, dated to about 400 B.C. This type of structure, surrounded by a row of columns, was a particular favorite of fourth century B.C. architects. Any possible opposition between diverse elements having been eliminated, it could thus enjoy a theoretically infinite number of viewpoints, totally becoming a part of the surrounding space. Thus tholoi sprang up at Olympia, Epidaurus, and Delphi. However, at Delphi there existed an older precedent, a tholos erected between 586–548 B.C., which it has been possible to reconstruct by examining architectural elements taken from it and used in the foundation of the treasury of the Sicyonians. The interior chamber of this older tholos was surrounded by thirteen slender Doric columns surmounted by a low architrave. In the Doric frieze, the triglyphs and metopes, divided by a constant pattern, were distributed uniformly, without any relationship to the supporting elements. In this way the entablature and the stylobate became two similar elements, emphasizing the very cadences of the circular plan. This was a singular edifice in which problems Greek architecture would pose only centuries later were apparently solved as if by chance.

Despite this achievement, the tholos dating to about 400 B.C. (Figure 36) is much richer in its effects. The outside colonnade of twenty Doric columns found its counterpart in a colonnade of nine half-columns set against the inside wall of the interior chamber, itself located at the center of the interaxes of the twenty columns. The delicate Corinthian capitals of this interior colonnade were derived from those created by Iktinos for the temple at Bassae, while the Athenian experience was enriched also in the use of materials of diverse colors, somewhat in the manner established by Mnesicles for the Propylaea of the Acropolis of Athens. In contrast with the white marble of the exterior of the tholos, black marble was used for the interior walls, for the base of the Corinthian half-columns, and for the floor of the chamber (except for the central circle). The metopes of the friezes had sculptured decorations, further enhancing its rich visual appeal.

Delos and the World to the East

In the early Greek world, Asia Minor seems to have played a secondary role compared to the Aegean islands; perhaps this was simply because they lay on the major trade routes between Greece and Egypt and Syria, economically and culturally advanced countries at that time. The obligatory function of these islands as part of a sea lane imparted a dynamic impetus to the environment, transforming the small landowners and fishermen into merchants and traders. And because of the continuous relations with the Near East, the artistic patrimony of these islands was enriched by the new motifs and stimuli furnished by Egyptian, Assyrian, Canaanite, Phoenician, and other cultures. There thus flourished, especially at places like Rhodes, Crete, and Aegina, a complex Orientalizing art that remodeled the foreign contributions into an imaginative and harmonious Greek language.

Eventually, though, it was the cities along the coast of Asia Minor and its offshore islands — comprising the region known as Ionia — that assumed the leading role in shaping Greek civilization. On the island of Samos, the one closest to Asia Minor, the great sanctuary of Hera was established as far back as the Mycenaean age. Here, said tradition, the goddess herself was born. The most ancient altar dates from the middle of the tenth century. The cult image, which Pausanias saw in the second century A.D., was a simple tree trunk; in the first half of the sixth century this was replaced by a wooden statue dressed in real clothes, the work of Smilis of Aegina. The antiquity of the cult is also indicated by the rite of the Hera feast, the *Tonaia*, celebrating the sacred marriage of the goddess with Zeus, which is said to have taken place on the island; in this ceremony, the cult idol was carried to the water's edge, purified, and then wrapped in tree branches.

By the end of the eighth century, the sanctuary of Hera on Samos had already attained a state of great splendor; precious bronze and ivory handicraft objects came from Phoenicia, Egypt, and Syria, and the heterogeneous source of these votive offerings gives an idea of the extent of the island's trading contacts and the sanctuary's renown. A native of Samos was said to have been the first Greek sailor to reach Spain, around 640 B.C., bringing back ivory works and other precious goods to Samos. In the meantime, on the coast of Asia Minor just a bit southeast of Samos, the city of Miletus had undertaken a policy of expansion, creating

37. **Delos: The Oikos of the Naxians seen from the east. Like the other temples in the sacred enclosure of Apollo on Delos, this structure faced the west, although Greek temples normally faced east.**

38. Delos: The sacred way that led from the sanctuary of Apollo to the sacred lake. Lining a sacred way with a series of animal statues was a tradition common in Egypt and the Near East; such sacred ways had probably been viewed by men from the Cyclades on their voyages there.

numerous colonies around the Black Sea and its approaches. That part of the world boasted a rich fishing trade; moreover, some of the new colonies were located near the metal deposits that for centuries had fed the economies of the Hittites' realm and Mesopotamia, and to this extent contributed to the cultural development of those regions. In this way, Miletus set itself up in competition with the Greek ports of call in Syria, which had been the first to enter this metal market.

By the end of the seventh century, the cities of Ionia had a permanent base at Naucratis on the Nile Delta. The ascent to power of the Pharaoh Amasis (570–526 B.C.), who married a Greek princess from Cyrene and was well disposed toward the Greeks, consolidated the Ionians' position in Egypt. At Naucratis, the people of Samos erected a Temple of Hera, and the Milesians erected a Temple of Apollo. Such contacts with Egyptian civilization played some part in the formation of Ionian monumental architecture: the great temples at Samos, Miletus, Ephesus, and Sardis, in

which great masses of columns thronged and alternated with light and shadows, revealed a knowledge of Egyptian hypostyle halls. This knowledge gave rise to the custom of giving greater breadth in the peristyle to the intercolumniations along the fronts of temples and also a larger diameter to the columns, almost as if to create an opening in the impenetrable mass of the supporting elements. The Egyptian influence is also seen in the forms of the capitals and in the decorative elements of the molding. The entablature, which in Doric architecture was linear and defined the structure's volume, was enriched in the Ionian temple with intaglio-decorated molding on which the light formed a fringe effect, thus eliminating the more decisive geometric profile. The structural function of the single parts, the contrast between supporting elements and the downward thrust of the entablature, so essential to the dynamics of Doric architecture, were concealed and attenuated by the interposing of decorative elements between the columns and the stylobate, and by the insertion of moldings that transfer a chromatic to the inside of the entablature. In effect, the Ionic temple of the Ionian Greek setting negated the geometric treatment of volume and space developed by other Greeks.

The theoretician of this new Ionic architecture was Theodorus of Samos who, together with Rhoicos, planned the first monumental Temple of Hera at Samos in the second quarter of the sixth century B.C. Just as with the contemporaneous Temple of Artemis at Ephesus, the peristyle consisted of a double row of columns; a third row was added on the ends, and other supporting elements were massed in the interior of the pronaos and naos. The altar of Rhoicos, replaced during the Roman epoch by an exact copy, gives us today a better idea of the decorative exuberance of this style than do the few other remains. The Temple of Hera, destroyed by fire about 530 B.C., was rebuilt immediately afterward with even more colossal dimensions, under the auspices of the Samian tyrant, Polycrates. Despite its great fame, the Hera sanctuary at Samos remained only a religious center; it did not serve any political function, as did the other great sanctuary of the Cyclades, Delos.

At Delos, a nature goddess — that primitive lady of the wild beasts so dear to the Minoan world — seems to have been the most ancient inhabitant of the sterile island. Identified with Artemis, she had her own sacred enclosure in the northwestern corner of what became the sanctuary of Apollo. Her temple was rebuilt many times in the same place, and the various edifices were set one upon the other, evidence of the continuity of a cult so typical of the most sacred sites. The amphiprostyle temple with six Ionic columns, erected after the island's independence (314 B.C.), was built over the site of an edifice of the late eighth or early seventh century. The foundation treasury, found under the northeastern corner of the more ancient temple, contained some precious gold and ivory objects that had belonged to a Mycenaean-age temple, the foundations of which were recognized in the lowest stratum. The Artemis cult must have linked itself with an older structure, similar to a Mycenaean tholos-tomb, near which images of Artemis were found; among these was the statue dedicated by Nicander in the middle of the seventh century B.C. and the work of an artist from Naxos. When Apollo became lord of the island of Delos, the tholos was considered the tomb of Opis and Arge, two of the Hyperborean girls who had helped Leto give birth to Apollo. As has been observed by various scholars, such well-built edifices with their precious objects provide strong arguments in favor of the hypothesis that Delos had a religious character in the Mycenaean age. This religious function would seem to be the only plausible explanation for the obvious importance of an island otherwise so sterile and unproductive.

With the advent of the supremacy of a patriarchal society, Apollo cast the ancient female divinity of Delos into the background, but the sacred character of the island remained intact. The author of the *Homeric Hymn to Delian Apollo* recalled how in his day, in the seventh century B.C., Delos was the religious center where the Ionians of the islands met in order to honor the gods and celebrate with Olympic-type games. Probably it was its unproductive character that allowed the island to remain common property, suitable as a meeting place and for the exchange of products

THE ESTABLISHMENT OF THE DELIAN GAMES

Hail, bless'd Leto! who to Zeus of yore
Apollo and the immortal huntress bore;
Her in Ortygia, him on Delos' shore.
Stretch'd 'neath a palm by Cynthus' rugged brow,
Where the clear waves of smooth Inopus flow. . . .

Leto, teeming with the Archer-god,
Sought mid these scenes her future son's abode.
Each seat, though plenty there its blessings shower,
Shrinks fearful to receive the mighty power.
But Delos' favor'd isle she first explores,
Addressing thus the Genius of the shores —
  "Delos! if thou become my son's domain,
If here Apollo fix his splendid fane,

"Sacred alone to him thy seats shall be,
From other lords and mortal tyrants free.
What though nor flocks nor herds thy pastures feed,
No harvest ripen, and no vintage bleed;
Yet if thy shores his sacred temples grace,
From each assembling tribe of human race
Shall hecatombs with pious zeal be given,
The smoke of offer'd victims climb to heaven,
While every God protective influence yields,
And foreign plenty crowns thy barren fields."

. . . King of the argent bow, thy feet now climb
Of Cynthus' rugged mount the height sublime;
Now many an isle around and peopled shore
Wandering thy desultory steps explore.
For on the mountains near, that proudly rise
And shoot their azure summits to the skies,
By every stream the lowly plain that laves,
Rolling to Ocean's bed its winding waves,
Thy hallow'd groves their sacred umbrage spread,
The frequent temple rears to thee the head.

Yet, Phoebus! still the loved parental isle
Wins from an envious world thy favoring
  smile;
Where with their lovely dames and infant
  train,
Seeking protection of thy holy fane.

Ionia's war-like heroes crowding round,
Sweep with their lengthen'd stoles the sacred
  ground;
To thee devoted, festal games belong,
The lyre, the dance, the cestus, and the song;
While life and youth eternal seem to grace
With never fading charms the votive race.

Hymn to Delian Apollo

Delos: Plan of the sanctuary of Apollo
  1 Propylaea
  2 Altar of Zeus Polieus
  3 Temple of the bulls
  4 Portico with bulls' heads
  5 Temple of Dionysus
  6 Rectangular portico
  7 Temple of Aphrodite and Hermes
  8 Agora
  9 Treasuries
10 Northern propylaea
11 Temple of Apollo
12 Colossus of Apollo
13 Small portico
14 Processional way
15 Southern propylaea
16 Portico
17 Archaic Temple of Artemis
18 Exhedra
19 Portico of Philip
20 Terrace
21 Later Temple of Artemis
22 Porinos Neos
23 Port plaza
24 Sacred port

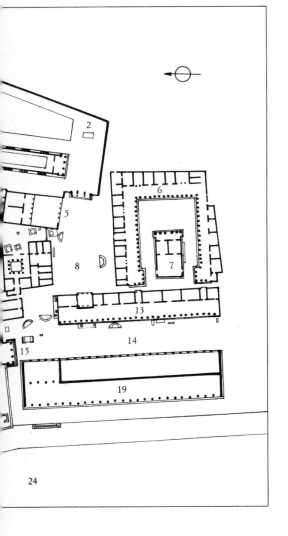

and the celebration of the cults; as in the Mycenaean age, its economic resources derived entirely from its role as a sacred island. This is confirmed by the promise that Leto, in the *Homeric Hymn*, searching for a place to give birth to Apollo, makes to the island: ". . . but if you will have the temple of Apollo who shoots arrows from afar, all men, gathering here, will continuously bring you great sacrificial offerings."

From the middle of the seventh century, the sanctuary of Delos came under the protection of Naxos, which made its presence felt by exercising cultural hegemony over Delos. The bond with Apollo played an important role in the struggle for dominion of the Cyclades, which saw Naxos and Samos opposed to Paros and Miletus. The first sign of the presence of Naxos was the dedication of a colossal statue of Apollo near an ancient and narrow edifice divided into three naves with two rows of wooden supports. At the end of the seventh century, this construction was replaced by a splendid marble edifice, which at the end of the archaic epoch was the most imposing sanctuary of the whole island. The *oikos* of the Naxians (Figure 37), perhaps a treasury or a meeting place, included an elongated rectangular hall preceded by a vestibule, which one entered originally through a simple door. The main hall was divided into two naves by the single row of eight slender Ionic columns that rose up out of simple disc bases and were surmounted by small Ionic capitals with jutting echinis. Later, the hall had a marble floor that incorporated the bases of the columns; the pronaos was turned into a distyle in antis; and an opisthodomos with four Doric columns was added.

Meanwhile, a monumental character was lent to the road that started at the sacred zone, passed in front of the little temple of Leto, built at the beginning of the sixth century, and went toward the sacred lake (which no longer exists). On the edge of the terrace overlooking the road were lined up nine lions with gaping jaws (Figures 38), taut and tense as if protecting the sacred lake. They were carved from Naxos marble at the end of the seventh century. As occurs with Naxian works, the bodies of the great felines are made up of sharply juxtaposed planes that meet in conspicuous angles. Unlike the Peloponnesian sculpture, it was not the rhythm of the volumes, the insistent prominence of the structure, that interested the sculptor of such works: considered from this viewpoint, the lions, vaguely inspired by late-Hittite prototypes, appear somewhat incredible. Their expressive value lies in the dynamic charge, in that bursting strength, full of modern connotations, which gathers around the taut and elastic contours: there immediately comes to mind the comparison with the silhouettes painted on the Orientalizing vases of Attica and the Cyclades. Only five of these lions remain intact in the barren setting of Delos, but they still exercise their powerful charm.

All these works were constructed at a time when Naxos was attempting to emphasize its relationships with Apollo, with the aim of consolidating its prestige. In those same years, Naxos dedicated at Delphi, in the sanctuary that most authoritatively influenced the politics of the Greek cities, a marble sphinx atop a high column. It was no coincidence that the sphinx was situated in the most sacred area, as if to guard the sacred spring and the oracular cavity of Apollo.

Athens, in its desire to establish itself as the homeland of the Ionians, soon directed its attention toward the Delos sanctuary. In Solon's time, and perhaps even earlier, representatives of Athens took part in the festival by sending a sacred ship to Delos; until the ship returned to Athens, punishment was suspended. Pisistratus, who had sought in vain to secure the benevolence of the Delphic Apollo (who was favorable to the Alcmaeonidae), wanted to consolidate his prestige among the Ionians by presenting himself as the patron of the Delian Amphictionic League. In homage to the Oracle, he had the island partially purified about 543 B.C. by removing its sepulchers, which were no longer considered compatible with the sacred character of the place. Undoubtedly Athens' role in the sanctuary at Delos helped to expand the city's trade in eastern Greece and the islands. After the above-mentioned purification, the archaic temple of Apollo was built; this Ionic-style temple was called the Poronos Neos (after the type of limestone used), or "the temple in which

39. Eleusis: Relief of Demeter, Persephone (Kore), and Triptolemus. Persephone, holding a long torch in her left hand, introduces the youth Triptolemus to her mother Demeter, who holds a scepter in her left hand. Demeter gives the youth a stalk of wheat so that he can go all over the world and spread the cultivation of grains, and thus spread civilization. This Attic relief, dating from about 440 B.C., is part of an Athenian tradition that makes the myth of Triptolemus a central theme of their political propagandizing. (National Museum, Athens)

HADES SEIZES PERSEPHONE

Demeter, to thee belongs the votive lay,
Whose locks in radiance round they temples play,
And Persephone whom distant from thy sight,
Fierce Hades bore to realms of endless night.
For thus decreed the god, whose piercing eyes
Trace every act, whose thunder shakes the skies,
That she, whose hands the golden sickle bear,
And choicest product of the circling year,
Rich fruits, and fragrant breathing flowers, should know
The tender conflicts of maternal woe.
  In Nisia's vale, with nymphs a lovely train,
Sprung from the hoary father of the main,
Fair Persephone consumed the fleeting hours
In pleasing sports, and pluck'd the gaudy flowers.
  The fair Narcissus far above the rest,
By magic form'd, in beauty rose confess'd.
So Zeus, to ensnare the virgin's thoughtless mind,
And please the ruler of the shades designed.
He caused it from the opening earth to rise,
Sweet to the scent, alluring to the eyes.
Never did mortal, or celestial power,
Behold such vivid tints adorn a flower.
From the deep root an hundred branches sprung,
And to the winds ambrosial odors flung;
Which, lightly wafted on the wings of air,
  The gladden'd earth and heaven's wide circuit share.
The joy-dispensing fragrance spreads around,
And ocean's briny swell with smiles is crown'd.
  Pleased at the sight, nor dreaming danger nigh,
The fair beheld it with desiring eye:
Her eager hand she stretch'd to seize the flower,
(Beauteous illusion of the etherial power!)
When, dreadful to behold, the rocking ground
Disparted — widely   yawn'd   a   gulf   profound! —
Forth rushing from the black abyss, arose
The gloomy monarch of the realm of woes,
Hades, from Saturn sprung — the trembling maid
He seized, and to his golden car convey'd.
Borne by immortal steeds the chariot flies:
And thus she pours her supplicating cries —
"Assist, protect me, thou who reign'st above,
Supreme and best of gods, paternal Zeus!"
But ah! in vain the hapless virgin rears
Her wild complaint — nor god nor mortal hears! —
Not to the white-arm'd nymphs with beauty crown'd,
Her loved companions, reach'd the mournful sound.

Hymn to Demeter

the colossus lies," because it housed a colossal wooden and gold statue of Apollo. The temple was the work of the Naxians, Tektaios and Angelion.

With the establishment of the Attic-Delian League in 477 B.C., Delos, like all the islands of Ionia, fell victim to the ever-growing oppression of Athens. The treasury of the League was placed in the Poronos Neos, following the custom of making sanctuaries into economic centers. With the League's money, the construction of a new and larger temple of Apollo was undertaken. Originally planned as an Ionic peripteral, the construction was interrupted in 454–453 B.C., when Pericles — in an undeniable abuse of his powers — had the treasury transported to the Parthenon in Athens. It was only toward 314 B.C., when the recently liberated island became the center of the new island league sponsored by Antigonus II Gonatus and his son Demetrius, that the construction work was resumed and the temple completed; but the original project was abandoned and preference was given to a Doric-style temple.

The oppressive policy of Athens toward its allies finally proved to be just as dangerous to the oppressor city itself. Following the smashing defeats of the first years of the Peloponnesian War, the loyalty of Athens' allies grew more and more unreliable. A sensational instance may be seen in the revolt of Lesbos in 428 B.C. Although it inflicted heavy punishment on this island, Athens was forced to mitigate its despotic attitude. It was during these times of political turmoil that the second purge of Delos took place, due to the piety of the city (426 B.C.). The construction of a new temple, called the Temple of the Athenians, was begun on Delos. This repeated in the colonnade the proportional relationship used in the Parthenon, and this fact has led some to believe that the architect was the same Callicratis. Hexastyle colonnades appeared only on the two ends of the Temple of the Athenians; the pronaos, between the doors, had four slender pillars in place of the columns. In the wall that divided the pronaos from the naos, on the sides of the door, there were two windows, as in the Propylaea at Athens; these gave light to the naos, where seven gold and ivory statues, dedicated by Pisistratus, had been transferred from the archaic temple, the Poronos Neos. To this extent, the sanctuary at Delos proved to be stronger than the pressures of Athens.

Private Religious Rites: Sanctuary of Eleusis

The author of the *Homeric Hymn to Demeter* of the seventh century B.C. told how the goddess, angry with the gods who had helped Hades in his abduction of her daughter Persephone, spurned high Olympus and went off to the cities and fertile fields of mankind. She thus arrived at Eleusis, and "with her heart full of sorrow, she sat at the side of the road near the Well of the Virgins from which the women of the city drew water." The daughters of King Celeus consoled her, and the king received her as a guest in his house. Isolated in her grief, the goddess "provoked for men, on the earth that nourishes all, the most horrible and frightful year; the earth did not allow any seed to sprout." Finally Zeus sent Hermes to order the god of the infernal regions to give Persephone back to her mother. Hades, "who is lord of the dead," laughed to himself, but he did not refuse to obey the sovereign Zeus' order; however, he did give his wife a pomegranate seed to eat so that she might be forced to stay with him four months of every year. When Demeter, now placated by Persephone's return, consented to go back to Olympus, she showed the form of her rites to Diocles the horse-tamer, to Celeus the ruler of the people, and to his son Triptolemus, as a token of gratitude to Eleusis, the city that had received her so graciously.

This particular myth was the expression of an agricultural society that drew its basic sustenance from the cultivation of grain and cereal grains. In the figures of the two goddesses, mother and daughter, as Sir James Frazer long ago pointed out, are resolved two personifications of grain: the mother representing the old wheat of the year before, Persephone representing the young wheat of the new year. Scholars still differ in analyzing the details of this myth, even if they all agree that Persephone's return to the earth represents the growth and flourishing of the crops, after the seeds lay hidden for a long time in the bosom of the earth. For Frazer again, the myth seemed identical with the Syrian myth involving Aphrodite (Astarte) and Adonis, the Phrygian myth of Cybele and Atys, and the Egyptian myth of Isis and Osiris. But was it entirely coincidental that in all these Near Eastern examples the couple consisted of a male and a female, while the Greek myth had two females? The Greek myth, therefore, would seem to have roots in an ancient matriarchal society; only later does there appear next to Demeter numerous male figures, whose function was more or less defined but whose position remained subordinate.

The cult of the Eleusinian divinities was widespread in Attica, but the many sanctuaries, called Eleusinia, did not have the character of the Eleusinian Mysteries, which remained an exclusive feature of the city that had welcomed the goddess. At Eleusis, in the same place where the Mysteries were celebrated during the archaic and classical periods, there had existed a cult edifice as far back as the Mycenaean age. Probably built during the late Helladic age (1500–1425 B.C.), it had the form of a megaron: a rectangular hall divided into two rooms and crossed by a middle row of three columns. On the front, two small stairways afforded access to the podium. The sacred zone of the Mycenaean sanctuary was separated from the community by a wall. After a gap from about 1230 to 1000 B.C., a new edifice — rather similar in plan to its predecessor — was constructed.

The Eleusinian cult had grown up as a propitiatory ritual of an

And now the all-seeing god, whose thunders shake
The aerial regions, thus to Rhea spake,
Around whose form her robes in darkness flew;
From whom her birth the queen of Seasons drew —
"Let Demeter hasten to the etherial plain,
And every honor she desires, obtain.
Her Persephone, with heavenly powers shall share
In joy, two parts of the revolving year:
The rest in realms of night." — The thunderer said:
The willing goddess his commands obey'd;
And from Olympus' cloud-encircled height
Bends to Callichorus her lofty flight:
O'er the drear region desolation frown'd,
So late with fruits and waving verdure crown'd.
But soon the earth its wonted power regains;
Again the harvest clothes the extended plains;
Increasing ploughshares turn the grateful soil,
And weighty sheaves reward the laborers' toil.

Hymn to Demeter

40. Eleusis: The Telesterion as we see it today is the version designed in the second half of the fifth century B.C., perhaps according to the plans of Iktinos, the architect of the Parthenon; in any case, even this version was somewhat modified in later eras.

agrarian character. But the crisis that shook the agricultural society in Hesiod's time — that is, approximately in the eighth century B.C. — not only placed the farmers in precarious and often dramatic conditions but with the growth of vast differences in individual wealth, it shook the values of a society that was still based on family relationships. In this context, we can understand how the myth of Demeter and Persephone took on new meanings. The ritual, represented in the Eleusinian Mysteries as a sacred drama, no longer celebrated only the hope for a good harvest; the return of the young goddess from Hades' world also contained the promise of another life that would compensate for the unhappy earthly existence. "Happy is he among the men that populate the earth, who saw these things," sang the author of the hymn, "because he who was not initiated into the Mysteries and did not take part in them will not share the same fate when he is dead in the obscure Darkness."

Originally, participation in the Mysteries did not require the observance of any particular moral code; it was sufficient to be an Athenian citizen and not to have been guilty of homicide. Moreover, merely by being open to citizens of every social class, the Eleusinian religion, with its collective rites and its promises of salvation in the afterlife, contained considerable egalitarian significance. It must have contributed in no little measure to the maturation of the uprooted and poor people's consciousness of their rights. But we must not imagine that the religious ideology of the Eleusinian rites served as a direct spur to a class that was inert and unaware of its position. The new aspect of the Eleusinian religion, rather, accompanied the social ferment that was agitating Attica between the eighth and sixth centuries B.C.; this new religiosity, in turn, became the

41. Eleusis: The Great Propylaea, the monumental entranceway to the sanctuary of Eleusis, was built of Pentelic marble shortly after A.D. 129, under the auspices of the Roman Emperor Antoninus Pius. It is his portrait bust that peers from the medallion that ornamented the pediment over the main gate.

41

ideological expression of the ferment and served as its stimulus.

By the fifth century, the initiate in the Eleusinian Mysteries was distinguished by his particular moral behavior (*ethos*) if we may judge, for example, from the song in Aristophanes' *The Frogs*: "We, as we have been initiated, behave in a pious manner toward foreigners and the common people." This last category, remarks Nilsson, even included the slaves, who in classical society were considered mere means of production and were deprived of an expression of personality.

In fact, as early as the age of Pisistratus, the possibility of becoming an Eleusinian initiate had been extended to the citizens of every state that had dealings with Athens; from the fifth century B.C. on, to *any* Greek, including the slaves; later on, even to non-Greeks willing to undergo the initiation ceremonies. It was certainly no chance occurrence that the Eleusinian Telesterion, the hall used for the celebration of the Mysteries, was built in the sixth century B.C. by the tyrant Pisistratus, who considered himself the interpreter of the will of the mass of urbanized farmers uprooted from their natural social environment. The two principal construction phases of the mighty sanctuary, moreover, were connected with two democratic leaders, Themistocles and Pericles. And this was true even though the highest religious offices in the sanctuary always remained a prerogative of the local noble families, the Kerikes and the Buzyges. The Telesterion, or initiation room, built by Pisistratus, was a vast quadrangular hall, surrounded inside, on three sides, by seven steps to seat those who participated in the Mysteries. Five rows of Ionic columns were amassed in this large room, enriching it with an evocative half-light. The front, facing the southeast, was preceded by a portico. It has been observed that in the Pisistratean edifice, and in all its successive transformations, the most important element of the older megaron was preserved — the adyton, the impenetrable room situated at the back of the edifice. This would have been the *sancta sanctorum* that the ancient sources refer to, where the ancient wooden idol of Demeter was kept.

This Telesterion was destroyed during Xerxes' expedition, but when the Persians were repulsed, a newer, much more ambitious structure was conceived. The new edifice was planned to be four times larger than its predecessor, and the leveling of the rocky coast was undertaken to make more space for the project. During the course of the work, however, a more modest solution had to be found. The Telesterion, actually built during the time the first League of Delos was established, was twice the size of the one built during the reign of Pisistratus. It was an elongated rectangular hall with seats on three sides and crossed by three rows of columns. In the meantime, the myth of Demeter and Persephone had taken on a definitely Attic aspect, thanks to the figure of Triptolemus (Figure 39). He was supposed to have revealed to Herakles, and to the Dioscuri at Athens itself, the mysteries he had learned from Demeter, thus bringing to the Peloponnesus the goddess' precious gift of wheat. Athens, in other words, took credit for having spread a new civilization over the world, enriching it with two important gifts: the hope of an afterlife, and the cultivation of the fields. The celebrated Athenian orator Isocrates (436–338 B.C.) was among those who proudly asserted this fundamental theme of Athenian propaganda, and it was widely echoed in red-figured Attic pottery. It was also the theme of one of Sophocles' tragedies, *Triptolemus*, staged in 468 B.C., which received the first prize from the Council of Generals presided over by Cimon.

When Pericles undertook the colossal public works enterprise that changed the face of Athens, he entrusted the project of the new grandiose Telesterion to Iktinos, the Parthenon architect (although some scholars question whether Iktinos was actually involved). However, this new project was never realized, even though the natural rock on the site had been prepared. This preparation allows us to reconstruct the plan with a certain degree of precision. The architect aimed at transforming the hypostyle hall, filled with columns, into a circular plan that would exploit fully the possibilities of trilithic architecture, which did not use the arch but utilized solely the elementary solution of an architrave resting on two supporting elements. The enormous hall, 170 feet by 160 feet on

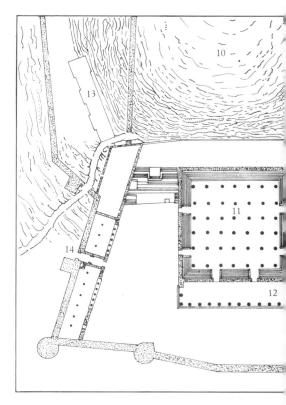

Eleusis: Plan of the sanctuary
1. *Arch*
2. *Temple of Artemis*
3. *Sacred way*
4. *Great Propylaea*
5. *Kallichoron*
6. *Arch*
7. *Small propylaea*
8. *Ploutonion*
9. *Roman storehouses*
10. *Acropolis*
11. *Telesterion*
12. *Portico of Philo*
13. *Museum*
14. *Southern gate*

Eleusis: Plan of the Telesterion in its two major phases; the smaller phase (in dark black) was that of Pisistratus; the larger was that of the mid-fifth century B.C. The Portico of Philo, along the southeast end, was added in the second half of the fourth century B.C.

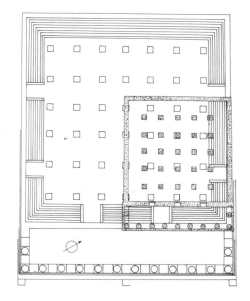

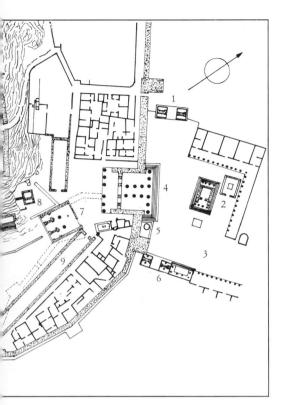

the inside, must have been covered with the aid of only two peristyles: the outer one held up a gallery, while the inner one marked out a central rectangular space, above which the roof must have let in light. The perfect equivalence of the walls was highlighted by the uniform repetition of the seats and the openings on all four sides. The problems presented by the circular plan were not entirely unknown to the Athenian architects, who could look to the example of the tholos built in their Agora about 470 B.C.: there, the interior columns, with their elliptical cadence and staggered interaxes, introduced an element of tension in relation to the perfect geometry of the round wall.

The clear-cut and spacious structure that Iktinos — assuming he was the architect — had conceived for the Telesterion reflected a new conception of the Eleusinian religion. Within the framework of fifth-century radical democracy, the initiation had become a tradition for Athenian youth; the Mysteries had lost much of their revolutionary character and took on more and more of an official nature. But the patrician families of Eleusis who still controlled the sanctuary administration evidently did not look favorably upon such innovations. Thus, in the final reconstruction of the Telesterion, although the arrangement of the seats and doors was preserved as Iktinos had planned, the interior space was broken up by seven rows of columns, preserving the traditional evocative atmosphere created by the play of light and shadow. The Telesterion (Figure 40), which could by now seat four thousand people, must have looked from the outside like a secluded, almost forbidding structure, an impenetrable cube made of dark stone, barely linked to its surroundings by a portico with twelve white marble columns. Even if the Eleusinian religion, whose rite was restricted to a few initiates, had already become the common patrimony of Athenian citizens, the secret surrounding the rites was no less rigorously kept. We need only mention the case of Aeschylus, who risked being condemned by the Areopagus judges because he was suspected of having alluded to some details of the Eleusinian ritual in one of his tragedies.

A road went from the Telesterion to the northern gate of Pisistratus' wall, where the Small Propylaea was built during the Roman epoch. This sacred way was marked by sites associated with the wanderings of the grief-stricken Demeter. Outside the enclosure, near the corner of Pisistratus' wall later occupied by the Great Propylaea (Figure 41), there was a well, perhaps that of the "lovely dances" (*kallichoron*), but more probably the Well of the Virgins where the broken-hearted Demeter was consoled by the daughters of Celeus. If this was so, then the kallichoron, above which the goddess ordered the Eleusinians to build her temple and altar, should be sought near the Portico of Philo, which in the fourth century B.C. replaced the Periclean portico along the front of the Telesterion. Meanwhile, "the stone that knew no laughter" (*aghelastos petra*), on which the grief-stricken Demeter sat, has been identified near the corner staircase leading to the terrace. Behind this, to the west of the small Propylaea, was the Ploutonion, the grotto sacred to Hades (Pluto), in which the ancients recognized the entrance to the underworld that Hades used to take Persephone to his abode. The sacred area was closed off by a wall in the fourth century B.C.; the little Roman-age temple that is there today was preceded by a much older temple built in the time of Pisistratus.

The sanctuary of Eleusis was an object of great veneration throughout antiquity. About 54 B.C., the first monumental entranceway (Small Propylaea) was built with Ionic columns and Caryatids, thanks to the munificence of the Roman Appius Claudius Pulcher; it was set above the simple passageway in the archaic wall, protected by a jutting tower. A new, more splendid entranceway was built at the end of the second century A.D. by the emperor-philosopher Marcus Aurelius when he restored the sanctuary.

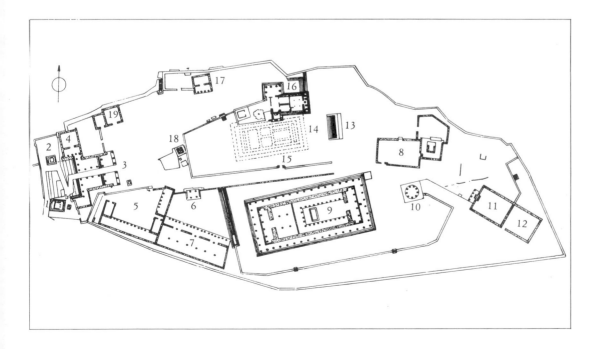

Athens: Plan of the Acropolis
1 Temple of Athena Nike
2 Monument of Agrippa
3 Propylaea
4 Pinakoteka
5 Sanctuary of Artemis Brauronia
6 Propylon of the Parthenon
7 Chalkotheke
8 Sanctuary of Zeus Polieus
9 Parthenon
10 Temple of Roma and Augustus
11–12 Pandionion
13 Altar of Athena Polias
14 Archaic Temple of Athena Polias
15 Propylon of Athena Polias sanctuary
16 Erechtheum
17 Houses of the Arrhephoroi
18 Athena Promachos statue
19 Storehouses

Limits of Athenian Radical Democracy

The battle of Salamis in 480 B.C. marked a decisive turn in Athenian life, among other ways, as a glorious test of the policy of Themistocles. When, after Marathon and the accession of Xerxes, a new conflict with the Persians appeared inevitable, this strategist made a choice with political consequences that went far beyond the occasion that determined it. In 483 B.C., the discovery of new silver mines at Maronea, at Lavrion near Cape Sounion, put great wealth at the disposal of Athens. At the risk of making himself unpopular, Themistocles opposed those who wanted to distribute this money among the citizens; he had it spent, instead, on the construction of a powerful fleet of one hundred triremes, as well as on the construction of naval ports and defenses for Athens and its port, Piraeus. It was probably on this point that Themistocles' conflict with Aristides took place, ending with the temporary banishment of the latter in 482 B.C.

However, it was Aristides who returned to help Athens in its moment of danger, and who sanctioned (after the victory over Xerxes) the establishment of an alliance between Athens and the Ionian Greeks headed by

42. Athens: The Acropolis seen from the southwest. In the background (right) is Mount Lycabettus. In the foreground (left) is the Odeon of Herodes Atticus; running off to its side is a long portico that ends above the theater of Dionysus, just visible against the slope (lower right). On the Acropolis, from left to right, are the Propylaea, the small Temple of Athena Nike (on the near bastion), the Erechtheum, and the Parthenon.

Chios and Samos — the Delian League of 477 B.C. This alliance was a defense against the Persians; the great victories of Salamis, Plataea, Mycale, and Mantinaea only marked a pause in the struggle, which lasted until the peace treaty with the Persians effected by Callias in 448 B.C.

The administration of the Delian League, which involved the maintenance and strengthening of the fleet on the part of Athens, produced a great change in the relations among the social classes within Athens. The fleet not only continually absorbed a part of the urban proletariat but it was also decisive in creating a new political consciousness. Meanwhile, the political power in Athens was entirely in the hands of the great aristocratic families. Cleisthenes' reforms, although he had swept away the residue of a state organization based on the nobility, had kept intact the political privileges of certain families: suffice to say that Cleisthenes' gens, the Alcmaeonidae, could count on positions of power in three or four of the ten new tribes after his reforms.

In the long period from Marathon to 462 B.C., if one looks at the list of the most important administrations (and also at the number of noted statesmen ostracized into temporary exile), one will see the exclusive alternation of the members of a few great patrician families: the Kerikes (Aristides) and the Buzyges (Xanthippus) of Eleusis; the Philaidae (Miltiades and Cimon); and the Lycomidae (Themistocles). Aristotle (or an author close to him) disclosed the sense of the political struggle in Athens about 425 B.C. Alluding to the time when, after the death of Pericles, Cleon took over the administration of the popular government, he complained that things were much worse because now, for the first time, the populace had selected as its chief one who did not enjoy the favor of the respectable classes that had always led the people.

On one hand, the members of the aristocratic families who took over the leadership of the people limited the power of the old surviving noble institutions such as the Areopagus; on the other hand, they helped to orient Athenian politics in such a way as to release social tensions without disturbing existent privileges, directing the interest of the people toward foreign policy. The Delian League soon emerged from a defensive alliance among Greeks to an instrument of imperialism that impinged on Athens' old allies. The crucial episode that marked the qualitative change of the alliance — the siege of Thasos — was the work of the son of Miltiades, Cimon, who certainly could not have been suspected of having democratic tendencies. All this demonstrates the convergence of common interests among aristocratic leaders, be they exponents of radical democracy or self-styled moderates. Thasos, the richest island in the northern Aegean, had tried to rebel against Athens' interference in its commercial interests. After two years of struggle, Cimon crushed the island's resistance in 463 B.C. The punishment inflicted by Athens on its rebellious ally was severe; the large Thassian fleet, the gold mine near Mount Pangaeus, and its other possessions in Thrace were confiscated and the island's walls were destroyed. The fruit of this drastic transplant operation was harvested by the leaders of Athens' democratic party in 454 B.C., when the League treasury, kept in the archaic Temple of Apollo on Delos, was transferred to Athens.

Athens justified the new aspect of the alliance with an historic right: the city was the mother-country of the Ionians, and the Ionian cities of the Aegean islands had to consider themselves colonies of the city in all respects. This thesis, later enunciated to the same Athens in the last scene of Euripides' *Ion* and in Aristophanes' *Lysistrata*, dated perhaps as far back as Solon's time; in any case, the claim was certainly being asserted in Ionia and Athens by about 500 B.C. Thucydides (I, 95, 1) made this one of the motives that drove the Ionians, who were hostile to Sparta, to ask Athens to form the alliance. Nor should we forget that the proposal to transfer the treasury was put forward not by Athens, but by the then faithful Samos, which was quite zealous in confirming such ideology even on a religious level.

The same year in which the treasury was transferred, the Panathenaea — a festival which Athens celebrated with a procession, sacrifice, and games — was observed. Shortly after this, Athens conceded

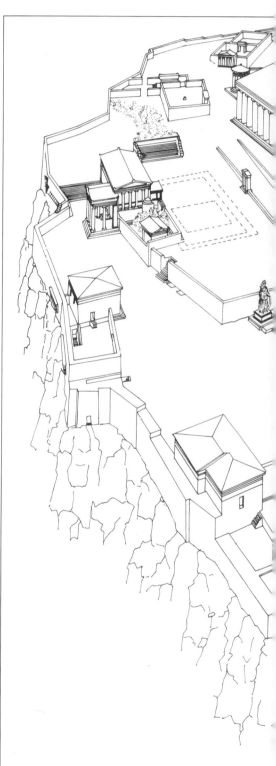

Athens: The Acropolis. A reconstruction according to G. P. Stevens.

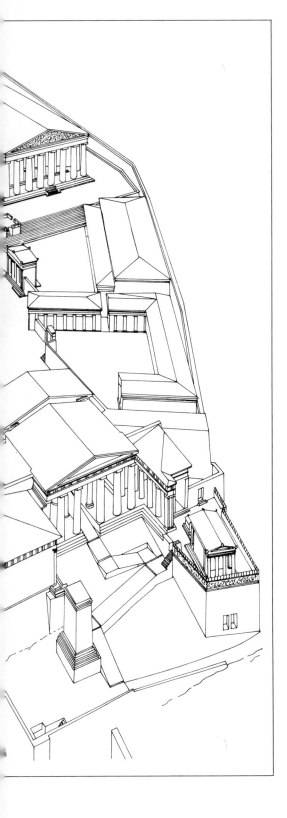

to some privileged allies the right to send to every Great Panathenaea, held every four years, a cow and a trophy, deemed suitable for the colonies that respected the powerful goddess of the Acropolis, Athena Polias. Thus in Pericles' city, the Great Panathenaea became the triumphant expression of the Athenian empire.

Toward the middle of the fifth century B.C., after the constitutional reforms of Cleisthenes and Ephialtes, Athens had, from an institutional viewpoint, the structure of a radical democracy. The decision-making organ was the assembly of all the citizens, the *ecclesia*, while the high council, the *boule*, had the task of arranging the agenda for the assembly. The College of Archons, which served as the executive branch, had lost much of its authority since 487 B.C., when it had been established that the office was no longer to be elective, but that the archons had to be chosen by lot on the basis of a list prepared by heads of the populace at large. This also diminished the prestige of the Areopagus, which was made up of ex-archons. Thus the executive functions tended to pass on to the generals.

Moreover, this completely formal democracy did not include the equal right of all citizens to participate in the political life of the city. Of the upper classes, only the two richest ones could provide the archons; and if from 488 B.C. this right was extended to the third class, the "commoners" always remained excluded. Even the generals were chosen by custom only from among the members of the highest classes. The people — those who belonged neither to the landholding aristocracy nor to the new urban commercial class — may have had some power of control over the political life of the city, but they did not have any power of initiative. Even Pericles, the most renowned exponent of radical democracy, was a nobleman: on his mother's side, he was Cleisthenes' grandson; his father was Xanthippus of the Buzyges family and a friend of Pisistratus. Yet Pericles, whose person aroused so much hatred, nonetheless seemed moderate when, shortly after his death, the leadership of the people passed into the hands of those who claimed popular extraction.

With the emerging influence of the urban proletariat masses, whose consent had determined his own rise to power, Pericles brought the policy of his predecessors to its extreme consequences. At Athens, the urban entrepreneur class had based its activities on trade. However, manufacturing activity that would allow for a great absorption of labor was not developed; with rare exceptions, the handicraft activities were still carried on by individuals, or at best in small workshops. The only production that had assumed any importance in the realm of international export was painted ceramics, which reached the most remote corners of the Mediterranean in great quantities. It was therefore necessary for the imperialist policy to guarantee to the Athenian proletariat great working opportunities and better living conditions, usually at the expense of allied cities. This was a fragile economy, whose precarious equilibrium remained totally dependent upon the political power of the city-state. Pericles tried to consolidate his balance by ending the war with the Persians and trying to eliminate Sparta as a rival. On the domestic front, he tried to create new work opportunities financed by the state, thus involving a large number of citizens in the well-being of the polis.

The judiciary reform and the replacement of the ancient court (the *heliaea*) by numerous popular courts (*dikasteria*) should be viewed within this framework. The popular judges, for the most part "commoners," succeeded in gaining, according to Aristophanes, a salary for about three hundred days a year. Many lower-class people, meanwhile, were permanently employed in the crews of the sixty triremes in the Athenian fleet. In this way, about twenty thousand citizens got at least some salary from the government. Others found work abroad in the military missions sent to the strategic points of the empire. Naturally, such measures could not but arouse the discontent of Athens' allies. The military colonies took over the best lots of land; moreover, they did not content themselves with the small single lots characteristic of Aegean agriculture, but occupied the large lots held in common by groups of farmers.

And this was not the only way in which the Athenian proletariat made

itself a responsible "partner" in the exploitation of the city's allies. After the transfer of the Delian League's treasury to Athens, the monies collected became an integral part of the Athenian budget. Pericles used a lot of this money to finance another of the foundations of his policy: the ambitious building program that would change Athens in the space of a few years. The city, by now the capital of a veritable empire, had to reflect this new role in its very appearance; this ideological weapon was to be no less effective in impressing potential enemies and allies than the triremes and the military colonies. But the colossal building ventures also had a primary economic purpose. As Plutarch acutely observed, the construction projects insured a salary and a job to all artisans who could not find work in the military and court enterprises.

In one sense, then, the flourishing of Athens under Pericles was truly a miracle. The city had a fragile and hazardous economy; the aggressive and despotic policy toward the city's allies irremediably corroded the foundations of the empire; continual provocations to Sparta only made

43. Athens: The Parthenon seen from the northwest. If we would have some idea of how the temple originally appeared, we must remember that the colonnade along the north side was much darker, since it was backed by the cella wall, most of which no longer stands; moreover, the peristyle was completely covered. But if the interior was relatively dark, the exterior was gleaming and articulated, with its sculptured frieze and pediment, of which only fragments remain today.

the final conflict all the more inevitable, a conflict that the city seemed to run toward with that pride (*hubris*) that sooner or later must provoke the envy and vengeance of the gods. The last opposing voice, that of Thucydides (son of Milesias) was silenced by his ostracism in 442 B.C. Despite all these provocations of fate, Athens continued to prosper. The people at large, given more freedom by government compensation, could take an active part in the political life of their city. The seeming elimination of social conflicts, at least in Attica, through the discussion within the assemblies, generated unbounded confidence in the *logos*, the word taken as a measure of things. In this climate, Socrates and the Sophists grew up; the former, the symbol of Pericles' Athens; the latter, the symbol of the foreboding storms that were forming on the horizon. This tragic, serene, Olympian illusion of Athenian invulnerability found its highest expression in the art of Phidias, who knew how to capture in stone the ideology of Pericles' Athens.

The Parthenon as an
Expression of the City-State

When Pericles initiated his building program, peace reigned. The terrible memory of the Persian sacking of Athens had been mitigated; the city preferred to remember the victory at Salamis — the triumph of Athens over the Persians had taken on a legendary character. In 449 B.C., the so-called Treaty of Callias had put an end to the war with the Persian Empire to the east, removing every appearance of justification for the Delian League; but Athens had its claws so firmly implanted in its allies that this event had no effect. And having made peace with Sparta as well, Athens could enjoy the fruits of its policy. A treasury of 9,700 talents was deposited on the Acropolis — an enormous sum when we consider that toward the middle of that century a trireme cost three talents. A large part of this sum, 8,000 talents, came from the treasury of the Delian League, and it was essentially with this money that Pericles financed his building program. About 2,012 talents were used for the expenses of the Propylaea and other edifices, including the Parthenon; the statue of Athena Parthenos alone cost 700 talents.

Pericles entrusted to Phidias, his friend and collaborator, responsibility for directing the reconstruction of the entire Acropolis. Many sculptors and architects worked there, of course, but there was one coordinating mind that, in continual rapport with Pericles, could adapt the conception of the whole — the architectural and sculptural style and expression — to the total context of the contemporary political experience (Figure 42).

44. Athens: The Parthenon seen from the east, the main entrance end. The frieze had metopes with the battle of the Amazons. On the pediment, left side, was the chariot of Helios and Dionysus; on the right, the chariot of Selene.

45. Athens: The Parthenon. Behind the western colonnade we see the front of the opisthodomos, surmounted by a frieze (barely visible in the shadows, upper right), and the door that led into the inside chamber with its four Ionic columns.

46. Athens: The western frieze of the Parthenon seen in close-up. Slabs XII, XIII, and XIV represent the preparations of the young knights for the procession.

THE SPEECH OF ATHENAGORAS
THE SYRACUSAN

Some one will say that a democracy is neither a sensible nor an equitable thing, but that those who have property are also most competent to rule best. But *I* say, in the first place, that "democracy" is a name for all, but "oligarchy" for only a part; and, in the second place, that though the rich are the best guardians of property, the intelligent would be the best counselors, and the mass of the people the best judges after hearing measures discussed; and that all these things, both severally and collectively, have their due share allotted to them in a democracy. An oligarchy, on the other hand, admits, indeed, the many to a share of dangers, but of advantages it not only enjoys the larger part, but even takes away and keeps the whole. And this is what the powerful and young among you desire — a thing impossible to attain in a great city.

THUCYDIDES: *History* (VI: 39)

PERICLES' ORATION
ON ATHENIAN DEMOCRACY

For we enjoy a form of government which does not copy the laws of our neighbors; but we are ourselves rather a pattern to others than imitators of them. In name, from its not being administered for the benefit of the few, but of the many, it is called a democracy; but with regard to its laws, all enjoy equality, as concerns their private differences; while with regard to public rank, according as each man has reputation for anything, he is preferred for public honors, not so much from consideration of party, as of merit; nor, again, on the ground of poverty, while he is able to do the state any good service, is he prevented by the obscurity of his position. We are liberal then in our public administration; and with regard to mutual jealousy of our daily pursuits, we are not angry with our neighbor, if he does anything to please himself; nor wear on our countenance offensive looks, which though harmless, are yet unpleasant. While, however, in private matters we live together agreeably, in public matters, under the influence of fear, we most carefully abstain from transgression, through our obedience to those who are from time to time in office, and to the laws; especially such of them as are enacted for the benefit of the injured, and such as, though unwritten, bring acknowledged disgrace on those who break them . . . . Again, the same men can attend at the same time to domestic as well as to public affairs; and others, who are engaged in business, can still form a sufficient judgment on political questions. For we are the only people that consider the man who takes no part in these things, not as unofficious, but as useless; and we ourselves judge rightly of measures, at any rate, if we do not originate them; while we do not regard works as any hinderance to deeds, but rather consider it a hinderance not to have been previously instructed by word, before undertaking in deed what we have to do.

THUCYDIDES: *History* (II: 37–40)

For those who today face the Propylaea, after the tiring ascent up the western slope, the Acropolis is like a bald limestone hill from which there dramatically emerges the Parthenon on the right and the articulated volume of the Erechtheum on the left. But when Pericles' project was completed, the approach to these monuments was quite different. The panorama, for instance, was screened off by a series of "wings" that led the visitor into a progressive discovery of the monuments from the different points of view according to which they had been conceived. The central part of the hill was closed off by the Mycenaean bastion wall, later used as a terrace for the Athena Polias sanctuary. On this was placed Phidias' statue of Athena Promachos, "first to fight" in defense of the citadel and the first work that appeared to those who crossed through the Propylaea. To the right, a short distance from the Athena Polias enclosure, ran a long wall which marked off the two little courts that belonged to the sanctuary of Artemis Brauronis and the Chalkotheke, the edifice in which the weapons were kept. Whoever wanted to approach the Parthenon had to go along the corridor formed by these two enclosures, catching a glimpse of the northwestern corner of the temple in a foreshortened view that highlighted the fullness of its volume.

Opposite the Chalkotheke (to the north), there was a small propylon, an entranceway with columns which led into a trapezoidal courtyard bounded along the side toward the Parthenon by a large staircase. By the time a person had gone this far, the temple dominated the spectator in all its strength (Figure 43): from pure mass it was transformed into a complex web of columns and architectural elements, further extended by the sculptured decorations. The west facade (Figure 45) must have appeared unusually overwhelming with its animated mass of columns. The eight columns on the peristyle ends, normal in the large Ionic temples of Asia Minor where the breadth was compensated for by the slenderness of the tall columns, were exceptional in Doric architecture. Behind this wide facade, and set on a two-stepped base, were the six smaller columns that formed the front of the opisthodomos; these columns were at least partially visible because they were slightly staggered in relation to the eight columns of the facade. Proceeding farther along the exterior of the Parthenon, a viewer would have found the interior of the peristyle blocked by the end wall of the opisthodomos. The architectural volume on this side thus appeared quite confined, even if the vertical thrust of the columns was taken up again by the metopes and the frieze, which only now was visible, so high was it compared to the peristyle architrave.

Once up the stairway, the viewer took the path along the narrow space between the enclosure wall and the north side of the temple. The Panathenaic procession represented in the frieze along the sekos accompanied the onlooker in his gradual discovery of the monument. Along the west end, he may already have caught a glimpse of the preparations and of the youths on horseback (Figures 46, 48, 49), where the bodies tended to coagulate in groups, favoring the upward rhythm of the columns. On the long sides, the procession is animated by chariots, sacrificial animals, bearers of offerings, all culminating on the east end, where the virgin bearers of the sacred garment (the *peplos*) offered to Athena across the boundary — which at that time appeared quite tenuous — between Athens and Mount Olympus. The gods, seated among the ten eponymous heroes of Cleisthenes' tribe here, seemed to have found their natural earthly place on the Acropolis.

Here, too, for the first time, from an open area in front of the east end, the viewer could once more appreciate the edifice as an architectural organism, which opened out toward the world beyond (Figure 44). Through the columns of the peristyle and the pronaos, the eye could get a hint of the inside colonnade of the naos, which with its double row of Doric columns effected a notably upward impetus. This effect, now lost in the Parthenon because the naos is seen as a limitless square of marble, can still be appreciated at Paestum, Italy, in the so-called Temple of Neptune. The repeated rhythm of the interior colonnade accentuated the depth of the naos and led the eye to the pivotal point of the monument: Phidias' shining gold-and-ivory (or chryselephantine) statue of Athena Parthenos. Its barbaric richness, in which was condensed all the pomp and splendor

47. Athens: The Parthenon, looking toward the east from its interior. On this end, only the peristyle is well preserved. Of the six columns on the front of the pronaos, only a few drums remain, while nothing remains of the inside colonnade that ran inside around three sides of the naos.

The Doric order
 1 *Euthynteria*
 2 *Crepidoma*
 3 *Stylobate*
 4 *Echinus*
 5 *Abacus*
 6 *Architrave*
 7 *Guttae*
 8 *Regula*
 9 *Taenia*
10 *Frieze (metope and triglyph)*
11 *Guttae*
12 *Mutule*
13 *Cornice (geison)*
14 *Tympanum*
15 *Sloping cornice*
16 *Sima (gutter)*
17 *Acroterion*
18 *Pediment*

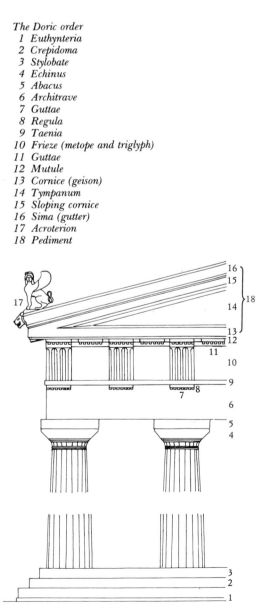

of Athenian imperialism, would disturb us too much to permit a true appreciation these days; the gold and ivory had cost the equivalent of 230 triremes, and from 210 to 270 pounds of gold alone were used on this sculpture. It is impossible to comprehend what must have been the effect of this great sculpture, about fifty feet high, including the base; and yet Phidias' fame in antiquity rested largely on this work. All we can do today is to try to imagine the implacable and remote force of the expression of Phidias' statue by looking at such works as the gem of Aspasios, a red jasper Augustan-age stone that had the face of the statue engraved on it.

The plan of the Periclean Parthenon reflected the pattern of the temple that preceded it, the one begun by Cleisthenes and interrupted by the Persians' sacking of the city. It also echoes the plan of the Athena Polias temple of Pisistratus' time. In the last analysis, too, the original inspiration dated from the Temple of Apollo at Corinth. But all the older formulas were liberally elaborated upon by the two architects, Iktinos and Callicratis, with whom Phidias probably collaborated, even in the planning stages. Although it has been adopted as the canon of Greek Doric architecture, the Parthenon deviates from the normal pattern in every detail, with a freedom of expression and a sensitivity to the environment that might well scandalize pure classicism. The Doric temple was basically a closed structure, visible only from the outside, dominated by a rigid symmetry that emphasized its character of pure volume: by the contrast between the peristyle, where the empty spaces prevailed over the volume, and the naos in which the solid wall predominated. The sekos of the Doric temple, therefore, had a simple plan, with a median room, the naos, between two vestibules with columns (pronaos and opisthodomos) which served to connect the naos to the peristyle.

In the Parthenon, the symmetry was broken up by the different aspect of the two end rooms: the one closed off and the other open toward the outside. The inside of the naos, with its double-order Doric colonnade that formed an ambulatory around the statue of the Athena Parthenos, had its own spatial area and interfered with the view of the east front of the temple (Figure 47). Behind the naos was another room, reached through the opisthodomos only, with its roof held up by four Ionic columns. Originally, only this room was called the Parthenon, or "Hall of the Virgins," the name that was later extended to the whole temple. The use of Ionic columns in a Doric edifice was to become a peculiar feature of Periclean architecture, which used these elements for their dynamic contrasts. In the Parthenon, this solution was rendered necessary by the lack of available space in the western hall; the Ionic columns, being much more slender, could reach the ceiling in one clean vertical line. A series of devices — such as the the curving of the horizontal lines, the inward inclination of the corner columns — reveals the level of refinement the artists had attained, and helps to consolidate the organic unity of the edifice.

Sculptures of the Parthenon

The plan of the sculptural decoration of the Parthenon was determined by one person, Phidias, even if he entrusted much of the work to a group of mason-artists, who in turn used a larger group of assistants in the execution of the frieze and metopes. The overall plan was based on ideal polarities, represented by the two ends of the temple: the west facade was dedicated to the heroes and myths of Athens, the east facade consecrated to the gods. The metopes along the west end represented the defense of the Acropolis against the assault of the Amazons, who had come to liberate their queen Antiope, whom Theseus had abducted and taken to Athens. This typically Athenian myth, which spoke of the citadel defended against the barbarians by its founder, Theseus, was greatly popular in the period following the Persians' sacking of Athens. It was celebrated in the second quarter of the same century in two paintings by Micon, the first in the so-called Theseum and the other in the many-colored Poikile portico in the Agora of Athens. If Theseus had been the founder of Athens, Pericles had given it a second life; so that in a second battle with the Amazons, that Phidias had sculptured on the shield of the

48. **Athens: The Parthenon, western frieze, slabs III, IV, and V, showing the departure of the horsemen in the procession.**

ATHENA AND POSEIDON CONTEND FOR ATTICA

Cecrops, a son of the soil, with a body compounded of man and serpent, was the first king of Attica, and the country which was formerly called Acte he named Cecropia after himself. In his time, they say, the gods resolved to take possession of cities in which each of them should receive his own peculiar worship. So Poseidon was the first that came to Attica, and with a blow of his trident on the middle of the acropolis, he produced a sea which they now call Erechtheis. After him came Athena, and, having called on Cecrops to witness her act of taking possession, she planted an olive tree, which is still shown in the Pandrosium. But when the two strove for possession of the country, Zeus parted them and appointed arbiters, not, as some have affirmed, Cecrops and Cranaus, nor yet Erysichthon, but the twelve gods. And in accordance with their verdict the country was adjudged to Athena, because Cecrops bore witness that she had been the first to plant the olive. Athena, therefore, called the city Athens after herself, and Poseidon in hot anger flooded the Thriasian plain and laid Attica under the sea.

APOLLODORUS: *The Library* (III: XIV, 1)

THE ARISTOCRATS AND THE PEOPLE

So long, however, as Pericles was leader of the people, things went tolerably well with the state; but when he was dead there was a great change for the worse. Then for the first time did the people choose a leader who was of no reputation among men of good standing, whereas up to this time such men had always been found as leaders of the democracy. The first leader of the people, in the very beginning of things, was Solon, and the second was Pisistratus, both of them men of birth and position. After the overthrow of the tyrants there was Cleisthenes, a member of the house of the Alcmaeonidae; and he had no rival opposed to him after the expulsion of the party of Isogoras. After this Xanthippus was the leader of the people, and Miltiades of the upper class. Then came Themistocles and Aristides, and after them Ephialtes as the leader of the people, and Cimon son of Miltiades of the wealthier class. Pericles followed as leader of the people, and Thucydides, who was connected by marriage with Cimon, of the opposition. After the death of Pericles, Nicias, who subsequently fell in Sicily, appeared as leader of the aristocracy, and Cleon son of Cleaenetus of the people. The latter seems, more than any one else, to have been the cause of the corruption of the democracy by his wild undertakings; and he was the first to use unseemly shouting and coarse abuse on the Bema and to harangue the people with his cloak girt up short about him, whereas all his predecessors had spoken decently and in order.

ARISTOTLE: *Atheniensium Respublica* (28)

Following pages:
49. **Athens: From the western frieze of the Parthenon, slabs V, VI, and VII.** In this western frieze, and probably in the metopes as well, Phidias' closest collaborators made clay models of his drawings and then the execution of these was given over to a group of sculptors. The difference in quality of execution can be noted, for example, by comparing the inert and angular figure of the horseman with the breast-armor and helmet (second from left) with the horseman following him, a totally realized sculpture.

statue of Athena Parthenos, ancient tradition recognized the portraits of Pericles and Phidias. Scholars today usually recognize these central figures as Theseus and Daedalus.

The west pediment showed a struggle between Poseidon and Athena for possession of Attica, won by the goddess when she made the olive tree sprout up. This divine conflict, signs of which are said to survive still in the sanctuary of Athena Polias, was witnessed by the families of the mythical progenitors of the Athenians, the Cecropidae and the Erechthides. King Erechtheus was accompanied by his daughter Creusa and her son Ion. The figure of Ion, mythical progenitor of the Ionians, as we have seen, was closely linked with the imperialistic propaganda of Athens. For this reason, it was set in a prominent position by Phidias, on the northern side of the west pediment, among the first sculptures that appeared to the visitor's eyes.

Theseus provided the unifying motif between the western and southern metopes, the latter depicting the battle between the Thessalian Centaurs and the Lapiths. As we have already seen on the west pediment at Olympia, the Athenian hero had come to the aid of his friend Pirithous in the battle that ensued after the Centaur Eurytion attempted to violate Pirithous' bride Hippodameia. In the center of the battle of the Centaurs there was inserted a group of reliefs with a different subject, the legends of the Attic heroes Cecrops, Erechtheus, and Pandion. The exaltation of the glories of Athens was again made explicit, as must certainly have been the case with the central metopes on the northern side between the scenes about the conquest of Troy and those that narrated the tremendous night of the sacking of the city.

We do not know if the choice of the destruction of Troy was dictated exclusively by the desire to represent once again the victory of the Greeks over the barbarians. In any case, this theme lent itself to the glorification of the power of Athena; here too, as in the painting of Polygnotos in the Lesche of the Cnidians at Delphi, attention must have been concentrated on the dramatic episode of Ajax's abuse of Cassandra. The young prophetess, daughter of King Priam of Troy, on the tragic night when Troy was destroyed, had taken refuge near the statue of Athena Pallas. But "Little Ajax" took her from there by force and violated her, thus committing a sacrilege, since whoever took refuge in a sacred place was under the protection of the gods. The tremendous punishment inflicted on the triumphant Achaeans by the goddess must have seemed like a great warning to every Greek. Among other things, in Polygnotos' painting there was Aethra, Theseus' mother; and ancient Greeks would not have forgotten that Theseus' sons, Acamas and Demophon, were said to have brought the venerated statue of Athena back to Athens.

The east pediment was dominated by the birth of Athena. However, Phidias, making innovations in the traditional iconography, did not represent the moment in which the goddess bursts forth armed from the head of Zeus after Hephaistos' hammer blow. The archaic complexity of such an incident did not suit his eminently human art. He preferred to represent the moment after the birth, when the goddess appeared alongside the supreme Zeus in all her unexpected splendor. Bernard Schweitzer, the great scholar of the Parthenon sculptures, has remarked: "The corner figures of the Sun being born and Selene at sunset indicate the birth of the day. With the birth of the divine protectress, there begins a new day, a fatal day, a cosmic day." Meanwhile, the eastern metopes represented the victory of the gods over the Titans, the episode that had occupied the east pediment of the Temple of Athena Polias; in the Parthenon metopes it was reduced to a series of duels rhythmically divided by the gods' chariots.

Work on the Partheon lasted from 447 B.C. — shortly after the peace with the Persians — to the beginning of the Peloponnesian War (433–432 B.C.). Much of the credit for having clarified the history of the sculptural decoration is due to Bernard Schweitzer, who has shown how the chronology of its several parts reflects the slow maturation of an artistic and human experience. In the metopes, for instance, completed before 442–441 B.C., or in the western frieze of the sekos made before

That which gave most pleasure and ornament to the city of Athens, and the greatest admiration and even astonishment to all strangers, and that which now is Greece's only evidence that the power she boasts of and her ancient wealth are no romance or idle story, was his construction of the public and sacred buildings. Yet this was that of all his actions in the government which his enemies most looked askance upon and cavilled at in the popular assemblies, crying out how that the commonwealth of Athens had lost its reputation and was ill-spoken of abroad for removing the common treasure of the Greeks from the isle of Delos into their own custody. . . . [saying] that "Greece cannot but resent it as an insufferable affront, and consider herself to be tyrannized over openly, when she sees the treasure, which was contributed by her upon a necessity for the war, wantonly lavished out by us upon our city, to gild her all over, and to adorn and set her forth, as it were some vain woman, hung round with precious stones and figures and temples, which cost a world of money."

Pericles, on the other hand, informed the people, that they were in no way obliged to give any account of those moneys to their allies, so long as they maintained their defense, and kept off the barbarians from attacking them; while in the meantime they did not so much as supply one horse or man or ship, but only found money for the service; "which money," said he, "is not theirs that give it, but theirs that receive it, if so be they (perform the conditions upon which they receive it." And that it was a good reason, that, now the city was sufficiently provided and stored with all things) necessary for the war, they should convert the overplus of its wealth to such undertakings as would hereafter, when completed, give them eternal honor, and, for the present, while in process, freely supply all the inhabitants with plenty. With their variety of workmanship and of occasions for service, which summon all arts and trades and require all hands to be employed about them, they do actually put the whole city, in a manner, into state-pay; while at the same time she is both beautiful and maintained by herself. For as those who are of age and strength for war are provided for and maintained in the armaments abroad by their pay out of the public stock, so, it being his desire and design that the undisciplined mechanic multitude that stayed at home should not go without their share of public salaries, and yet should not have them given them for sitting still and doing nothing, to that end he thought fit to bring in among them, with the approbation of the people, these vast projects of buildings and designs of work, that would be of some continuance before they were finished, and would give employment to numerous arts, so that the part of the people that stayed at home might, no less than those that were at sea or in garrisons or on expeditions, have a fair and just occasion of receiving the benefit and having their share of the public moneys.

The materials were stone, brass, ivory, gold, ebony, cypresswood; and the arts or trades that wrought and fashioned them were smiths and carpenters, molders, founders and braziers, stone-cutters, dyers, goldsmiths, ivory-workers, painters, embroiderers, turners; those again that conveyed them to the town for use, merchants and mariners and shipmasters by sea, and by land, cartwrights, cattle-breeders, waggoners, rope-makers, flax-workers, shoemakers and leather-dressers, road-makers, miners. And every trade in the same nature, as a captain in an army has his particular company of soldiers under him, had its own hired company of journeymen and laborers belonging to it banded together as in array, to be as it were the instrument and body for the performance of the service. Thus, to say all in a word, the occasions and services of these public works distributed plenty through every age and condition.

As then grew the works up, no less stately in size than exquisite in form, the workmen striving to outvie the material and the design with the beauty of their workmanship, yet the most wonderful thing of all was the rapidity of their execution.

Undertakings, any one of which singly might have required, they thought, for their completion, several successions and ages of men, were every one of them accomplished in the height and prime of one man's political service. Although they say, too, that Zeuxis once, having heard Agatharchus the painter boast of despatching his work with speed and ease, replied, "I take a long time." For ease and speed in doing a thing do not give the work lasting solidity or exactness of beauty; the expenditure of time allowed to a man's pains beforehand for the production of a thing is repaid by way of interest with a vital force for the preservation when once produced. For which reason Pericles' works are especially admired, as having been made quickly, to last long. For every particular piece of his work was immediately, even at that time, for its beauty and elegance, antique; and yet in its vigor and freshness looks to this day as if it were just executed. There is a sort of bloom of newness upon those works of his, preserving them from the touch of time, as if they had some perennial spirit and undying vitality mingled in the composition of them.

Phidias had the oversight of all the works, and was surveyor-general, though upon the various portions other great masters and workmen were employed. For Callicratis and Iktinos built the Parthenon; the chapel at Eleusis, where the mysteries were celebrated, was begun by Coroebus, who erected the pillars that stand upon the floor or pavement, and joined them to the architraves; and after his death Metagenes of Xypete added the frieze and the upper line of columns; Xenocles of Cholargus roofed or arched the lantern on top of the temple of Castor and Pollux; and the long wall, which Socrates says he himself heard Pericles propose to the people, was undertaken by Callicratis. . . .

The Odeum, or musicroom, which in its interior was full of seats and ranges of pillars, and outside had its roof made to slope and descend from one single point at the top, was constructed, we are told, in imitation of the King of Persia's Pavilion; this likewise by Pericles' order. . . .

The propylaea, or entrances to the Acropolis, were finished in five years' time, Mnesicles being the principal architect. A strange accident happened in the course of building, which showed that the goddess was not averse to the work, but was aiding and cooperating to bring it to perfection. One of the artificers, the quickest and the handiest workman among them all, with a slip of his foot fell down from a great height, and lay in a miserable condition, the physicians having no hope of his recovery. When Pericles was in distress about this, Athena appeared to him at night in a dream, and ordered a course of treatment, which he applied, and in a short time and with great ease cured the man. And upon this occasion it was that he set up a brass statue of Athena, surnamed Health, in the citadel near the altar, which they say was there before. But it was Phidias who wrought the goddess' image in gold, and he has his name inscribed on the pedestal as the workman of it; and indeed the whole work in a manner was under his charge, and he had, as we have said already, the oversight over all the artists and workmen, through Pericles' friendship for him; and this, indeed, made him much envied, and his patron shamefully slandered with stories, as if Phidias were in the habit of receiving, for Pericles' use, freeborn women that came to see the works. . . .

438 B.C., the artist revealed a sure knowledge of the world outside; he searched for the representation of a controlled dynamics, which even in the tension of the bodies did not infringe upon the measure of the Doric architecture. The ample and linear composition of the western frieze does not obscure the accents created by the axes of the columns, and the figures tend to coagulate in almost metope-like groups, with a regular alternation of knights and figures on foot. The relief unfolds on a single plane, with compact figures standing out on a broad background. The variety of the patterns, in contrast with the frequency of repeated figures in the later parts, shows that Phidias was here establishing a new theme and vision. But some figures, in a nervous and unsteady pose — such as the youth tying his sandal (Figure 49) — already go beyond this vision.

The eastern and western sections of the frieze, as Schweitzer has demonstrated, were sculptured in the Parthenon workshops before being put in their places. This helped to create perceptible breaks and "pauses" between groups of slabs entrusted to different masters and masons (Figure 48). The stylistic level of the masters in charge of the preliminary designs, sketched out by Phidias, is inconsistent; one often notes a strong contrast between the boldness of a compositional pattern and the opacity of its rendering, and the qualitative lack of balance is quite considerable from one block to another. For example, the group made up of two knights and the youth tying his sandal (Figure 49) is close to Phidias' personal style; while the knight with helmet and cuirass, in his inert marionette-like pose, indicates how little that particular stonecutter knew how to interpret the compressed energy that animates the frieze.

In the eastern section of the naos, above all in the central part (Figure 50), the sculptures were entirely executed by the chiefs of the stonecutters' crews, Phidias' closest collaborators, and therefore the qualitative deficiencies almost disappear. Here, where the rising rhythm of the edifice was already emphasized by the double colonnade that was dimly seen in the naos, the frieze did not take up the architectural rhythm with rigor; instead, the composition became more flowing and fused. At the same time, the light became more important in the definition of the figures, which lost some compactness of volume in order to emerge more totally into space. The different manner of interpreting the drapery contributed to this; in the crowding together of the broken folds, of the arched and drooping backs, the light was broken up and gathered together again in a complex variety of effects.

This first phase of the Parthenon sculptures culminated with the figure of Dionysus who occupied the corner of the east pediment (Figure 51). "The motif of the spread limbs," as Schweitzer has put it, "dominated the formal language here, acting as the expression of a concentrated strength and a limitless grandeur, of the free manifestation of being and of the extreme mastery of space." The style of the drapery, which manifested itself in the eastern frieze, reached its extreme expressive possibilities in the group of Dione and Aphrodite, brought to the limit between virtuosity of light effects and the dissolution of the sculptured surface.

Where the frieze ran along the top of the sekos, no relationship with the supporting elements had to be established, and the composition thus sprang up free from any architectural binds. The blocks were sculptured on the spot, perhaps after Phidias himself had traced the design on the surface of the marble. The style, therefore, proved to be more immediate and spontaneous. The continuity of work between the stonecutters and masons who worked side by side here eliminated those breaks and the slight incongruities of pattern that we have noticed in the sections sculptured by different crews. The contrast between background and figure, still noticeable in the eastern frieze, has now dissolved (Fgure 52); the representation unfolds on different planes, and the contrasting tensions that animate the bodies come together where the movement is most lively. Take, for example, the warrior leaning out of his moving chariot (Figure 53); he emerges from the great hollows of shadow in the shield and, although standing, echoes in his pose, with his limbs spread apart, the Dionysus on the east pediment. But the pose is unstable in the frieze; the large semicircle of the figure is connected by means of the opposite

curve of his short cloak to the even more closed arch of the round shield. The torso modeling no longer tends toward the construction of a firm volume; the anatomical markings become the pretext for deep grooves of shadow which make the surface fluid.

Even where the figures were arranged on one plane, set at a distance from one another, as in the procession of the urn-bearers (Figure 54), the skin reveals a mobility unknown in the frieze along the narrow ends of the temple. This is true even if at times the artist's chisel was not quite up to the task of rendering the stylistic subtleties of Phidias. This process — of stone-carving moving toward virtuoso modeling — attained its extreme in the west pediment, the last of the sculptural works prepared for the Parthenon. Here again, according to Schweitzer, "the marble draws away from the final compactness of the finished form; the tension of the sinews and the animated play of the muscles are reflected on a fluid, unstable surface full of unexpected and sudden passages. The work of the chisel helps to give us this impression, as it does not strive to realize the finish and the smoothness of the stylistic form on the east pediment." This pictorial sculpture, which is expressed through the opposition of powerful undefined masses in an unresolved and restless antagonism, is the language of a formal world in crisis (Figure 55). What there had been of a defined, domineering corporeal presence in the previous figures was here seen as a limit; the certainty of Pericles' *polis* was now inadvertently changing, and that world, which had seemed to be complete in itself, now revealed itself in all its fragility. Thus, the objectified form dissolved, due to the need for a more persistent expression of the individual.

The fragile Athenian empire, which had seen the Parthenon begun at the moment of its greatest splendor, now saw the first cracks spreading.

When the orators, who sided with Thucydides and his party, were at one time crying out, as their custom was, against Pericles, as one who squandered away the public money, and made havoc of the state revenues, he rose in the open assembly and put the question to the people, whether they thought that he had laid out much; and they saying. "Too much, a great deal," "Then," said he, "since it is so, let the cost not go to your account, but to mine; and let the inscription upon the buildings stand in my name." When they heard him say thus, whether it were out of a surprise to see the greatness of his spirit or out of emulation of the glory of the works, they cried aloud, bidding him to spend on, and lay out what he thought fit from the public purse, and to spare no cost, till all were finished.

PLUTARCH: *Life of Pericles* (XII-XIV)

50. Athens: The Parthenon, eastern frieze. The gods of Olympus — Poseidon, Apollo, and Artemis. According to one authority, this is one of several slabs executed by one of Phidias' closest collaborators. (Acropolis Museum)

51. Athens: The Parthenon, southern corner of the east pediment showing the chariot of Helios and Dionysus. In this figure, the motif of the spreading of the limbs introduces a restless, dynamic element that will be fully exploited in the figures of the west pediment.

Pericles' prestige had been slowly corroded by the long years of his government. The aristocracy and the small landowners could no longer pardon the statesman for his continual provocation of Sparta, for they knew quite well that such a campaign would have everything to lose in a mortal struggle that, after 435 B.C., seemed almost inevitable. Even in the city itself, among the urban proletariat so carefully looked after by Pericles, discontent was beginning to spread; his economic policy, which had failed to create jobs in more productive fields by basing everything on the public building program, the state compensations, and the fleet — this policy was displaying more and more its inherent deficiencies and faults. Even before the outbreak of the Peloponnesian War, Pericles' esteem in the *ecclesia* must have undergone a severe blow, and his political opponents lost no time in attacking those closest to him — the philosopher Anaxagoras and the sculptor Phidias. Accused of having stolen precious material that was to have been used for the statue of Athena Parthenos, Phidias had to go into exile in 432 B.C., just when the Athenians could finally contemplate, on the west pediment of the Parthenon, his figures of their heroes erected as a symbol of the new imperial Athens.

Erechtheum and Propylaea

The Parthenon, conceived as the apex of attention on the Acropolis, was the first edifice of Pericles' plan to be realized. Then, while the sculptured decorations of that temple were still being finished, the Propylaea (437–432 B.C.) and Erechtheum were begun. Work on the latter was interrupted for many years because of the Peloponnesian War, and was resumed only after the restoration of democracy in 409 B.C.; even this time, though, it remained unfinished. Thus, we must recognize that the profound stylistic and moral crisis that had such an effect on Phidias' work did not arise from his experience as an individual but, as we have seen, from deep-rooted, historical situations. And the artists who, like Phidias, worked for the completion of Pericles' plan of the Acropolis, and who had among other things a common "client" in the city-state, could not but notice the complex and contradictory dimensions of the situation in Athens. Their stylistic problems were akin to those of Phidias'. In a certain sense, the Erechtheum and the Propylaea posed once again the problem set by Phidias in the Parthenon, polarizing the search for opposite heights represented by the sculpture of that great temple's pediments: the east pediment, where the form, albeit in an antagonism of tension, was recomposed in a restless equilibrium; the west pediment, where this equilibrium was broken up with the liberation of the masses and the tensions.

In both the Propylaea and the Erechtheum the monolithic unity of the Greek temple — pure self-sufficient volume in which every dynamic thrust was reabsorbed within the two perfect horizontals of the stylobate and the entablature — was cast aside. For that matter, the Parthenon had already betrayed dissatisfaction with this form. Now it was broken up and the architectural organism was articulated in opposing masses that open out to space; the suggestion offered by the surroundings, by the irregularity of the ground, was taken up as the theme of this architectural discourse, which qualified it by interpreting it. It was no longer an arbitrary horizontal plane on which a pattern, already complete in itself, was placed, but rather the attempt to interpret the natural factor by linking the architectural form to it in an indissoluble manner. This problem, felt with the same urgency, was solved in different ways by Mnesicles, the architect of the Propylaea, and the unknown creator of the Erechtheum. In the latter structure, the architectural masses, although clearly differentiated and molded on the irregular profile of the rock, were finally recomposed in a contained equilibrium. With the Propylaea, on the other hand, Mnesicles availed himself of the contrasts, the discontinuities, in order to emphasize in every way, at the risk of breaking up the form, the open dynamics generated by the different levels and by the different formal value of the architectural masses.

For as long as he was at the head of the state in time of peace, he governed it with moderation, and kept it in safety, and it was at its height of greatness in his time: and when the war broke out, he appears to have foreknown its power in this respect also. He survived its commencement two years and six months; and when he was dead, his foresight with regard to its course was appreciated to a still greater degree. For he said that if they kept quiet, and attended to their navy, and did not gain additional dominion during the war, nor expose the city to hazard, they would have the advantage in the struggle. But they did the very contrary of all this, and in other things which seemed to have nothing to do with the war, through their private ambition and private gain, they adopted evil measures both toward themselves and their allies; which, if successful, conduced to the honor and benefit of individuals; but if they failed, proved deterimental to the state with regard to the war. And the reason was, that he, being powerful by means of his high rank and talents, and manifestly proof against bribery, controled the multitude with an independent spirit, and was not led by them so much as he himself led them; for he did not say any thing to humor them, for the acquisition of power by improper means; but was able on the strength of his character to contradict them even at the risk of their displeasure. Whenever, for instance, he perceived them unseasonably and insolently confident, by his language he would dash them down to alarm; and, on the other hand, when they were unreasonably alarmed, he would raise them again to confidence. And so, though in name it was a democracy, in fact it was a government administered by the first man. Whereas those who came after, being more on a level with each other, and each grasping to become first, had recourse to devoting not only their speeches, but even their *measures,* to the humors of the people.

THUCYDIDES: *History* (II: 65: 5-10)

52. **Athens: The Parthenon. The young man directing someone with his gesture is evidently one of the organizers of the Panathenaic procession represented in the frieze. (Acropolis Museum)**

The Erechtheum — only in more recent times was the name used for the entire edifice — rose up at the center of the northern side of the Acropolis, where the palace of the Mycenaean kings had once stood. This was the place where the most ancient traditions of Athens were concentrated, the first signs of divine benevolence toward the city, and the memories of the mythical kings that Phidias had sculptured so many times on the Parthenon. Here were the signs of the conflict between Athena and Poseidon for control of Attica: the olive tree, which had given the victory to the goddess, and the spring of salt water that had gushed forth when Poseidon struck the rock with his trident. Here the serpent, the sacred custodian of the rock, had lived. The tomb of Cecrops and the enclosure dedicated to his daughter Pandrosos were venerated here as well, thus keeping alive an ancient myth. King Cecrops' three daughters had received in custody from Athena a basket containing the baby Erichthonios, part human and part serpent (and later the fourth king of Athens), with strict orders not to open it. Herse and Aglauros could not resist the temptation; only Pandrosos was able to conquer her curiosity, and for this was rewarded with the veneration of the Athenians.

It is difficult today to establish with any certainty the location of these relics — especially the very ancient statue of Athena — that were waiting to be gathered together. We only know that the eastern part of this area, where the "chamber of Athena" arose, was on a higher level, somewhat like a low hillock. Apparently the architect "forced" the natural site, including it in a more ample structure made homogeneous by the single foundation and by a continuous entablature, and kept this architectural structure contained in a compact volume. However, the difference in height remained the dynamic element of the structure; this central body was divided into two independent halves, with floors on different levels.

54

55. Athens: The Parthenon, west pediment.
In this representation of the Ilissos River, one
of two in Athens, the restlessness that was already spreading into the figures of the east
pediment has finally broken up the compact
solidity of the sculptured surfaces. (Acropolis
Museum)

The two facades were intentionally differentiated, too: the eastern one, prostylic, while in the western one, Ionic columns rising up from a high base were transformed into wall elements connected partly by walls and partly by latticework. Since the western side had its lower part hidden by the Athena Polias enclosure, the base of the columns was raised right where the ground descended.

As in the Parthenon, the two ends of the Erechtheum were different: the eastern, the principal one, was open to the world outside; the western one, closed and compact. In the latter, the resistant surface, made vibrant by the projection of the Ionic columns, was then framed by two architectural masses set on different levels (Figure 56). There was the ample northern portico with its wide intercolumniations, made more delicate by the refined frame of the doorway as well as by the decoration of the Ionic columns; and there was the compact Portico of the Caryatids, animated by the mute presence of the female figures (Figure 57). The complex dynamics of these articulated volumes, differing in quality and in light, was condensed above all on the western side of the Erechtheum, exactly that side best visible to the visitor coming onto the Acropolis.

The interior of the Erechtheum was also articulated in a complex way. From the pronaos, on the east facade, one entered the naos dedicated to Athena. The three western rooms, set on a lower level, were reached by means of the northern portico; this led into the room with the view framed by Ionic semicolumns, probably that mentioned in an inscription as the prostamiaion. In fact, it seems that the *prostomion*, an opening in the floor, was located here; from this opening one could see the spring of salt water supposedly tapped by Poseidon's trident. From here, one passed on to two flanking chambers, consecrated to Erechtheus and the hero Butes. From the prostomiaion, a small door led to the Pandrosos enclosure and to the tomb of Cecrops; a second door, hidden from the outside, gave access to the Portico of the Caryatids (Figure 58).

In the Erechtheum the use of the dark blue marble of Eleusis as a support for the frieze figures, in contrast to the white marble elsewhere in the temple, not only served a decorative function but also joined the architectural elements in a single organism. The expressive value of such chromatic contrast, however, was carried out with still greater dramatic intensity in the Propylaea. There the steps and stone moldings marked the fundamental pauses of the architectural "discourse," freeing the columns that rested on them in an accentuated rising sweep. A row of vertical slabs made of dark Eleusinian marble emphasized in the interior the different levels on which the colonnades on the two facades of the Propylaea rested. A passageway cut into the rock — for the passage of the sacrificial animals — cut transversely through the marble base (Figure 59); while on the facades, the Doric columns, because of the effect of this rather wide opening and the contraction of the end intercolumniations, crowded together into two groups with diminishing light.

As one ascended the steep western incline of the Acropolis along the ramps, the intense value of the "initiation" was constantly evoked and reinforced by a succession of pauses and ascending movements. Behind the Doric columns that formed the outside view, there were two rows of Ionic columns, much higher and more vibrant, which flanked the central opening; higher up was the dark stone threshold that divided the city from the rock; and in the background were the interior Doric columns that, set on a higher level and shorter than the Ionic columns, seemed to project farther away toward the sky.

The Propylaea also confronted the problem of connecting to its central body two terraces — different in breadth, level, and function — which flanked the entranceway of the Acropolis. The southern terrace, slightly lower, was from time immemorial consecrated to the cult of Athena, who here took on the character of a more ancient divinity connected with fertility and life after death. This bastion in the form of a tower, oriented on an east-west axis, was among the most sacred spots on the Acropolis because of the antiquity of the cult that went back to the Mycenaean period, that world into which the Athenians liked to project their heroes. The other, northern terrace, was free and available for Mnesicles' imagination to exploit.

56. Athens: The Erechtheum seen from the southwest. (In the background is Mount Lycabettus.) The lower part of the front was hidden by the Pandroseion enclosure wall. The articulation of the total structure into its three elements is here evident: on the left, the northern portico; on the right, the Caryatids Porch; between them, on a different level from both of these, were the central places of worship.

57. Athens: The Erechtheum seen from the southeast. In the cella, the floor was slightly higher than the stylobate on which rested the Ionic columns of the pronaos.

58. Athens: The Erechtheum, Caryatids Portico. The sculptured figures, done a little before 413 B.C., are descendants of the *kourai*, the statues of young women placed, during the archaic age, on the same site around the Temple of Athena Polias. Here, though, the archaic cult motif has assumed a more sophisticated architectural function. (The second figure from the left is the cement cast of the original now in the British Museum.)

57

Athens: A reconstruction of the Erectheum viewed from the west.

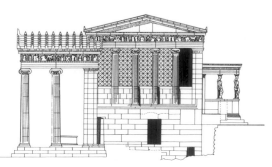

These two terraces were connected to the body by two short colonnades enclosed between segments of wall and pilasters that continued from the outer facade of the Propylaea. The colonnade on the north wing became the front of the Pinakoteka, the other led to the short terrace of the bastion tower on the south, at the point where the little Temple of Athena Nike was eventually built. The free choice of symmetry was emphasized by the homogeneous columns of the wings, which immediately afforded a visual comparison between the two terraces: the one closed off by the volume of the Pinakoteka, the other spacious and luminous because of the space that the little temple created around itself.

Sounion and Bassae

Pericles' building program also involved other sacred sites in Attica. At Eleusis, he had built the new Telesterion, while a new temple of Poseidon rose up at Sounion. The latter sanctuary stood on the southernmost point of Attica (Figure 60), in a rich and strategically important district. A few miles to the north lay the silver mines of Lavrion and Maronea, whose riches had permitted the construction of the Athenian fleet at the time of the battle of Salamis. Like the Acropolis, the Sounion promontory was consecrated to Athena and Poseidon; except for traces of Mycenaean and pre-Mycenaean cultures, the first evidence of a Poseidon cult dates from the beginning of the sixth century when, under Solon, Athens seemed to open up toward the sea. Some statues of youths, probably demolished during the Persian devastation, date from this period; the foundation of an older temple, from the end of the sixth century, has also been identified under the Periclean edifice.

The Temple of Poseidon at Sounion must have been visible from quite some distance at sea by those sailors sailing between Greece and Euboea and points to the east. Begun perhaps before the Parthenon, the Periclean temple was set directly over the archaic one, which had occupied the highest point on the promontory. The wall of the sacred enclosure included this part of the steep hill and, on the northern side parallel with the side of the temple, the propylaeum. For those approaching from the propylaeum on the lower level, the temple — detached from the rock by the clear-cut geometry of its stylobate — must have appeared to be rising toward the sky. This effect seems to have been intentionally accentuated by the architect: the closed volume of the sekos was much reduced in relation to the peristyle, while behind the colonnades of the facades was a spacious ambulatory. The prevalence of empty spaces over volume and the slender form of the columns must have rendered the structure even more easily recognizable for the sailors looking up at the promontory from the sea. The Sounion temple, because of its proportional relationships, has been attributed by some to the same architect who designed the Temple of Hephaistos and the Temple of Ares, both in Athens.

According to Pausanias, Iktinos, the architect of the Parthenon, also designed the Temple of Apollo Epikourios at Bassae in Arcadia. It sits at the top of a steep and rugged slope, and the limited flat space available determined its unusual orientation, with the ends on the north-south axis. This was an objective difficulty for the ancient architect: the orientation of the facade toward the east, toward the rising sun, not only had a ritual value but it also provided the condition for a controlled light in harmony with the architectural scheme of the Greek temple. The light, penetrating the temple through the pronaos, accentuated the perspective effects and created a natural relation between interior and exterior. The lack of this dominant feature at Bassae induced the architect to discard any idea of that exterior differentiation of the various parts of the edifice, which Iktinos had realized, for example, in the Parthenon.

The peristyle, with its rather stout columns set far apart, had a somewhat schematic character; enclosed between the two geometric planes of the stylobate and the entablature, it was set on a barren countryside like a neat, rational decision (Figure 61). The ambulatories on the ends are deep, just as at Sounion; however, the interior structure, with its elon-

59

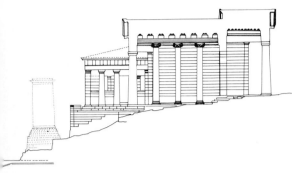

Athens: A schematic drawing of the Propylaea, seen from the north.

59. Athens: The Propylaea, western wing. The two large columns on the right without bases are the Doric columns of the front. On the left are the slender Ionic columns on high bases, set on the sides of the ramp that cuts through the foundation of the Propylaea. In the background, between these columns, is the Temple of Athena Nike on its bastion.

gated proportions, had a marked importance in the composition of the whole. From the outside, almost nothing of the naos interior was seen, and yet it was exactly here that the architect's attention was concentrated. It is probable that, because of the desires of those who commissioned the work, he had to keep in mind the Temple of Hera at nearby Olympia; there, in the naos were Doric semicolumns anchored to the lateral walls by segments of wall that made up a series of niches. At Bassae, the architect upset this static pattern, replacing the Doric columns with thin Ionic columns that emerged from boldly molded bases, and arranging at the end two wedgelike elements at the sides of the free columns. In the very center of the naos, at this end, was one free-standing Corinthian column — the earliest known example of such a column in Greece. The result was a centripetal disposition that set up an interior space full of tension. The light penetrated the naos from the end, through a door that is not visible, at the end of the eastern wall, creating an unpredictable tonal inversion in the room. The complex interplay of niches and supporting elements was enriched by a mysterious suggestiveness, almost as if the light came from the idol of the divinity, a bronze statue some twelve feet high.

Since the center of interest at Bassae was the interior of the naos, the figured frieze ran along the walls of the naos on the architrave that surmounted the Ionic columns. The sculptures (now in the British Museum) represent the battle between the Centaurs and the Lapiths and the battle between the Amazons and Herakles. These reliefs, in the Peloponnesian tradition, were executed by many artisans; allowing for certain differences among the various stonecutters, however, their fundamental stylistic characteristics are homogeneous. The figures, in the heavy fullness of their bodies, remind us in some ways of the sculptures at Olympia. Yet a closer look reveals the agitated opposition of the gestures, the exaggerated torsion of the bodies, the curling of the edges of the cloaks, the stretching of the clothes: every gesture and detail seems pushed to the limit of its expressive possibilities, and this strikes us even more when compared with the solid structure of the figures. The lesson afforded by the Parthenon was profoundly understood by the creator of the frieze, who embodied in his art Phidias' compositional secrets: the conflict motif, indicated by the knot of arms linked in rectangular form between two figures with opposite dynamics; the "spreading limbs" motif; the stretching of the clothes into thick areas separated by gathered folds, here simplified into backs with deep grooves. Nor is there any lack of bold touches, such as the warrior immersed in the background, covered by the foreshortened shield. The rigor of the compositional patterns, which bind the bodies in intricate geometric forms, marks the surfaces with thick, crossing lines amplified by the torsion of the bodies and the drapery. This manner was to become very popular, in that it allowed for the expression of an accentuated, often unresolved pathos; it was the language of Sophocles' *Antigone*, reflected in this sculptured world with its profound juxtapositions.

The group of Lapith women who draw back from the fury of a Centaur (Figure 62) was inspired by the reliefs executed by Phidias for the throne of Zeus in Olympia; this was particularly evident in the group of Niobe's two daughters, one of whom, pierced by arrows, leans on her still unharmed sister for support. In Phidias' relief, the group, as if set in a triangle, found its equilibrium in the balance of the volumes and the gestures; in the Bassae frieze, the standing figure opened out to a dramatic cross-pattern that vigorously created its own space. The pain-filled body of the fallen Lapith shifts the center of the composition toward the middle of the block, where the entanglement of the struggle condensed itself in the hand of the Centaur that seizes the cloak; at this point meet the two crossing diagonals that dominate the composition of the whole block.

At Bassae, the metopes on the front and back of the naos and the pediments also bore sculptured decorations. In one of the pediments, full-relief figures probably depicted the massacre of Niobe's children, pierced by Apollo's and Artemis' arrows at the request of their mother,

61

61

60. **Cape Sounion: The promontory at the tip of Attica is here viewed from the east, with Patroklou Islet just offshore. The Temple of Poseidon has twelve of its original columns standing, and they appear probably even taller and more airy than they would have when supporting the temple roof.**

61. **Bassae: The Temple of Apollo Epikourios seen from the northwest. This temple faced the north, a unique exception to the normal axis of Greek temples. The six columns on the front end are larger than the others, while the lateral columns are closer together.**

Leto. Niobe had dared to boast of her many children, thus incurring the wrath of the goddess, who was the mother of only those two. Almost certainly the celebrated Niobe piece found at Rome (in the Orti Sallustiani) came from this pediment; it is very close in character and technique to the dying Lapith in the frieze. The quality of these two particular sculptures is higher than that of many figures in the frieze, and it is probably that the master who conceived the entire sculptural decoration of the Bassae temple had reserved for himself the execution of the pediment figures, while he worked only occasionally on the frieze, less visible in the dim light of the interior.

The temple at Bassae was dedicated to Apollo Epikourios ("ready to protect"), and the sculptured decoration celebrated his terrible power; together with his sister Artemis, Apollo participated in the massacre of Niobe's children, and he took part in the battle with the Centaurs on a chariot drawn by a deer. Pausanias recalled that the Arcadians erected the temple in order to give thanks to the divinity who had defended them against the plague that struck the land in the second year of the Peloponnesian War (430 B.C.); however, as a date for this temple, that has not been unanimously agreed upon. It has seemed unlikely that Iktinos, after his Parthenon experience, could have conceived this edifice in which the interior space is unrelated to the exterior views; moreover, some elements of archaic tradition — such as the narrowing of the intercolumniations on the long sides of the peristyle — have been preserved. But since the style of the frieze is so close to the Parthenon sculptures, it has been suggested that the temple was begun before the Parthenon but was not finished, due to some interruption, until the last quarter of the fifth century B.C. None of these observations, by the way, take into account the particular problem posed by the topography of the site, and it is exactly here — in his ability to create in relationship to the environment — that the architect demonstrated how he profited from the Athenian experience. The solution adopted for the interior of the naos, indeed, seems directly descended from the Parthenon, so that Pausanias' attribution to Iktinos and the date assigned may reflect the architectural novelty here introduced in an Arcadian temple.

Athenian Mannerism: Cleon and the Crisis of the Consensus

The Periclean building program on the Acropolis came to a sudden halt with the beginning of the Peloponnesian War (431 B.C.). The conflict with Sparta, which was to decide which power would enjoy hegemony in the Greek world, was the logical outcome of Athenian policy, with its remote causes dating from at least as far back as the time of Themistocles and Cimon. But focusing, for the moment, on Pericles' Athens, we have seen how this city-state, even in the midst of its splendor, bore within itself the causes of its decline. The ranks of the populace had grown continuously, both because of the normal increase in population and because of the progressive exodus of the farmers from the Greek countryside, which no longer yielded enough to support the growing population. Increased trade and the relative facility in importing wheat and other foodstuffs from abroad had brought about a decrease in the price of agricultural products, and this phenomenon damaged the small and medium landowners most. Pericles' own policy, aimed at giving some kind of state compensation to the entire urban populace, had probably contributed to the growth in the number of persons not engaged in productive activity. This pressure necessitated new outlets; it was necessary to employ an ever-growing number of people in the army and the fleet, and this force then became a potential to be used to enlarge the empire.

Meanwhile, Sparta represented a real and constant threat; it had always boasted of having liberated the cities of Greece from tyrants, and it could use this tradition as a formidable propaganda tool with regard to its antagonist, Athens, which threatened to suffocate it. Pericles pursued his aim of a decisive confrontation with icy determination, openly violating the Thirty Years' Peace that had been concluded in 446 B.C.; when the war broke out, he had his strategy clearly worked out. The Spartan army, he realized, was stronger than the Athenian one in field battles; it was therefore necessary to abandon Attica to the enemy. But the Athenian fleet was far superior to the Spartan fleet, and could inflict heavy losses on the Spartans and their allies, devastating their territory with sudden, overwhelming attacks. Such a policy, however, sharpened the contrast between city and countryside; it might at best meet with approval of the *ecclesia,* most of whose members were urban proletariat. However, for the proletariat the policy seemed too weak on one hand, and repugnant on the other hand in its realistic evaluation of the Athenian army. In this respect, the heated words of the demagogues of popular extraction had a greater hold over the assembly.

The declared and open opponents of such a policy were the farmers, both large and small landowners who saw their land being left to the mercy of the enemy army; the moderate opposition, with the caustic Aristophanes as their spokesman, took up their desire for peace. During the Spartan siege, the farmers found refuge in the city and could thus make their voice heard in the *ecclesia.* This was a rude awakening for the Athenian city-state, which rapidly moved into a general crisis of the consensus that had held it together. A tremendous plague broke out in 430 B.C. in the city full of refugees, dealing a severe blow to the morale of the Athenians. It also killed a great number of people, including Pericles himself, and his death in 429 B.C. marked the end of an epoch for Athens. With him disappeared the last head of the radical-democratic

Bassae: Plan of the Temple of Apollo Epikourios

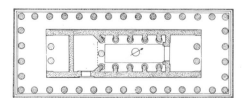

62. **Bassae: A slab from the temple frieze, showing the Lapith women being attacked by a Centaur. The battle of the Centaurs decorated the western and northern sides of the temple, while the battle of Herakles and the Amazons occupied the eastern and southern sides, covering the interior colonnade of the cella. (British Museum)**

party, who, because of his aristocratic blood and breadth of political vision, had succeeded in maintaining the consensus among the antagonistic components of the Athenian city-state.

The populace, in the meantime, had acquired an awareness of its own strength and was no longer willing to continue the game of a "protected" democracy. The leadership passed into the hands of statesmen of popular extraction, branded by aristocratic tradition as "demagogues," and they put a decisive end to the policy of Pericles and his predecessors of glossing over class differences. The space left unoccupied by Pericles was filled by Cleon, the leather merchant who was without a doubt the cleverest and most upright of the new politicians. Despite this, he was unable to propose a new policy that would give up the dream of empire in order to remedy the internal ills of the city. He merely pushed Pericles' policy to its extreme and thus became, thanks to Aristophanes and the aristocratic historians, the scapegoat for the great crisis of Athens. Cleon fell in 422 B.C., at Amphipolis, in the defeat suffered at the hands of the Spartan Brasidas.

When, after varying successes and failures on both sides, the two powers contending for hegemony in the Greek world made peace in 421 B.C., they were both exhausted and in distress. The Attic farmers had been ruined by the continual devastations of the Spartan armies; in particular, the large landowning class had been withered by the death of many of their young men who had served as knights or hoplites, as well as by the tributes imposed on them by the exigencies of the war. This situation, however, was the fruit of their own myopic policy: since Solon's time, they had provided the leaders for the democratic party, channeling the pressure of the masses into urbanization, the fleet, the empire — in short, toward any direction that did not endanger their caste privileges.

The Peloponnesian War had a profound effect upon Athenian culture. For one thing, because of its fratricidal character, the war could not find an ideal justification that would dress it up in epic overtones, as had been the case with the Persian wars. Pericles, in the funeral oration for those who had died in 431 B.C., had tried to make it appear as a necessary defense of democratic values against the Spartan oligarchy. But those

GREECE FROM HESIOD TO THUCYDIDES   121

63. Athens: The Temple of Athena Nike. The foundation of this edifice was hidden under a Turkish bastion and only brought to light in 1835, at which time the temple was reconstructed. Then between 1936–1940 it was necessary to take it apart again, and during this process traces of the Mycenaean cults were discovered on the site.

64. Athens: Nike tying her sandal, from the Balustrade of the Athena Nike bastion. The balance between bodily structure and drapery, so carefully preserved in the classic work—as, for example, in the transparent drapery of Phidias — here appears more like folds set in relief over a nude body. (Acropolis Museum)

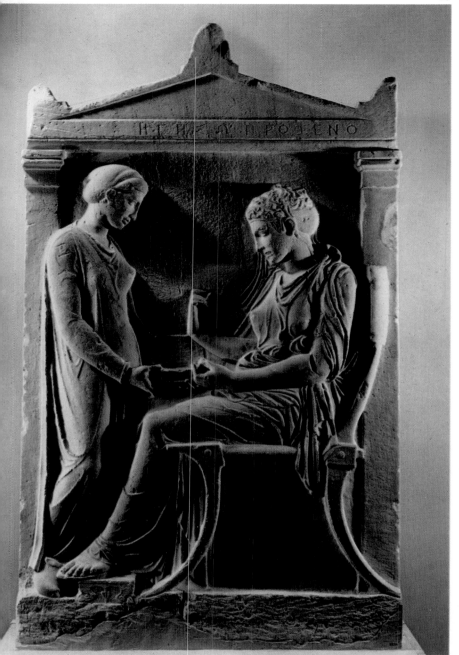

values ran no real risk in Pericles' Athens, and his justification was too feeble to cover up the true nature of the struggle. For other reasons as well, the war cut deeply into the tradition of the city-states. It had been marked by an unprecedented ferocity, and the massacre of civilians had many times obeyed nothing but the ruthless logic of reprisal.

The moral values that had until that time sustained Greek society were now in crisis, and the problem of human destiny was posed in all its dramatic and tragic overtones: man, in his disheartening individuality, seemed to be less and less a part of a social group, and more and more the tragic protagonist of his own personal fate. The profound moral and religious crisis struck the well-to-do most of all, those who could devote more time to reflection and could afford the luxury of an education in the school of the Sophists. These Sophists expressed in the most complete manner the moral atmosphere of the moment. Their thought was skeptical in regard to any preconceived truth of a moral, religious, or social character. Sophists placed their faith exclusively in an exaggerated rationalism: what can be demonstrated by means of discourse is true and real, but there can be two opposing cases or discourses concerning everything. In this way, rationalism was transformed into relativism. As Protagoras, one of the most illustrious Sophists, said: "I can affirm neither

124   GREECE

65. Athens: The funerary stele of Hegeso, from the Eridanos cemetery. The contained sadness of this late-fifth-century stele will be replaced shortly by a more blatant pathos, as the role of the polis declines and private life takes on greater importance. (Athens, National Museum)

66. Athens: The stele of Dexileos in the Eridanos cemetery. Dexileos was the son of a prominent family who died in the Corinthian War (394 B.C.). In this same cemetery there is also preserved the official monument erected by Athens for those who died during this war, and even this stele echoes something of the old spirit of the Periclean polis.

AFTER THE BATTLE OF PLATAEA
(August 1, 479 B.C.)

A general assembly of all the Greeks being called, Aristides proposed a decree that the deputies and religious representatives of the Greek states should assemble annually at Plataea, and every fifth year celebrate the Eleutheria or games of freedom. And that there should be a levy upon all Greece for the war against the barbarians of ten thousand spearmen, one thousand horses, and a hundred sail of ships; but the Plataeans to be exempt, and sacred to the service of the gods, offering sacrifice for the welfare of Greece.

PLUTARCH: *Life of Aristides* (XXI)

the existence nor the nature of the gods; in fact, there are many difficulties that obstruct me in this regard."

An analogous thought was maintained by Socrates, who, however, was an adamant adversary of Sophism, both because of its relativism and because the Sophists had turned philosophy into a profit-making profession. Although he was most respectful of the laws and gods of Athens, Socrates set the human intellect above every dogma. His thought was, from this point of view, aristocratic in its inextinguishable faith that the truth derives from reason, while the consensus of the multitude cannot make the wise man foolish nor the foolish man wise. Also close to the Sophists in some respects was Euripides. According to an ancient saying, he showed men what they are and not what they should be, placing all his interest in the realistic representation of characters and sentiments: above all, those that traditional ethics considered "unseemly," even categorizing them as forms of madness. The Homeric gods, whom Euripides had appear often in his plays, were made to seem archaic and distant, and their very wisdom was debated: Orestes, who had killed his mother in order to obey Apollo, could freely doubt the god's wisdom.

This culture had an essentially aristocratic basis. Even though Euripides' verses were familiar to the masses, — the Athenian prisoners in Sicily were said to have saved their lives by reciting to the Syracusans long passages from his tragedies — his world was no less distant from the primitive religiosity of the poorer classes. The heads of radical democracy played on the traditionalism of the lower classes, as they considered the new culture the sign of the oligarchical spirit. In 422 B.C., Cleon accused Euripides of impiety, and Alcibiades paid heavily for having been a student of Socrates, a fact that must have contributed to the creation of his notoriety as an "impious" person, who was tried in 415 B.C. and exiled. On the other hand, even an aristocratic spirit like Aristophanes, associated with the class of knights, could hurl himself against the new culture, against Socrates himself, in his criticism directed against the leaders of radical democracy and the Athenian political line of the day. From these criticisms, though they might originate from opposite ends of the political spectrum, there emerged as a constant the longing for the Athens at the time of Marathon, which corresponded in the literary sphere to the dramatic poetry of Aeschylus.

The antagonism between two cultures — the traditional one, and the one embodied in Sophism, Socrates, and Euripides — was aggravated by the propaganda of the democrats and the moderates. The new culture was to become, to some degree, the matrix for the oligarchical movements that would disrupt Athens at the end of the fifth century B.C. Sophocles himself, although he had been a friend of Pericles, was to side with the oligarchical party when eighty years old. And after the restoration of democracy in 410 B.C., and Alcibiades' return in 407 B.C., Euripides went into exile in Macedonia. Despite this great crisis, which already at the Peace of Nicias foreshadowed the irreversible decline of the city, the public finances were overflowing because of the money obtained from Athens' allies. The tributes imposed had reached their greatest sums in the last five years of the war, when Athens was already exhausted and the military operations required the greatest effort. In any case, between 421 and 415 B.C., the proceeds from the Athenian empire were greater than at the outbreak of the war.

Temple of Athena Nike

It was against the background of such struggles that the little Temple of Athena Nike was erected, the last of the edifices planned for the Acropolis. It was located on the southern bastion opposite the Propylaea; as mentioned, from the Mycenaean age this site had been consecrated to a goddess connected with fertility and the afterlife, a goddess whose powers were later assimilated by Athena. On the bastion there was an altar and, later on, a small temple built on the occasion of the victory at

Plataea (479 B.C.). It is probable that the bellicose nature of Athena had by then prevailed over the original aspect of the cult, and the goddess was being celebrated as the goddess of victory, Nike.

The project for the new temple had been conceived shortly after the Peace of Callias (449 B.C.) by Callicratis, one of the architects of the Parthenon. However, the work was not executed at that time, even though it was taken into account in the construction of the colonnade of the southern wing of the Propylaea. Callicratis constructed in another place, on the bank of the Ilissos River in Athens, the small temple he had planned for the Acropolis bastion. This was based essentially on the contrast between the massive wall and the spacious and vibrant wing of Ionic columns. Given the requirements of the space available, the sekos had been reduced to its essentials: a naos with a pronaos having two columns between the antae; the opisthodomos was barely hinted at by two prominent pillars that marked the end of the lateral interior walls to the west.

When the Temple of Athena Nike was finally erected after 428 B.C., the original plan was modified by the elimination of the pronaos. In the meantime, Callicratis' formal research had found its complete expression in his little temple on the Ilissos and possibly also in the Erechtheum. Compared to these more advanced achievements, the Nike temple assumed the character of a first experiment in another direction: the columns appeared lower, the entablature relatively massive. Or perhaps the upward thrust of the supporting elements was contained because the dimensions of the edifice had been reduced, and a disequilibrium between the vertical development and the dimensions of the plan would then have resulted. In any case, the effect of this monument is that of fragile yet complete balance (Figure 63). One must remember that it was usually viewed from below, from the steep access ramp of the Acropolis, and isolated on its three-step stylobate; seen from there, it seemed to project itself into the limpid Attic sky. The Ionic style peculiar to Attica attained its most finished embodiment in this little temple.

Above its architrave, divided into three courses, there ran a figured frieze; although the exact subjects and figures cannot be known for certain, the western, northern, and southern sides evidently represented various battles of the Greeks, including the battle of Plataea. The sculptured decoration took on a polemical political aspect in the light of historic events. Plataea was the glorious city (near Thebes) where the Persian army had been definitively destroyed by the united forces of one hundred thousand Greeks in 479 B.C. The cities united in the Hellenic League had established that on the anniversary of this victory, every year, their representatives would meet there in order to sacrifice to Zeus the liberator, and that the people of Plataea would be dedicated to the gods as sacred and inviolable. The first temple on Athens' Acropolis' south bastion had been erected evidently in commemoration of this event. But in 428 B.C., Plataea, under seige by the Thebans, was razed by the Spartans and its citizens massacred. This event must have caused a terrible sensation among the Greeks who still recalled their recent past, and the reconstruction of the Nike temple thus took on meaning as effective anti-Spartan propaganda. The frieze representing the first battle of Plataea was also important from another point of view; it was a rare precedent, in the classical Greek age, of those historic reliefs that were to become so popular and widespread in Hellenistic and Roman art.

During the course of the Peloponnesian War, while Athens' vision of hegemony over Greece seemed more and more remote, Athenian interest in its neighbors and colonies to the west — already manifest in various aspects of Pericles' policies, from the alliance with Segesta in 458 B.C. to the foundation of Thurii in 444 B.C. — was reawakened. The Athenians' first intervention in Sicily (427–425 B.C.) had aroused the hostility of Syracuse and activated its alliance with Sparta. After the Peace of Nicias, Athens — under the influence of Alcibiades, a genial and unscrupulous aristocrat — used all its resources and energies in an attempt to annihilate Syracuse and thus obtain control of Sicily. Among other things, the island offered the possibility of large grain provisions, and during the first phase of the Peloponnesian War, the contribution of

THE PELOPONNESIAN WAR AS VIEWED BY THE CONSERVATIVES

Spectators, be not angered if, although I am a beggar, I dare in a Comedy to speak before the people of Athens of the public weal; Comedy too can sometimes discern what is right. I shall not please, but I shall say what is true. Besides, Cleon shall not be able to accuse me of attacking Athens before strangers; we are by ourselves at the festival of the Lenaea: the period when our allies send us their tribute and their soldiers is not yet. Here is only the pure wheat without chaff; as to the resident strangers settled among us, they and the citizens are one, like the straw and the ear.

I detest the Lacedaemonians with all my heart, and may Poseidon, the god of Taenarus, cause an earthquake and overturn their dwellings! My vines also have been cut. But come (there are only friends who hear me), why accuse the Laconians of all our woes? Some men (I do not say the city, note particularly that I do not say the city), some wretches, lost in vices, bereft of honor, who were not even citizens of good stamp, but strangers, have accused the Megarians of introducing their produce fraudulently, and not a cucumber, a leveret, a suckling pig, a clove of garlic, a lump of salt was seen without its being said. "Halloa! these come from Megara," and their being instantly confiscated. Thus far the evil was not serious and we were the only sufferers. But now some young drunkards go to Megara and carry off the courtesan Simaetha; the Megarians, hurt to the quick, run off in turn with two harlots of the house of Aspasia; and so for three gay women Greece is set ablaze. Then Pericles, aflame with ire on his Olympian height, let loose the lightning, caused the thunder to roll, upset Greece and passed an edict, which ran like the song. "That the Megarians be banished both from our land and from the sea and from the continent." Meanwhile the Megarians, who were beginning to die of hunger, begged the Lacedaemonians to bring about the abolition of the decree of which those harlots were the cause; several times we refused their demand; and from that time there was a horrible clatter of arms everywhere. You will say that Sparta was wrong, but what should she have done? Answer that. Suppose that a Lacedaemonian had seized a little Seriphian dog on any pretext and had sold it, would you have endured it quietly? Far from it, you would at once have sent three hundred vessels to sea, and what an uproar there would have been through all the city! there 'tis a band of noisy soldiery, here a brawl about the election of a Trierarch; elsewhere pay is being distributed, the Pallas figureheads are being regilded, crowds are surging under the market porticoes, encumbered with wheat that is being measured, wineskins, oar-leathers, garlic, olives, onions in nets; everywhere are chaplets, sprats, flute girls, black eyes; in the arsenal bolts are being noisily driven home, sweeps are being made and fitted with leathers; we hear nothing but the sound of whistles, of flutes and fifes to encourage the work-folk. That is what you assuredly would have done, and would not Telephus have done the same? So I come to my general conclusion; we have no common sense.

ARISTOPHANES: *The Acharnians* (496–556)

THE COUP D'ETAT OF JUNE 7, 411 B.C.

A proposal too had already been openly set on foot by them, that no others should receive pay but such as served in the war; and that not more than five thousand should have a share in the government, and those such as were most competent to do the state service both with their property and their persons.

Now this was but a specious profession for

the people at large, since the same men would really hold the government as would bring about the revolution. The people, however, and the council of five hundred still met notwithstanding, though they discussed nothing that was not approved of by the conspirators, but both the speakers belonged to that party, and the points to be brought forward were previously discussed by them. Indeed no one else any longer opposed them, through fear, and from seeing that the conspiracy was extensively spread; and if anyone did speak against them, he immediately came to his end in some convenient way, and there was neither any search made for those who had perpetrated the deed, nor were they brought to justice if they were suspected; but the commons remained still, and in such consternation that everyone thought himself fortunate who did not meet with some violent treatment, even though he held his tongue. From supposing, too, that the conspiracy was much more general than it really was, they were the more fainthearted, and were unable to ascertain its extent, being powerless in consequence of the size of the city, and their not knowing one another's views. And on this same ground also it was impossible for a man to bemoan himself to another in his indignation, so as to repel one who was plotting against him; since he would either have found a person he did not know, to whom to speak his mind, or one whom he knew but could not trust. For all the members of the popular party approached each other with suspicion, supposing everyone to have a hand in what was going on. For there were amongst them some whom one would never have supposed likely to join an oligarchy; and it was these that produced the greatest distrust in the many, and that contributed most to the safety of the few, by confirming the people's want of confidence in each other.

Pisander and his colleagues therefore having come at this critical time, immediately addressed themselves to the remainder of the work. In the first place, having assembled the people, they moved a resolution for electing ten commissioners with absolute powers for compiling laws, and that after compiling them they should lay before the people, on an appointed day, their opinion as to the manner in which the state would be best governed. Afterward, when the day had arrived, they enclosed the assembly in the Colonus (a temple of Poseidon outside the city, at the distance of about ten stades), and the compilers brought forward no other motion, but simply this, that any of the Athenians should be at liberty to express any opinion he might please; and if anyone either prosecuted the speaker for illegality, or otherwise injured him, they imposed upon him severe penalties. Upon that it was at length plainly declared, that no one should any longer either hold office or receive pay, according to the present constitution.

THUCYDIDES: *History* (VIII: 65–67)

Following page:
67. Athens: The theater of Dionysus viewed from the southeast. What we see today is the fourth-century reconstruction executed entirely in stone; it was at this same time that Lycurgus had the statues of the three great tragic poets placed here.

Page 129
68. Epidaurus: The theater. At the end of the tiers we see one of the two doorways through which the spectators entered.

Pages 130–131:
69. Syracuse: The theater in its version built during the time of Hieron II. Note that the tiers are divided by a wide passage (known as the *diazoma*).

Sicilian provisions had been essential for Sparta.

Aristophanes warned the Athenians that this venture was overly ambitious — although it did not seem so absurd to Thucydides, the historian. But during the actual grave crisis for his city, Aristophanes restrained himself in his tragi-comic allegory, *The Clouds*, produced in 414 B.C. Although the undertaking provoked the Spartans into intervening, the Athenians came close to winning at several points. But the Athenian expedition ended tragically in the 413 B.C. disaster when over two hundred ships were destroyed and over forty thousand men died. Two of the Athenian commanders, Nicias and Demosthenes, were executed by the victorious Syracusans.

The blame for all this was laid on those who had led Athens along democratic lines, and the oligarchical party, which had already consolidated its strength during this period of crisis, gained the upper hand. Its coup d'état of June 7, 411 B.C., was effected in an atmosphere of terror; the oligarchs had taken advantage of the absence of the fleet that, with its crew of commoners, was then at Samos. But this plan went awry; with the support of the fleet, Alcibiades cleverly succeeded in reestablishing the democratic government. But the oligarchs did not abandon their struggle. In the meantime, the Peloponnesian War was drawing to its tragic conclusion. After the definitive Athenian defeat, in April 404 B.C., the Spartan Lysander began to demolish the long wall that connected Athens with its port, Piraeus; since the wall was the symbol of its power, Lysander ordered the task to be done to the sound of flutes, because he believed, as Xenophon said, "that the day would mark the beginning of liberty for Greece." Strengthened by the Spartans' support, the oligarchs imposed the government of the Thirty Tyrants on Athens. Only in October of 403 B.C. did the democrats, who had (and not by chance) entrenched themselves in Piraeus, reenter the city and restore democracy after a bitter struggle.

The first democratic restoration — led by Alcibiades — was facilitated by a great naval victory won by Thrasybulus in 410 B.C. Perhaps in memory of this event, which had earned great prestige for the Athenian fleet, a sculptured balustrade, or parapet, was erected on the bastion that served as the terrace for the Temple of Athena Nike. The reliefs represented a procession of Winged Victories preparing to sacrifice to Athena Nike, and this sculptured parapet, which looked over the Pnyx Hill (where the *ecclesia* gathered), the Areopagus, and the access to the Acropolis, marked perhaps the last and most authentic moment of vitality of a democracy whose significance for the world would extend far beyond the liberties it had been able to realize for itself. The echo of the Parthenon sculptures is still to be seen in the spreading of the limbs, in the instability of the poses (Figure 64); but the breaking up of the folds, the deep furrows of shadow, the swirling of the draperies around the bodies, finish in a virtuosity that touches on mannerism — as when the reliefs indulged in such effects as the supple adherence of wet draperies to human bodies. The total involvement of Phidias and his colleagues to the life of the *polis,* which made it possible to transform their works into the complete expression of the labor of a collective body, was now no more than a memory. The profound moral and political crisis had by this time corroded the ideal of the city-state, and the lack of content is now to be noted under the smooth sculptured forms.

As always, the prevalence of pure form marks a moment of separation between the artist and his world. Man, as a social animal, became reduced to an individual, and the private sphere took on an ever greater importance. It was not by pure coincidence that in the second half of the fifth century B.C. — especially as the impact of the art of the Parthenon was being absorbed — that the funerary stele, which had almost disappeared at the end of the sixth century, once more became fashionable. Next to the deceased, usually seated, were represented relatives, servants, and animals dear to him in his earthly existence. Although generally reserved for only two personages, often the scenes became crowded with figures and lost their symbolic character in order to unveil with less and less restraint the delicate and touching episodes of family life. Still at the beginning of this tendency was the Hegeso stele, dated to the end of the

fifth century (Figure 65). Here the calligraphic virtuosity was contained in a clean-cut definition of the surfaces, and the urgency of the sentiments was barely suggested by the intensity of the glances. The stele of Dexileos (Figure 66), commemorating one of the Athenians who fell in battle during the Corinthian War (394–393 B.C.), stands alone in celebration of a public action among the many strictly private monuments that surround it in the Eridanos cemetery. This young warrior, who seems to have descended from the western frieze of the Parthenon, was by this time merely a memory of the old spirit of the *polis*.

Theater of Dionysus: Control of the Consensus

In the Greek city-state, the theater was one of the major means of mass communication, and the very origin of tragedy reveals its deep roots in the exigencies of social and political life. The first tragedy has traditionally been dated to 534 B.C., when Thespis, the poet of Icaria (in Attica), placed an actor next to the chorus, which had for some time dominated the ritual by singing Dionysian hymns, or dithyrambs. Thespis' innovation, which was to be of decisive importance for the history of Western civilization, appeared within the complex framework of religious and cultural renewal fostered essentially by Pisistratus. This tyrant established his power over the populace, and had to consolidate and increase the base for this power in order to keep the traditional governing class — the aristocratic families of great landowners — out of politics. At the same time, he had to find new elements of cohesion between the different classes so that their antagonisms would not endanger the very unity of the state he was promoting. With this end in mind, Pisistratus encouraged the cult of the Homeric gods and the egalitarian cult of the Eleusinian Mysteries and its divinities.

But Pisistratus concentrated most of all on the introduction of a new cult of Dionysus, which would make it possible for him to disperse the rising conflict between the city and the rural areas. The Dionysian cult, with its rural character, was solidly entrenched in Attica, where the Dionysian rustic festivals had long been taking place. Pisistratus renewed this cult, giving it a more solemn character. In fact, he did not im-

mediately connect it to the local tradition, but preferred to import from Eleutherae — a village near the border of Boeotia and Attica — the cult of Dionysus Melanaigis ("black goat skin") that, with its more mysterious nature, was better suited to a form of official religion. Tragedy then found a place in the new ritual, and thus Pisistratus, by instituting a splendid urban Dionysia, with a dithyramb contest and a tragedy competition, realized his aim of uniting the classes in one essentially religious festival.

The first function of tragedy, therefore, was that of making all the classes, especially the popular masses, participants in the common past embellished with myths and marked by the presence of the gods, but not for this reason any less real in the eyes of the ancients. "The world of ancient history, the world of myths," as Mazzarini has said, "always moved along the paths of difficult reconstruction, in which poets and historians collaborated, without there existing between them — as regards the credibility and destiny of their opinions — any distinction in values." The theater became the most effective means of propagandizing ideas; at the same time, the monopoly of culture and political power remained, up to the last quarter of the fifth century, the prerogative of the well-to-do classes, particularly the old landed aristocracy. Thus the great tragic authors assumed firm, if moderate, positions often critical of radical democracy.

The political importance of the theater was seen for the first time when the poet Phrynicus portrayed in his play, *The Conquest of Miletus*, the final disaster that put an end to the Ionian revolt against the Persian occupation. Athens did not have a clean conscience in this matter; after having backed the revolt, it had abandoned the Ionians to their fate. The play was probably staged when Themistocles was the eponymous archon (the supreme magistrate who gave his name to the year) in 493–492 B.C.; Phrynicus was a close friend of the statesman, who wanted to remind the Athenians that the tragic fate of Miletus could be shared by Athens if the city did not concentrate its energies on defending itself against the forthcoming Persian invasion. But the reaction of the populace was so strong that the poet was fined one thousand drachmas.

About the time of Themistocles' ostracism (472 B.C.), Aeschylus staged *The Persians*, reminding the ungrateful Athenians of the glorious victory at Salamis for which the city was indebted to the genius of the great general. The expenses for the preparation and staging of the chorus were paid by the young Pericles. But Aeschylus' political passion is to be seen most clearly in the *Oresteia*. This was staged in 458 B.C. shortly after the reform of Ephialtes (462 B.C.), who circumscribed the powers of the Areopagus — the ancient aristocratic court — by limiting it to jurisdiction in cases of bloodshed, and transferring all the other powers to the popular courts. But in the last of the *Oresteia* trilogy, the *Eumenides*, Aeschylus exalted the greatness of the Areopagus, maintaining that it was exactly there that Orestes, pursued by the Furies for having killed his mother, was absolved of guilt. It was Athena herself who intervened in the judgment, and the addition of her vote broke the tie in favor of his salvation.

Triptolemus, the play that earned Sophocles his first victory in 468 B.C., illustrated one of the fundamental motifs of Athenian imperialistic propaganda. In this play, Sophocles showed how the hero took the cultivation of grain, the gift of Demeter at Eleusis, and went forth from Athens in his winged chariot and transmitted civilization throughout the world. Yet, in order to assure Sophocles the victory in the dramatic contest, which saw him vying against Aeschylus, his protector Cimon had to arrange matters in such a way that the contest was no longer decided upon by the usual college of judges but by the political authority, the college of archons.

Athenian propaganda also animated such patriotic works of Euripides as *The Herakleidae, Herakles,* and *The Suppliants*, written during the first years of the Peloponnesian War. Setting himself against the accusations that came from all over against Athens, considered by enemies and allies alike an unscrupulous imperialistic power, Euripides represented the city as the champion of the persecuted and the helpless; in particular he spoke of the aid Athens had given to the Peloponnesos. And yet some verses of his *Bellerophon* seem to express open condemnation of the op-

Creusa,
Go with your son to Cecrops' land, and then
Appoint him to the royal throne; for since
He is descended from Erechtheus, he has
The right to rule my land: and he shall be
Renowned through Greece. His sons, four branches from
One stock, shall name the country and its peoples,
Divided in their tribes, who live about my rock.
The first shall be named Geleon, the tribe
Of Hopletes second, then Argades, and one
Aegicores, the name from my own aegis.
At the appointed time, the children born
Of them shall colonize the Cyclades,
Possess the island cities and the coasts.
And thus give strength to my own land of Athens.
They shall live in the two broad plains of Asia
And Europe, which lie on either side the straits,
Becoming famous under this boy's name,
Ionians. Moreover, you and Xuthus
Are promised children. First Dorus, whose name
Shall cause the Dorians to be hymned throughout
The land of Pelops. Then Achaeus, king
Of that sea coast near Rhion, who shall mark
A people with his name.

EURIPIDES: *Ion* (1571–1594)

70. Delos: The theater. Whereas at Delphi the theater was situated inside the sanctuary, with which it had an intimate connection, at Delos it was far from the sanctuary, over in the Hellenistic quarter.

71. Athens: Theater of Dionysus. The marble seats of the place of honor (*proderia*), where the high dignitaries sat, were placed here between the end of the second and the beginning of the first century B.C.

71

pression exercised over Athens' allies; it is probable that those verses (423 B.C.) were written with an eye to the Lesbos incident (428 B.C.) when Cleon, having crushed the rebellion of Athens' island ally, wanted to put its citizens to death. Hence Euripides did not criticize Athenian imperialism as such, but its excesses; furthermore, when the power of the city was tottering, between 412 and 408 B.C., he furnished, in his *Ion*, a mythical, genealogical justification for Athenian hegemony over the other Ionians and also for the attempt then underway to undermine the Dorians and Achaeans. Meanwhile, in those very years, an aristocratic spirit like Aristophanes, who most certainly did not indulge in patriotic propaganda, ended by justifying the domination of the allies in his *Lysistrata*, written with the purpose of promoting an agreement between the contending cities in order to achieve a Panhellenic peace.

But peace was the principal theme of Aristophanes' works. The poet was well acquainted with the profound dissent that the Peloponnesian War policy had aroused in the Attic countryside. He was sympathetic toward the hardships that made the small and medium landowners the natural allies of the landed aristocracy. And his works, in their continual insistence on the theme of peace, became political propaganda, an explicit invitation to dissent. With Aristophanes the theater became ferocious political satire, attacking persons and events by name. Underlying this was the poet's nostalgia for the Athens of Aeschylus' time, before Sophism, when the masses had a voice in the government but when the political management remained in the hands of the upper classes. Therefore his barbs were pointed especially at Cleon, who, in his opinion and in that of Thucydides, had the basic defect of being a commoner who had become rich through the leather-tanning industry. In *The Babylonians* (426 B.C.) and, even more so, in *The Knights* (424 B.C.), Aristophanes attacked the demogogue with unheard-of violence, lampooning his behavior and his conduct as a strategist, administrator, and private citizen. But in his polemic, Aristophanes felt himself protected, at least, by the class of knights.

When Athens undertook the Sicilian expedition, even Aristophanes did not dare to satirize directly such an enterprise, which, after all, was led by none other than the moderate Nicias. But in his *Birds*, in Pisistratus' dream of building a city among the clouds in order to keep the gods from receiving the smoke from the sacrifices, Aristophanes derided the impossible delusions of grandeur hidden beneath an apparently lucid rationality. But the last plays of Aristophanes reflect the decline of vehement polemics among the Athenians. That type of theater, which thrived on contemporary problems, was born with the *polis* and required a public that participated in the political and cultural life of the city. Therefore it did not survive that climate. The comedy that took over the stage directed itself to the individual, to his affairs and sentiments.

But to return to the origins of Greek drama once again, the agrarian cults, such as those of Demeter and Dionysus, had been intimately connected with propitiatory ceremonies, which took the form of a choral dance and pantomime. These first forms of spectacle took place on the threshing floor, an earthen circular space on the open countryside; when placed properly, the natural slope of the land provided convenient seating and viewing. But the simple circular space was originally the orchestra, which we find again in the center of the Telesterion of the Eleusis, where a kind of pantomimed ritual for Demeter was performed. At Athens, there existed from 560 B.C., in the Agora, an "orchestra" connected with the Dionysian cult, in which the chorus sang dithyrambs, carrying out their movements before the faithful who sat on wooden platforms. When Pisistratus introduced the cult of Dionysus Melanaigis and had his sanctuary built on the slopes of the Acropolis, the orchestra in the Agora was transferred to the new sacred enclosure. (According to some scholars this move did not take place until about 498 B.C. after the collapse of the wooden platforms.) In any case, the theater of Dionysus on the southern slopes of the Acropolis originally consisted only of the orchestra, which had at its center the round altar of Dionysus. The auditorium was hollowed out of the hill, with tiers of wooden seats; the stage was a temporary wooden structure with a simple curtain as its back wall. In this simple setting the plays of the great dramatists were first performed. Only after the Peace of Nicias, in 421 B.C., were stone tiers built, with a series of radial walls on the slope of the hill. The wall of a portico, which marked off the sacred enclosure, was used as the stage backdrop, even though it was not centered in relation to the audience.

Meanwhile, in the Greek colonial world in the West, an autonomous theater tradition was also developing. Epicharmus, the greatest exponent of farcical comedy in the Dorian dialect, was born at Syracuse, Sicily, about 530 B.C. But aside from individual dramatists, it was the Deinomenidae who deserve the credit for having introduced the great Attic tragedies to the city of Syracuse. Aeschylus went several times to Sicily; his first trip, about 472 B.C., was due to an invitation from Hieron I, who had the theater of Syracuse built by the architect Damokopus. In 476–475 B.C. Hieron had forced the Chalcidian inhabitants of the nearby city of Catana (modern Catania) to go to Leontini, replacing them with Dorians from the Aetna area. In this way he hoped to establish some balance between Ionians and Dorians in Sicily; and to legitimize this policy, Aeschylus wrote *The Aetneans;* on that occasion he also staged his play, *The Persians*, in Syracuse.

With the crisis that struck the city-state at the end of the fifth century B.C., the vitality of the theater seemed to weaken. The tragic poets of the second half of the century had not contributed any further innovations, and Euripides' theater remained an unsurpassed high point for a long time. Only near the middle of the fourth century, as the shadow of Macedonian hegemony advanced threateningly toward Athens, did the city reawaken. The theater of Dionysus was then completely rebuilt, entirely of stone (Figure 67), and Lycurgus had the statues of the three great tragedians set up here, promoting new interest in the already "classical" tradition. The orchestra was moved more to the north, and in order to fill the space now created between the auditorium and the portico that had served as a wing, a new stage (*skene*) was built with projecting lateral structures decorated with columns. In the theater at Epidaurus, too (Figure 68), built about 350 B.C. by Polycletus the Younger, the stage had two similar side projections, evidently characteristic elements of the period.

Interest in the theater was rekindled in the second half of the fourth century when, due mainly to the genius of Menander (c. 342–290 B.C.), the New Comedy emerged. This new form of art inherited from Euripidean drama the concentration on individual psychology, the love of intrigue, and the use of dialogue to render the delicate play of emotions. By this time, a high stage over the orchestra was preferred, as it made the stage actions more visible and the dialogue more comprehensible. Originally the proscenium was wooden and could be removed for the performance of the classical plays. At Athens it was added on between 310 and 300 B.C., while the proscenium only appeared at Delos in 282–274 B.C. At Megalopolis, the theater erected toward the end of the fourth century was placed against the Thersilion, where the council of the Arcadian League met; thus the entire stage-structure was made of wood and set on wheels and could be placed in a sort of storeroom when access from the Thersilion to the auditorium had to be kept free. A permanent stage with fourteen Doric columns was built only after 222 B.C. — that is, after the Spartans devastated the city, and the Thersilion was already in ruins.

In the theater of Dionysus at Athens, a permanent marble proscenium was built about 150 B.C.; the delay in building such a structure was probably the result of the Athenians' profound attachment to the classical tradition. The proscenium had sixteen Doric columns, and the arcaded projections of the stage were set back to form two wings. The new theater at Syracuse (Figure 69), built by Hieron II (236–216 B.C.), had a permanent proscenium right from the outset, and a low *pulpitum*, or stage, was set against this for performances of the indigenous salacious farces then so popular. The high proscenium introduced for the New Comedy was set above the front of the scene, partially hiding it. Therefore the scene had to be raised, adding a second story (*espiscene*) to the structure. This

72. **Athens: The Silenus, a sculpture from the Roman proscenium of the theater of Dionysus. It dates from the time of Hadrian, in the second century A.D.**

73. **Miletus: The theater. In the center are two of the four columns that decorated the imperial box.**

Athens: Plan of the theater of Dionysus in its four principal phases
A In the age of Pericles
B In the age of Lycurgus
C During the Hellenistic age
D During the Roman age
1   Stage   2 Portico   3 Archaic temple
4   Odeon of Pericles   5 Orchestra

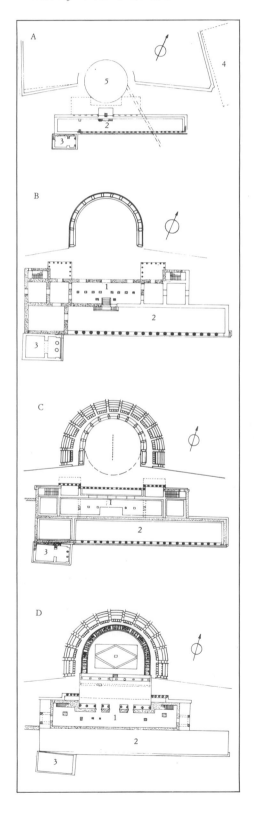

THE ARISTOCRATS' VIEW OF CLEON, "THE PAPHLAGONIAN"

I will begin then. We have a very brutal master, a perfect glutton for beans, and most bad-tempered; 'tis Demos of the Pnyx, an intolerable old man and half deaf. The beginning of last month he bought a slave, a Paphlagonian tanner, an arrant rogue, the incarnation of calumny. This man of leather knows his old master thoroughly; he plays the fawning cur, flatters, cajoles, wheedles, and dupes him at will with little scraps of leavings, which he allows him to get. "Dear Demos," he will say, "try a single case and you will have done enough; then take your bath, eat, swallow and devour; here are three obols." Then the Paphlagonian filches from one of us what we have prepared and makes a present of it to our old man. T'other day I had just kneaded a Spartan cake at Pylos, the cunning rogue came behind my back, sneaked it and offered the cake, which was my invention, in his own name. He keeps us at a distance and suffers none but himself to wait upon the master; when Demos is dining, he keeps close to his side with a thong in his hand and puts the orators to flight. He keeps singing oracles to him, so that the old man now thinks of nothing but the Sibyl. Then when he sees him thoroughly obfuscated, he uses all his cunning and piles up lies and calumnies against the household; then we are scourged and the Paphlagonian runs about among the slaves to demand contributions with threats and gathers 'em in with both hands. He will say, "You see how I have had Hylas beaten! Either content me or die at once!" We are forced to give, for else the old man tramples on us and makes us spew forth all our body contains. There must be an end to it, friend. Let us see! what can be done? Who will get us out of this mess?

ARISTOPHANES: *The Knights* (40–72)

was made of wood at Delos (274 B.C.) in the theater that had been reconstructed in stone in 279 B.C. (Figure 70); while a stone episcene with seven doors was added to the theater at Miletus at the end of the fourth century B.C.

The theater at Pergamum (Figure 74) is a rare example of a theater built entirely during the Hellenistic age; it therefore reflects the needs of that time, without any of the limitations and conditions derived from preceding structures. However, the orchestra's location on a terrace along a steep slope did not leave enough space for a permanent stage, as this would have interrupted the road that ran along the edge of the terrace. Therefore sixty-four holes or slots for poles, on which the wooden stage could be placed, were set up in this way, the possible architectural solutions for theatrical productions could be varied from time to time. The theater was built by Eumenes II (197–139 B.C.), who also restored the fourth-century theater at Delphi.

Sparta, a city noted for its austere customs, did not build a permanent theater until the second or third century B.C. As late as the Augustan age, when Rome ruled Greece, the stage was still wooden, set on wheels, and mobile; only in A.D. 78, when a fire destroyed Sparta's stage, did the Emperor Vespasian build an architectural facade, with columns rising from a high podium — to which a permanent proscenium was added in A.D. 200.

The Roman drama, with its tragedies so rich in characters, had different scenic requirements than those of Hellenistic comedy. The stage, for example, had to be low and deep. Thus, as the Romans took over the Greek world, the various Greek theaters underwent further transformations. At Athens, as at Miletus, greater depth was obtained by setting forward the front of the pulpitum until it reached the end of the auditorium's tiers. The stage-scene, decorated by columns with acanthus capitals, had two stories. The front of the pulpitum was decorated with imitation classical reliefs (Figure 72) — a style typical of Hadrian's age — representing the marriage of Dionysus. The last restoration of the theater at Athens, in which the materials and reliefs from preceding phases were used, dates from the end of the third or the beginning of the fourth century A.D., after the destruction of the city by the Heruli.

During the Roman imperial age, Graeco-Roman theaters took on a monumental aspect, still to be seen in the well-preserved theaters in Caria or in the Odeon of Herodes Atticus in Athens. The Miletus theater, as it

stands today (Figure 73), is a typical example of second-century A.D. architecture; the wall of the stage, three stories high, was animated by columns and niches, and the polychrome resulting from the use of red and black marble must have been especially effective. The seating was divided into three rings; while the two lower ones were cut out from the slope of the hill, the upper one was artificial. At the center of the lower ring was the imperial box, held up by four columns.

Various Greek theaters were thus adapted to the needs of Roman spectacles — at Pergamum, for instance, the orchestra was enlarged to accommodate the gladiatorial contests. But at Syracuse the classical tradition was still strenuously maintained; during the imperial age a subterranean tunnel was built to put the stage-scene in communication with the center of the orchestra. This was used for the sudden appearances of characters evoked from the underworld, so typical of ancient drama. It also, alas, may serve as a metaphor for what had survived from the great age of classic Greece: tragic drama had become melodramatic spectacle.

74. **Pergamum: The theater. The enormous, steep seating area, which could hold some fifteen thousand spectators, occupied the entire side of the hill overlooking the city's acropolis and the valley of the Selinus River.**

THE GREEKS IN THE WEST

Greeks in Sicily

The Greeks' colonial movement had emerged in the second half of the eighth century as a result of the crisis in the agrarian society in their homeland. This crisis drove not only the small farmers but also the members of the aristocratic families to seek new sources of income. Thus there were born the merchants and colonists who, often guided by the Delphic Oracle, looked elsewhere for those rich lands that the motherland lacked. The initiative started in various centers situated on key points of land and sea routes — Corinth, the cities of Euboea, the coastal and island cities of Ionia — that had been quick to realize how trade could take its place beside agriculture in the economy.

The traders were the first to explore those lands where colonization led them, establishing relations with the indigenous populations to whom they brought handicraft products in exchange for raw materials (preferably metals) and foodstuffs. This early type of contact, which relied on bases established in the most favorable trading points, is usually defined as "pre-colonization." But this name is still misleading, for the dynamics often differed from those of the colonial phenomenon. In fact, whereas the first merchants found their income in trade, the true colonists who followed were in many cases driven only by a desire for land to cultivate.

In the first half of the sixth century, the social conflicts that shook Greece became equally acute in the Greek colonial world to the west, specifically in Sicily. We cannot be as sure of the causes in that colonial world, however. Probably the great availability of servile or cheap labor, supplied by the indigenous populations, was more important than the lack of land in creating the social situation in Sicily. The natives had a firm hold on the interior of the island, with the Siculi in the eastern part, the Sicani in the west, and the Elymi at the northwestern point. But during this same period in which the Greeks were moving into Sicily, the Phoenicians were already well established. From their homeland along the coast of the Levant, this population of sailors and traders had gone to the northern coast of Africa and from there to Spain, following the route that connected with the tin (needed for making bronze) from the Cassiterides — the "tin islands," now believed to refer to Cornwall and the Scillies off southwestern England. Among the numerous colonies founded along this itinerary, the most important was Carthage, which immediately felt the need to assure itself of control of the Tunisian-Sicilian channel, so crucial for the voyages to Spain. So it was that the Phoenician-Carthaginian colonies of Sicily sprang up, concentrated along the northwestern coast of Sicily.

The presence of the Carthaginians on Sicily did not necessarily produce a state of conflict with the Greeks; on the contrary, Greek colonial cities that had little possibility of expanding along the eastern coast — such as Megara Hyblaea between Syracuse and Leontini, or Zancle perched on a rocky promontory — often were quite sympathetic toward the Punic world. About 650 B.C., Zancle (the future Messina) founded Himera along the northern coast; in 651 or 628 B.C., colonists from Megara Hyblaea founded Selinunte; neither of these moves provoked any reaction from the Carthaginians. Selinunte especially seemed to live in substantial concord with the neighboring Carthaginian colonists, and built its prosperity through the exchange of foodstuffs with the Punic cities of Sicily as well as with Carthage itself. Selinunte seems to

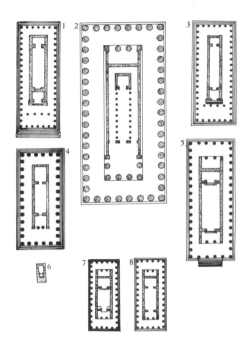

Selinunte: Plans of the temples
1 Temple C (550–30 B.C.)
2 Temple G (520–450 B.C.)
3 Temple F (525 B.C.)
4 Temple D (535 B.C.)
5 Temple E (480–60 B.C.)
6 Temple B
7 Temple A (460 B.C.)
8 Temple O (460 B.C.)

75

Following pages:

75. Selinunte: The ruins of temples F and G; along with Temple D, they are situated outside the acropolis, on a hill east of the ancient gate. Temple G was one of the largest Doric temples, exceeded in size in Sicily only by the Temple of Olympian Zeus at Agrigento. Its dimensions were 367 feet by 175 feet.

76. Selinunte: Metopes from Temple C, representing, from left to right: the chariot of Helios; Athens, Perseus, and Medusa; Herakles and the Kerkopes. Beyond the similarities in the sculpture, these metopes were integrated by the colors painted on them (and note the painted meander still visible, upper right). (Palermo, National Museum)

have begun truly to flourish when the Greek presence in its part of the island (the southwest) was strengthened by the foundation in 580 B.C. by Rhodians and Cretans of a colony just a bit to the east along the coast — Agrigento. Selinunte's heyday lasted until about 460 B.C. Within about one century, seven great temples were built at Selinunte, and the local artisan class reached its peak in the field of sculpture, architectural terra-cotta work, and terra-cotta sculptured figurines. The city must have been governed during this period by tyrants, as was Agrigento, where it is known that Phalaris held power from 565 to 549 B.C. Referring to how Phalaris took power, Polyaenus said that the tyrant had obtained from the city the contract for the collection of taxes so that he could supervise the construction of the Temple of Zeus Polias on the acropolis. With that money, Phalaris bought slaves and paid foreigners to do the actual construction work. This story is important not only because it illustrates the way an ancient Sicilian city went about constructing a public edifice; it also gives the impression that, at least in Agrigento, there did not yet exist in the second quarter of the sixth century B.C. an indigenous lower class like that in Athens, desperately seeking to sell its labor. In that case, the tyrant would not have been — as he was in Greece — the mediator between the two classes in social conflict but rather the expression of the landed aristocracy. But we certainly cannot presume to have disposed of this question on the basis of one isolated passage of uncertain authority.

The oldest temples at Selinunte, temples C and D on the acropolis and temple F (Figure 75) on the eastern hill (since it has been impossible to determine which gods most of the temples at Selinunte were dedicated

to, they are conventionally indicated by letters), descend from the most ancient Doric architecture of the Peloponnesos. Built about the middle of the sixth century B.C., they still preserve some archaic characteristics that had by then disappeared in Greece itself. In all of them, for instance, the sekos, narrow and elongated, was a closed, asymmetrical body. At the western end, the open form of the pronaos was not repeated; instead, there was a closed-off room, the adyton, reached only through the naos. A clear formal relationship between the sekos and the peristyle was lacking. Finally, the edifices assumed a frontal view, with the eastern and western ends clearly differentiated.

Temple C sits on a high stairway, and the considerable depth of its ambulatory was accentuated by a double wing of columns. Built between 550 and 530 B.C., the temple had a rich terra-cotta decoration that covered the wooden structures of the roof; the entablature bore sculptured metopes, done in an archaic tradition that, in Sicily, would remain peculiar to Selinunte. The three best-preserved blocks (Figure 76) represent Apollo's chariot between Artemis and Leto; Perseus helped by Athena in the killing of Medusa; and Herakles and the Kerkopes. This last subject was particularly favored by the Greeks in the West, where the only sculptured representations of the tale are found, perhaps because this episode in Herakles' life was set by some sources in the Tyrrhenian Sea, at Ischia. According to the legend, the two Kerkopes, liars and rogues who looked like little genii (or like monkeys, as their name indicates), had been warned by their mother to watch out for the hero "with the black bottom." However, when they tried to steal Herakles' bow, he was sleeping on his back in the darkest point of the pass at Thermopylae, and so the Kerkopes did not realize the danger they were in. But the hero awoke, seized them, and tied them upside down on a pole he carried over his shoulders. In this position the Kerkopes were able to see his hairy rump and recognized the warning sign spoken of by their mother; at this, they could not contain their laughter. Herakles, once he learned the reason, also began to laugh. According to one tradition he let them go free; according to another, he changed them into monkeys, setting them on Pithecusae (Ischia), the "isle of monkeys," in the Gulf of Naples.

77. Selinunte: Temple E as it has been reconstructed in modern times. From the pronaos, we are looking back toward the "screen" framed by the wall of the opisthodomos.

78. Selinunte: Temple E, the northeastern corner. Although this temple is almost contemporaneous with the Temple of Zeus at Olympia, the columns appear less slender, a not uncommon characteristic of Greek architecture in the west.

GREECE

79

The patterns of the composition, the accentuated rhythms of the anatomical structures, and the compact volume of the figures — all reveal the Peloponnesian influences on these metopes of Temple C. The large triangular heads, the facial planes set off by heavy hairdos, and the mechanical gestures, give these sculptures a rather archaic aspect, which contrasts with the wavy surfaces of the bodies and the drapery. The rigid frontal view of the faces seems to have frozen the expressive capacity of the artist-sculptors, who yet demonstrated in the playful faces of the Kerkopes that they were capable of rendering a certain narrative vivacity.

About 520 B.C., when Selinunte was governed by the tyrant Pythagoras, its most grandiose monument was begun on the eastern hill. Temple G perhaps drew its inspiration from the Temple of Artemis at Corfu, built at the beginning of the same century. On the enormous stylobate of Temple G (177 feet by 372 feet) there stood a peristyle with eight and seventeen columns on the short and long sides, respectively. The ambulatories were twice the normal width, while the main facade of the sekos opened onto a four-column portico. This solution, already suggested in Temple D, was seen again at the so-called Temple of Ceres at Paestum. However, it was created at Selinunte, where it answered the

79. Selinunte: Metope from Temple E showing the sacred marriage of Zeus and Hera. In this, as in the other metope sculptures on the temple, the faces and the bare limbs of females only were made of Parian marble and then set in the limestone slab. (Palermo, National Museum)

80. Selinunte: Metope from Temple E representing Artemis standing by as Actaeon is being torn to pieces by dogs. The Sicilian sculptor who executed these metopes around 470 B.C. gives evidence of his refined culture, despite his probable provincial origins, and certainly reveals an acquaintance with Attic art of the time. (Palermo, National Museum)

need of local tradition to accentuate the spaciousness of the main facade. Temple G was never really finished; the work went on till the middle of the fifth century, so that the older columns on the eastern end differed greatly from the more recent ones on the western end, both in shape and in the contour of the capitals. In the original plan, the sekos ended at the west with the adyton, but during the course of construction, the Greek tendency to consolidate the architectural organism by means of greater symmetry of its parts, asserted itself even at Selinunte. The adyton was incorporated into the interior of the naos, and the sekos ended with an opisthodomos that, however, did not repeat the form of the pronaos. The interior of the naos was articulated in three naves with two rows of columns that were of minute dimensions compared to the size of the edifice, in three superimposed orders. Temple G is a singular work of architecture, open to complex solutions because of its very dimensions; it reflects a moment of transition from archaic frontality to the search for greater coherence of volume. This immense construction — equaled in the Greek west only by the Temple of Olympian Zeus at Agrigento, built somewhat later — gives an idea of the wealth at Selinunte toward the end of the sixth century B.C. If this wealth derived largely from the sale of

IN PRAISE OF SYRACUSE AND SICILY

Grave child of the waters of Alphaeus,
leafed branch of glorious Syracuse, Ortygia,
resting place of Artemis,
sister of Delos, from you the sweetly spoken
hymn begins, to shape
the great strain of praise for horses with storm
 in their feet, by grace of Zeus on Aetna;
and the chariot of Chromios is urgent with me,
 and Nemea, to link the song of glory for
 triumph in contests.

The beginnings are cast down by the gods,
aided by that man's divine gifts.
The uttermost of reputation lies
in achievement; for high trials
the Muse would be remembered in singing.
Scatter, now, some glory on this island, that the
 lord of Olympus,
Zeus, gave Persephone, and bowed his head to
 assent, the pride of the blossoming earth,

Sicily, the rich, to control under towering cities
 opulent;
Kronion granted her also
a people in brazen warfare,
horsemen; a people garlanded over and again
 with the golden leaves of olive
Olympian.

PINDAR: *Nemea 1* (1–18)

THE VICTORIES AT HIMERA AND SALAMIS

Zeus accomplisher, beside the waters of
 Amenas forever
let all men's speech decree such praise on the
 citizens and their kings.
By your aid, this leader of men,
enjoining it upon his son also, might glorify his
 people and turn them to peace and harmony.
Kronion, I beseech you, bend your head in assent
that the Phoenician and the war-crying Tyrse-
 nian keep quietly at home, beholding the
 shame of their wreck by sea at Kyme,

the things they endured, beaten at the hands
 of Syracuse's lord,
how he hurled their young men out of their
 fleet-running ships on the sea,
gathering back Hellas from the weight of slavery. I am given
favor in requital from men of Athens for
 Salamis
battle, and in Sparta for the fighting before
 Kithairon, where the Medes, benders of the
 bow, went under;
so likewise for singing fulfilment
for Deinomenes' sons of their victory at the
 watered strand of Himera,
that which they won by valor
when their foemen were beaten down.

PINDAR: *Pythia 1* (67–80)

foodstuffs to the Carthaginians, the lack of enthusiasm shown by Selinunte a few decades later for the Greek cause is thus explained.

In temples E (Figure 77), A, and O (480–460 B.C.), with their austere style, the adyton was still present, perhaps because of some special religious needs of the Greeks in Sicily. The adyton, in these temples, was placed between the naos and the opisthodomos; the two ends of the temple were then exactly alike, with their ambulatories still longer than the lateral ones. Following the Athenian practice, adopted in those same years at Olympia for the Temple of Zeus, the sculptured metopes in Temple E were placed on the pronaos and the opisthodomos. With these sculptures, the Selinuntian school reached its peak. Each slab generally includes two figures, one female and one male. The rigorous composition is centered on one of the two figures, who marks a broad diagonal. The instability of certain of the central figures' pose is compensated for by the static solidity of the other figure, as is the case with the metopes depicting the sacred wedding of Zeus and Hera (Figure 79) and the torment of Actaeon (Figure 80), torn to pieces by hounds because he gazed upon the naked Artemis. In other cases, the unstable pose is justified by the total composition of the frieze. The intense faces and the profoundly individualized gestures inject a strong expression into the neat composition. Figures like that of Herakles battling with the Amazon remind us of the style and patterns of the Athenian sculptor Kritios. But a less talented master executed the western metopes at Selinunte's Temple E, where the instability of the poses runs the risk of being interpreted as a mere lack of articulation of the bodies, and where the inconsistent and stiff drapery reveals the figures to excess.

Syracuse and Agrigento

Selinunte seems to have declined long before its destruction at the hands of the Carthaginians in 409 B.C., perhaps because the balance of power had already greatly changed in Sicily in the first decades of the fifth century. An agreement, reaffirmed by matrimonial ties, had been established between the Deinomenidae, lords of Syracuse and Gela, and Theron, the tyrant of Agrigento; following this, both greatly extended the boundaries of their states. When Theron had wrested Himera from the tyrant Terillo in 483 B.C., only Selinunte and Messina remained independent. Terillo asked for help from the Carthaginians, perhaps with the backing of the Selinuntians. After having organized a huge army in the Phoenician provinces of North Africa, Spain, Sardinia, and Corsica, the Carthaginian leader Hamilcar invaded Sicily in 480 B.C.; but in the decisive battle near Himera (which according to some sources took place on the same day as the battle of Salamis), he was defeated and killed. His soldiers were sold as slaves, and were used in Agrigento for the construction of the Temple of Olympian Zeus. Selinunte had not shown any inclination to intervene on the side of the Carthaginians.

The victory at Himera was grandly celebrated by the Sicilian tyrants, and especially by the Deinomenidae, who did all in their power to compare it to the battle of Salamis, thus promoting themselves as the saviors of Greek civilization on the island. A temple was erected on the battle site at Himera, while at Syracuse the Temple of Athena was built. This victory, in any case, marked the crowning piece of the Deinomenidae's policy. Gelon, tyrant of Gela, had made himself lord of Syracuse by taking advantage of the social struggles that were tormenting the city. His intervention had been requested by the great landowners who had been forced to leave the city because of the insurrection of the popular classes. As an ally of the oligarchs, Gelon had pursued a policy of territorial expansion; and by that time, eastern Sicily from Naxos to Gela was in his hands. The availability of land and the removal of half of the inhabitants of Gela, along with the inhabitants of the destroyed town of Camarina, to Syracuse, must have thwarted the pressure of the popular classes. The victory at Himera in the final analysis eliminated the only serious danger to the new political order, which from that point on saw most of the island divided into two spheres of influence, Syracusan and Agrigentine.

The new Temple of Athena in Syracuse, an identical twin of the one at Himera, occupied the most sacred area of the acropolis, the site where the first colonists had placed, on the remains of Siculian huts, a sacred enclosure and an altar. The new temple stood beside the base of a great Ionic temple that had remained unfinished when Gelon had assumed power in the city. Gelon's temple (now completely absorbed by the Christian cathedral) did not strive for grandeur, but rather for solid mass and perfect form; its architectural expression was therefore closer to that of the Greek motherland. The gaudy display of boundless power was more typical of the great landowners around Selinunte and Agrigento — the expression of a socially and economically static setting. The Syracuse of the Deinomenidae was, on the other hand, a city open to the sea and in constant touch with Greece. Its spendor appeared in the more refined details of the Temple of Athena, such as the gold and ivory doors, or the statue of Athena on the top of the facade, armed with a golden shield and visible from afar at sea. One of the acroteria on the temple may perhaps be identified in the marble Nike in flight (Figure 81), sculptured probably at Chios.

With Hieron I (478–467 B.C.), the power of Syracuse expanded into the Tyrrhenian Sea, especially after the victory over the Etruscans at Cumae in 474 B.C. Nevertheless, it was in the two ruling cities of Sicily — Syracuse and Agrigento — that an important political change was maturing. At Agrigento the tyrant Thrasydeus was expelled and, with the help of the aristocrat Empedocles, a democratic regime was installed. A few years later, the last of the Deinomenidae, Thrasybulus, was forced to seek refuge in Locris by the Syracusans, supported by those who had been victims of the tyrants of Gela, Agrigento, Himera, and Selinunte, as well as by the indigenous Siculi. The same phenomenon took place soon after in all the Greek cities on Sicily.

In this democratic period, Agrigento seems to have taken the initiative,

82. Agrigento: The Temple of Juno Lacinia. The columns on the sides are more slender and closer together than those on the two ends. Even today this temple has some religious meaning for the inhabitants of Agrigento, and it is customary for newlyweds to visit there right after the wedding, perhaps to propitiate the ancient goddess of fecundity.

83

83. Agrigento: The Temple of Concord. Given the exceptionally fine state of preservation of this edifice, it is possible to get a good idea of the relationship between the peristyle and the cella; on the other hand, the effects of light and shadow are distorted because the roof is missing.

judging from the architectural remains. In 460 B.C. the Temple of Juno Lacinia (Figure 82) was built at Agrigento, and thirty years later the Temple of Concord (Figure 83) similar in dimensions and design, was erected. By this time, the architectural organism was being fully realized as a volume immersed in space, and subtle optical corrections contributed to this effect. There remained from the past, however, the greater depth of the ambulatories on the short sides. Likewise the entablature, high and massive, weighed heavily on the columns, restraining their vertical thrust and thus adhering to a common characteristic of Greek architecture in the West.

The sanctuary of the chthonic divinities, Demeter and Persephone, was the most ancient sacred ground in Agrigento. Polyaenus recalled that when Phalaris took power (571 B.C.) a few years after the city's founding, he took advantage of the fact that the women gathered together in order to celebrate the Thesmophoria, the feast in honor of the Eleusinian goddesses; Phalaris simply captured the women as hostages. The feast must have taken place in the sanctuary near the southern gate, which still has altars and remains of very ancient edifices. The construction of a temple was undertaken and interrupted twice, and only toward 430 B.C. was the temple — called the Temple of the Dioscuri — finally built. Of this there remain only the cuts in the rock base and a few foundation stones; the corner of the colonnade that has become the most famous ruin of this part of Agrigento is actually an arbitrary reconstruction, formed from some elements that did not belong to the original temple (Figure 85). But from the remains of the columns and of the entablature, it is possible to reconstruct its plan, similar to that of the Temple of Concord.

In those same years, Athens began to intensify its interest in Sicily, an interest that had already manifested itself during Pericles' government. During the first phase of the Peloponnesian War, Syracuse's contribution had been considerable; Sicilian grain had helped to feed Sparta and its

84. **Agrigento: The Temple of Concord, the southern ambulatory. The arcades cut into the cella wall (left) date from the sixth century A.D. when the temple was converted into a Christian church.**

85. **Agrigento: The sanctuary of the Chthonic divinities. In the background (left) is the somewhat fanciful reconstruction of part of the Temple of the Dioscuri — made up of fragments of several structures. In the foreground is a large circular altar, while scattered about are remains of other altars and other structures. This site had been used by the pre-Greek Sicilians, and always retained its associations with pre-classic divinities.**

Following pages:
86. **Segesta: The temple seen from the east, or main entrance. This temple was never completed. Thus the Doric columns were never "fluted," and they sit on what appear to be exceptionally high bases, because the stylobate and the step beneath were never completed.**

allies. Using as a pretext the alliance formed by Pericles with Leontini and Rhegium — both cities by then struggling with Syracuse — Athens sent the first expedition to Sicily in 427–425 B.C. The second intervention was solicited by Segesta, based on an alliance made in 458 B.C. The Elymian city was inspired by an old grudge against the Greek cities of Sicily and had succeeded in convincing the Athenians that it possessed enormous riches in the treasury of the famed Temple of Aphrodite at Mount Eryx. In this way, by promising to pay the expenses of the expedition, Segesta had convinced Athens to intervene. By this time the struggle with Syracuse could end only with the annihiliation of one of the two powers. The second expedition (415–413 B.C.), promoted by Alcibiades, ended tragically (in part due to the Spartans' intervention) with the disastrous battle at the Assinarus River.

The Temple of Segesta, which still stands largely intact in the barren, hilly countryside, dates from the period between these two expeditions. The temple, similar in plan and dimensions to those built for the commemoration of the victory at Himera, was without doubt the work of Greek artists; the optical corrections, such as the slight curve in the stylobate, reveal a knowledgeable experience of classical architecture. It is legitimate to suppose that the construction of this temple in a foreign architectural style, at a difficult moment in the life of Segesta, answered political needs. It could well have served the double purpose of connecting the city ideally with its Athenian protectors, while displaying that economic well-being it had used to convince the Athenians to intervene.

85

The edifice remained unfinished, perhaps because after the disaster at Assinarus it no longer served any purpose. The holes dug for the foundations of the sekos were never used, nor were the blocks of the stylobate ever finished. The thick shafts of the columns, without fluting, make the edifice, already weighed down by the high entablature, seem even more massive (Figure 86). What Segesta was not able to obtain with the help of the Athenians, it obtained a few years later because of the Carthaginians. In 409 B.C. Selinunte was razed and half the inhabitants of Himera were massacred. In 406 B.C. Agrigento, which owed its prosperity to a long period of neutrality, also fell. Segesta would survive for another century, but only at Syracuse and in the eastern fringe of the island did Greek culture live on in Sicily.

Magna Graecia: Greeks in Southern Italy

The interest of the Greek cities in southern Italy — the region that was to become known as Magna Graecia — was strong from the outset of the colonial movement, when the ships from the Cyclades, Euboea, Corinth, and Ionia cut through the Tyrrhenian Sea, carrying on trade with the indigenous peoples along the route that led to the metal-rich Etruria, as the central region of Italy was known. Yet already toward the middle of the sixth century, with the decline of the Corinthian trade, Magna Graecia organized itself into an autonomous region, in which only certain large cities — such as Tarentum, Rhegium, and Locris — maintained any international influence. This explains why the Greek historical references to this area are so scarce and incomplete, much more so than for Sicily. Archaeological evidence thus becomes the major source of information for this part of the Greek world.

Paestum (Poseidonia was its original name), which rose up at the end of the seventh century B.C. as the last extension of the Sybarite network of colonies, was closely connected in the sixth century to the Achaean and Ionic colonies in Italy — Sybaris, Crotona, Caulonia, and Metaponto. The architecture in the sanctuary of Hera at the mouth of the Sele River shows strong analogies with the few known remains in the territory of Sybaris. One notes, for instance, in both areas the same love for figures carved with series of ovules or rosettes that, set into the entablature, soften the rigid geometric cadences of the Doric temple, introducing an element of color more consonant with Ionic architecture.

The sanctuary of Hera, founded, according to tradition, by Jason and the Argonauts, rose up isolated at a considerable distance from the actual city. The older of the two structures there, an archaic treasury small in size and with no peristyle, must have seemed like a work of sculpture rather than architecture. At the top of the edifice there ran a Doric frieze with sculptured metopes, providing a narrative that linked groups of slabs and making this grandiose cycle of archaic sculpture similar to the running story line of an Ionic frieze. The reliefs seem to be inspired by the poetry of Stesichorus of Himera, and some subjects rarely represented in Greece — such as Herakles and the Kerkopes, or King Minos killed due to his betrayal by the Sculian king Cocalus — seem to directly reflect the Western setting. The thirty-seven or thirty-eight metopes preserved, either entirely or in fragments, were executed by various artisans and are distinguished also by the type of workmanship. While on some, the relief is barely outline, as if cut on a sandstone surface, others are carefully finished, even those parts that would remain completely hidden. Among the metopes most effective for their coherent composition and narrative intensity, are one with Odysseus gazing at the sea while sailing on a turtle's back, and another, stylistically similar, with Sisyphus pushing a massive rock up a steep incline (Figure 87).

THE RICHES OF SEGESTA

So many were the nations of Greeks and barbarians that inhabited Sicily, and such was the size of the island against which the Athenians were eager to make an expedition; being desirous (to mention their truest motive) of gaining dominion over the whole of it; but at the same time wishing, as a plausible pretext, to succour their own kinsmen, and the allies they had gained besides. Above all, they were instigated by ambassadors from the Segestans, who had come to Athens and invoked their aid more earnestly than ever. For being borderers of the Selinuntines, they had gone to war with them on certain questions respecting marriage rights, and for some debated territory; and the Selinuntines, having taken the Syracusans for their allies. were pressing them hard with hostilities both by land and sea. Consequently the Segestans reminded the Athenians of their alliance, which had been formed in the time of Laches and of the former war with the Leontines, and begged them to send a fleet and assist them; alleging many other things, and, as the sum and substance of all, "that if the Syracusans should be unpunished for the depopulation of Leontini, and, by ruining such of the Athenian allies as were still left should themselves obtain the whole power of Sicily; there would be danger of their some time or other coming with a large force, as Dorians, to the aid of Dorians, on the strength of their connection, and, moreover, as colonists, to the aid of the Peloponnesians who had sent them out, and so joining in the destruction of the Athenian power. It were wise therefore, in concert with the remaining allies, to resist the Syracusans: especially as they would themselves furnish money sufficient for the war." The Athenians, hearing these things in their assemblies from the Segestans and their supporters, who were repeatedly alleging them, passed a decree on the subject; sending ambassadors, in the first place, to see about the money, whether it were already laid up, as they asserted, in the treasury and in the temples, and at the same time to ascertain what was the state of the war with the Selinuntines. . . . And the Segestans had recourse to the following contrivance, at the time when the first envoys of the Athenians came to them to see the state of their funds. They took them to the temple of Venus at Eryx, and showed them the treasures deposited there, consisting of bowls, wine ladles, censers, and other articles of furniture in no small quantity; which being made of silver, presented, with a value really trifling, a much greater show of wealth. And in their private receptions of the triremes' crews, having collected the cups both of gold and silver that were in Segesta itself, and borrowed those in the neighboring cities, whether Phoenician or Grecian, they each brought them to the entertainments, as their own. And thus, as all used pretty nearly the same, and great numbers of them were every where seen, it created much astonishment in the Athenians from the triremes; and on their arrival at Athens they spread it abroad that they had seen great wealth. Those, then, who had been themselves thus outwitted, and had at that time persuaded the rest, were severely blamed by the soldiers, when the report went abroad that there was not at Segesta the money they had expected.

THUCYDIDES: *History* (VI: 6, 46)

88

THE STORY OF SISYPHUS

And Sisyphus, son of Aeolus, founded Ephyra,
which is now called Corinth, and married
Merope, daughter of Atlas. They had a son
Glaucus, who had by Eurymede a son Bellerophon, who slew the fire-breathing Chim-
era. But Sisyphus is punished in Hades by
rolling a stone with his hands and head in the
effort to heave it over the top; but push it as he
will, it rebounds backward. This punishment
he endures for the sake of Aegina, daughter of
Asopus; for when Zeus had secretly carried
her off, Sisyphus is said to have betrayed the
secret to Asopus, who was looking for her.

APOLLODORUS: *The Library* (I, IX, 3)

88. **Paestum: A metope from the sanctuary
of Hera at the mouth of the Sele River. This
metope, representing two dancers (or perhaps
the daughters of Leucippus) belongs to the
more recent cycle of metopes — about end of
sixth century B.C. — that decorated the large
Doric temple. (Paestum, National Museum)**

Pages 156–157
89. **Paestum: The Basilica, showing the columns of the peristyle to be of an archaic type,
with an accentuated entasis and a flat, bulging
echinus. Behind these columns are those belonging to the Temple of Neptune.**

Pages 158–159
90. **Paestum: The Temple of Neptune
(Poseidon). In fact, it is now known that this
temple was included, together with the
Basilica, in an enclosure dedicated to Hera.
Here the temple is seen from the southwest,
and we can clearly see the slightly convex
curve of the stylobate, designed to correct the
optical illusion of a sinking base caused by
the long horizontal and the massive super-
structure.**

The oblique figure of the hero, clinging to the slope, is bent over by his superhuman effort; Sisyphus presses against the immense stone, and his taut expression reveals the absurdity of his labor as he looks at the top of the hill. This drama has an element of horror because of the presence of a winged genie, a hybrid of man and beast with an emaciated body marked by protruding ribs. This demon, as graphically described by Zancani Montuoro, "rests on Sisyphus' right leg, has seized him by the right shoulder and the neck, and, pushing with his legs and beating his wings, he will force Sisyphus to straighten up and lose his grip: the massive rock, no longer held, will once again roll down to the valley." The compositional pattern in this and the other metopes of the oldest cycle at this sanctuary, datable to the second quarter of the sixth century B.C., often remind us of the contemporary Peloponnesian art. Yet a greater heaviness of volume and the attenuated articulation of the anatomies reveal the influence of the local culture in their search for the same values expressed in the rigid lines of Doric architecture.

The larger temple at the sanctuary of Hera, dated to the end of the sixth century B.C., accentuated the fusion of the Doric and Ionic styles, as seen, for example, in the multiple moldings of the entablature accompanying the Ionic columns set in the pronaos, a solution that would recur later in the Temple of Ceres at Paestum. Almost all the metopes represent the same theme: dancing couples in Ionic costume (Figure 88), led by a girl with her head turned toward her companions, as if inviting them to dance. The unity of the subjects brings these metopes even closer to a continuous Ionic frieze, where the narration was not interrupted by the triglyphs. In the older Doric frieze, an intimate compositional relationship often brought many metopes together; here, however, the repetition of the same self-sufficient pattern on numerous slabs ended by subordinating the sculptural decoration to the cadences of the architecture, isolating the single couples of dancers in the heavy framework of the entablature and the triglyphs. The figures are worthy of mention because of the delicate chromatic effects that animate the surfaces; the mantles, which hang down in heavy strips of symmetrical form, contrast with the tunics barely furrowed by broad folds; their counterpoint merges with the punctilious gestures, animating the narrative with an intimate vivacity. The style of these sculptures is Ionic, yet they are simplified and solidified by local taste.

We have no way of knowing the real architectural dimension of the edifices at this sanctuary at the mouth of the Sele River, but this is possible when we come to Paestum and the large temples that have survived there. The "Basilica" (Figure 89), as it is known, built a little later than the older of the two temples on the Sele, has a singular plan. There are nine columns on the ends, and the odd number is justified by the presence of a single row of supporting elements in the naos where they hold up the main roof beam. This plan, of an archaic character, has strong roots in Samos. Even the carved figures, which at Paestum were inserted in the Doric entablature, recall the moldings of the Ionic Greeks, particularly those at Samos.

In the Basilica, the ambulatories were double normal width, as in the Temple of Artemis at Corfu, where we also found the sculptured decoration on the connecting point of the capitals. But the most convincing comparison with the plan is with the Temple of Apollo Lyceum at Metaponto, where the affinities extend to the architectural terra-cotta coverings that both decorated and protected the wooden roof. The single parts of the Basilica — columns, capitals, entablature elements — were conceived as works of sculpture. This feature, common enough in the archaic Greek temples, was particularly evident here. The strongly tapered columns, with a pronounced swelling about halfway up, and the bulging, flat capital marked by a sharp, double-curved molding, visually express the weight of the entablature; the figures set in the entablature, meantime, swell because of the weight of the frieze. This play of sculptural tensions is enriched by the light that gathers around the moldings in the little floral frieze that crowns them, and in the incisions of the figures. This is an objective world in which every element had its own value, one

91. Ivory carving: This work, representing Lysippe and Iphianassa, dates from the second quarter of the seventh century B.C., and is thought to have been made in Tarentum in southern Italy. (New York, the Metropolitan Museum of Art)

ODYSSEUS MEETS SISYPHUS
IN THE UNDERWORLD

There, too, the hard-task'd Sisyphus I saw,
Thrusting before him, strenuous, a vast rock.
With hands and feet struggling, he shoved the
 stone
Up to a hilltop; but the steep well nigh
Vanquish'd, by some great force, repulsed, the
 mass
Rush'd again obstinate down to the plain.
Again stretch'd prone, severe he toil'd, the
 sweat
Bathed all his weary limbs, and his head
 reek'd.

HOMER: *Odyssey* (XI:593–598)

Minos, the king of the Cretans, who was at that time the master of the seas, when he learned that Daedalus had fled to Sicily, decided to make a compaign against that island. After preparing a notable naval force he sailed forth from Crete and landed at a place in the territory of Acragas which was called after him Minoa. Here he disembarked his troops and sending messengers to King Cocalus he demanded Daedalus of him for punishment. But Cocalus invited Minos to a conference, and after promising to meet all his demands he brought him to his home as his guest. And when Minos was bathing Cocalus kept him too long in the hot water and thus slew him; the body he gave back to the Cretans, explaining his death on the ground that he had slipped in the bath and by falling into the hot water had met his end. Thereupon the comrades of Minos buried the body of the king with magnificent ceremonies, and constructing a tomb of two stories, in the part of it which was hidden underground they placed the bones, and in that which lay open to gaze they made a shrine of Aphrodite.

DIODORUS SICULUS (IV:79)

Paestum: Plan of the Basilica

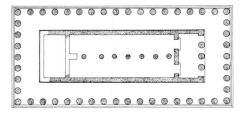

Paestum: Plan of the Temple of Ceres

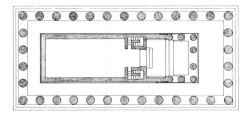

Paestum: Plan of the Temple of Neptune (Poseidon)

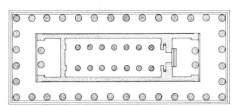

that was not subordinate to an external viewpoint. Even the walls and pillars of the sekos imitate the swollen profile of the peristyle columns.

In the Temple of Ceres (now considered to have been dedicated to Minerva), built about 510 B.C., the archaic taste for details was equally present, yet one notes a new interest in the edifice as an architectural organism. The tall columns with their slender profile effect a vertical thrust in the construction; the cornice descends from the slopes of the roof, continuing on to the long sides of the temple. All this emphasizes the three-dimensional character of the edifice; yet it does not create a geometric mass, since the articulated structure does not define — as will occur in later temples — a plane strictly parallel to the stylobate. In the interior of this Temple of Ceres, the naos, closed off by a wall, opens to the east via a spacious portico with Ionic columns. This is a residue of the archaic concern with a frontal view, which tends to accentuate the perspective depth of the main facade. Yet in the Temple of Ceres, the solid cohesion of the external colonnade impeded any fragmentation of the view, and the Ionic portico must have served as an element of transition from the exterior to the interior space, and the difference in quality and light. Stylistically this was without a doubt the loveliest of the three temples at Paestum, with its fragile equilibrium between an ancient mode of expression and the new elements that appear within it.

The Temple of Neptune — in fact, dedicated to Hera, as was the Basilica — is similar in its proportions to the Temple of Athena in Syracuse; both also have fourteen columns on the long sides. By the middle of the fifth century, the carved figures that softened the geometry of the most ancient temples on the plain of the Sele River had disappeared from the entablature. This severe and rather heavy entablature solidly embraced the peristyle, with its squat columns set close together (Figure 90) in a thick curtain that separated the interior from the surrounding countryside. The inclination toward the interior of the corner columns and the slight arch of the horizontal elements accentuated the cohesion of the architectural organism. Beyond the peristyle and beyond the front of the pronaos, appeared the naos, raised on a low podium and animated by two rows of thick columns. The dislocation of the pronaos and the naos on their two slightly raised levels added special emphasis to the transition to the interior space set between the thick walls of the sekos.

Leaving aside for the moment the architecture and the terra-cotta figurines, we must admit that the cities of Magna Graecia did not seem to have shown any great artistic initiative. The Ionian colonies were an exception — especially Locris and Tarentum — where the stronger and more frequent relations with Greece and the continual contributions of works from the mother country created a more dynamic cultural tone. The lovely ivory group representing Lysippe and Iphianassa (Figure 91), the daughters of Proteus driven mad by Hera because they said their home was richer than her sanctuary, is attributed to Tarentine artists. The exaggerated bodily structure, typical of Doric art, nearly distorts the figures; the long, thin legs end in the triangles of the short torsos and faces; the latter have lean, almost hollow cheeks, emphasizing the rather roughly carved profile. This aggressive and schematic rendering of the bodies is attenuated by the mantle, which with winding curves reveals the nude female underneath. This spiral rhythm, which adds tension to the figure, ends in the left arm crossed over the chest and the brusque turn of the face. The interpretation, origin, and chronology of this group is still being discussed and disputed. But if it is from Tarentum and dates from the seventh century, it reveals the existence, in this Spartan-Doric colony, of a particularly elevated and dynamic culture at an earlier period than one would have imagined.

In order to give an idea of the importation of Greek culture in the Tarentum area, we need only refer to one of the more recent discoveries in a minor center of the Salentine peninsula, as the "toe" of Italy is called: a bronze Poseidon from Ugento (Figure 92), dating from the last quarter of the sixth century B.C. The god lifts his right hand, ready to strike, while with his extended left hand he holds a fish; his crown, decorated with rosettes, partially covers the curls that fall over his forehead, and his

neck, and four long braids fall down over his shoulders. The subtle decoration of various details, seen not only in the face but in the rendering of anatomical details, softens the firm and rigorous fullness of the body. The work, executed in the Peloponnesos — perhaps in Corinth — is one of the most significant originals from late-archaic Greek bronze art.

THE GREEK WORLD
AFTER ALEXANDER THE GREAT

Hellenism:
Reconstructing the Classic World

After its profound crisis at the end of the fifth century B.C., Athens seemed to withdraw into itself in the fourth century. In the sculpture of Praxiteles, which marked the high point of that art in the latter epoch, the very gods, as if having come down from Olympus, seem to be caught by surprise in an individual attitude; their bodily presence was animated now by a subtle hedonism. Participation in the life of the polis was more and more limited. The citizen was transformed from a member of the *ecclesia* into a mere private individual. Certainly this phenomenon, this process, was gradual. And even in the middle of the fourth century, when the shadow of the Macedonian empire was falling over Athens, the conflict between Philip the Macedon's supporters, led by Isocrates, and the defenders of Greek liberty, headed by Demosthenes, involved most of the citizenry.

In 335 B.C., after the so-called Social War, the Athenian alliance dissolved. A similar fate occurred in the case of Sparta in its struggle with Thebes: after the battle of Leuctra (371 B.C.), Epaminondas, the leader of the Boeotian League's army, liberated Messenia — that region in the southwestern corner of the Peloponnesos — and built a heavily fortified capital at Messene. The conquest of Messenia in the second half of the seventh century had been the first step in the creation of Spartan domination, because — as Hammond has observed — "With this conquest the agricultural resources and labor force of the Spartan state had doubled." The Messenians, reduced to the condition of servants, had been serving as the cheap labor supply for the Spartans; now that economic base of the Spartan state had collapsed.

The walls of Messene (Figure 93), symbol of its independence regained under Epaminondas, reflect the progress made in military techniques by this time. The Arcadia Gate is a stupendous example of the most advanced military engineering of the day; it consisted of two entrances separated by an interior circular court, which funetioned as a partition and as the last line of defense. The outside main gate was flanked by two square towers (Figure 94).

The short-lived Theban supremacy — which, nonetheless, had succeeded in ending Spartan military hegemony — died out at its height due to the death of its protagonists: Pelopidas at Cynoscephalae in 364 B.C., after having won the battle for the Thebans, and Epaminondas two years later at Mantinaea, where he asked his fellow citizens to make peace with Sparta. The resulting political vacuum was quickly filled by the Macedonians, who under Philip II essentially forced the Greek city-states to end their centuries-long discord and establish, in 337 B.C., the League of Corinth, which included all the states south of Mount Olympus, except Sparta. The League was set up for the common defense of its members against external and internal threats; this also meant the safeguarding of the established privileges against the danger of new, more advanced social orders. The council of the League chose the ancient Panhellenic sanctuaries as their meeting places — Delphi, Olympia, Nemea, the Isthmus of Corinth — which, by themselves, had for many centuries kept alive the consciousness of the historic and cultural unity of all Greeks.

It was in this political and social climate that the Temple of Zeus at Nemea (Figure 95) was reconstructed in 340 B.C., probably by the same artists who had worked a few years before, under the guidance of the great sculptor and architect, Skopas, on the Temple of Athena Alea at Tegea. Both temples, for instance, reflected the tendency, typical of the fourth century, toward reducing the length of the edifice and the number of columns on the long sides (see plan, page 164). But whereas at Tegea the symmetry between the two end facades of the temple was

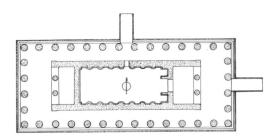

Tegea: Plan of the Temple of Athena Alea

93. Messene: The fortification wall, built about 369 B.C. when the city was founded after the liberation of the district of Messenia from its long domination by the Spartans. Square towers alternated with semicircular towers along the walls.

94. Messene: The Arcadia Gate, viewed from inside. We see part of the large circular court, with a diameter of some 65 feet, located between the interior and exterior gateways.

95.   Nemea: The Temple of Zeus. The Doric columns of the peristyle still preserved, as an archaic element, a strong entasis — a sculptural characteristic largely discarded by other architects of the time.

96.   Athens: The Choragic Monument of Lysikrates (also known as the "Lantern of Demosthenes"). Like the other choragic monuments, it stood on the "Street of the Tripods" that led to the theater of Dionysus on the slopes of the Acropolis.

97.   Pella: The mosaic from the palace of Alexander. The motif of the lion hunt, a favorite sport of ancient monarchs, was a favorite theme of Alexander the Great, who intended to assume the role and character of a Near Eastern potentate but was cut off in his prime. From that time on, however, the theme had something of a vogue in Hellenistic art.

98.   Didyma: The Temple of Apollo. From the adyton, here conceived of as a court, the broad staircase surmounted by two Corinthian columns led to the *chresmographeion*. On either side of the staircase are the doors for those who came from the pronaos through two tunnels.

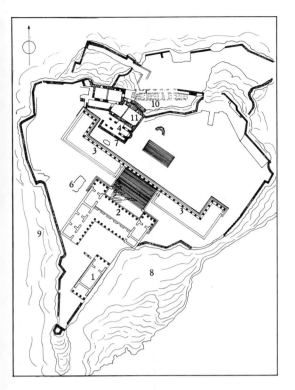

Lindos: Plan of the Acropolis
1 Temple of Athena Lindia
2 Propylaea
3 Great Portico
4 Medieval church
5 Archaic stairway
6 Large depository of votive offerings
7 Small depository of votive offerings
8 Caves and rock shelters
9 Waste dump
10 Relief with ship
11 House of the commander

preserved, at Nemea it was eliminated; the opisthodomos was abolished and the eastern ambulatory was twice as deep as the western one; the deep pronaos further helped to give great prominence to the main facade. The interior columns with Corinthian capitals, arranged in a U-shape as at Bassae, isolated a chamber at the end of the naos: perhaps this was a subterranean adyton. The slender peristyle columns, however, retained considerable entasis, which gave them an archaic heaviness. In the archaic Doric temple, sculptural values were the determining factor, as we have noted time and again; the capitals and moldings expanded, almost as if to materialize the weight of the entablature on the supporting elements. Gradually, in the classic age, the attention had shifted to the rendering of mass and space, where the capitals and moldings served a secondary function; their profiles became more and more vertical so that the eye could concentrate on the new architectural values. Even the entasis, so accentuated in the Basilica at Paestum (535 B.C.), had actually disappeared at Bassae. Its striking reappearance in the Nemea temple thus created a somewhat contradictory aspect.

It was in this period, too, that the Corinthian capital came into general use. It was used, perhaps for the first time on an exterior peristyle, in the tholos at Epidaurus, designed by Polycletus the Younger. Because of its design, equal from every vantage point, and — as Groeben pointed out — "because of its qualities of richness and lightness, its connective fluidity," the Corinthian capital was ideal for a circular edifice. Theodorus of Phocaea had earlier used just such a capital for the interior columns in the tholos at Delphi. And the monument that Lysikrates had built at Athens in 334 B.C. is essentially a miniature tholos (Figure 96). The preparation and rehearsal of the chorus in Athens was one of the obligations imposed on the upper classes; according to an ancient custom, the *choragus* (the person who had defrayed the cost of the chorus for a play), upon receiving first prize in a competition, would construct a little monument that served as the base for the victory tripod. In Lysikrates' monument, the Corinthian columns, in full relief, give the impression of being embedded in the upper tambour. The decorative effect is increased by the different colors of the stone: limestone for the square base, blue marble from Mount Hymettus on the steps above the base, and white marble in the upper tambour.

The Greek mainland was reduced to a secondary role in the new order of the Hellenistic world. There prevailed, however, a taste tied to the models of the classical age; this phenomenon reached its peak in Athens,

100

99. **Lindos: The Temple of Athena Lindia.** From the stairway that leads from the lower terrace to the sanctuary's terrace, we see the jutting eastern wing of the Great Portico.

100. **Priene: The Temple of Zeus, seen from the agora in the northwest. In the background is the valley of the Maeander River.**

in the last two centuries before Christ, in the rather cold, rigid neo-Attic style. Meanwhile, Macedonia has assumed a dominant role in the cultural field as well as in the political realm. The impressive mosaics in Alexander's royal palace at Pella (Figure 97) are enough in themselves to give an idea of the flowering of this Macedonian culture, which for centuries had remained on the fringes of the Greek world. The Athenians had viewed the Macedonian dynasty as the new barbarians come to crush the city that had thwarted the Persians. But Philip's son, Alexander the Great, presented himself as the legitimate heir of the Panhellenic tradition, and in this capacity he undertook the conquest of Asia. Alexander climaxed his four years of victorious campaigning in the Near East by his victory over the Persian Emperor Darius III Codomannus, who was killed in 330 B.C. The Greek coastal cities of Asia Minor, after an eclipse that had lasted almost two centuries, once again enjoyed a new period of prosperity. In the Persian empire, these cities had been like vassals, with no economy of their own; now that the doors to the East were opened to the Greek world, these cities once again became the ports of call of a rich and populous province.

The rebirth of Asia Minor was marked by the reconstruction of the colossal Ionic temples of the archaic age. Among the sanctuaries destroyed by the Persians after the Ionian revolt, the most important was the one at Didyma, near Miletus, along the coast of Asia Minor. Just as at Delphi, this temple this tunnel was linked to the oracular cult of Apollo, which here had a sacred spring where the laurel sacred to the god had first come to life. This was the central point of temple, which thus had, ever since the archaic age, a vast pillared court in place of the naos. The reconstruction of the Hellenistic Temple of Apollo at Didyma began about 313 B.C. and went on for five centuries without ever being completed. Although the new temple probably retained the fundamental relationships of the archaic plan, it expressed the new scenographic needs of Hellenistic architecture. The podium, elevated on seven steps, was clearly separated from the ground, and the line of the stylobate stood out quite prominently as the coordinating element in the huge structure. However, the adyton, the most sacred part of the temple, had to remain on the level of the archaic structure, since the spring and Apollo's laurel were there. This difficulty became the inspiration for a bold construction on three distinct levels. On the lowest level was a large court, closed off to the east by a large stairway (Figure 98), and backed by two semicolumns surmounted by Corinthian capitals. The staircase led to the uppermost level, to the *chresmographeion*, the "place where the oracles were written down"; in this room, set above the faithful who gathered in the pronaos and in front of the temple, the priest of Apollo stood to announce the god's oracle. From the pronaos, entirely filled by four rows of columns, one could not go to the oracular room; but two half-hidden, steeply descending tunnels allowed the few privileged people to pass into the adyton.

The sudden leap from the dazzling light of the Mediterranean sun to the darkness of the narrow, hidden passageway lent an intensity and suspense to the approach to the god's chamber. At the end of the steep descent, once past a dark subterranean propylon, the eye beheld the more blinding light of the large open court. Along its mighty wall were pillars with proto-Ionic capitals rising from a tall podium. The thrust of the pillars carried the eye to the *naiskos*, a chapel-like room, at the end of the court, which housed the spring with sulfurous vapors, the inspiration for the oracles. In the naiskos was also kept the bronze statue of Apollo Philesios, the work of Kanachos of Sicyon, stolen by Darius and brought back to the sanctuary by Seleucus I. "Thanks to the arrangement of the large pillars," as Groeben has pointed out, "thanks to the jutting architrave that ran all around the edifice and that seemed to hold up a nonexistent roof, the sky itself was called upon to serve as the roof for the pillared court." This court, filled with thick laurel shrubs, thus created the suggestion of an interior space shut off from the surrounding world, and attracted to itself the sense of mystery appropriate to an oracular cult. The architectural form thus was one with the religious conception, helping to clarify it with its own expressiveness. In this intimate fusion

DAILY LIFE IN ALEXANDRIA IN THE THIRD CENTURY A.D.

GORGO *(setting off for the Festival of Adonis)*
But come, my dear, get your cloak and gown. I want you to come with me to call on our high and mighty Prince Ptolemy to see the Adonis. I hear the Queen's getting up something quite splendid this year.

PRAXINOA *(hesitating)*
Fine folks, fine ways.

GORGO
Yes; but sightseers make good gossips, you know, if you've been and other people haven't. It's time we were on the move.

PRAXINOA *(still hesitating)*
It's always holidays with people who've nothing to do. *(suddenly making up her mind)* Here, Eunoa, you scratch-face, take up the spinning and put it away with the rest. Come, bestir yourself. Quick, some water! Pour out the water. *(E. washes her mistress' hands and face)* Oh, you wretch! What do you mean by wetting my bodice like that? That's enough. *(to Gorgo)* I've got myself washed somehow, thank goodness. *(to Eunoa)* Now where's the key of the big cupboard? Bring it here. *(Takes out a Dorian pinner — a gown fastened with pins or brooches to the shoulders and reaching to the ground, with an overfold coming to the waist — and puts it on with Eunoa's aid over the inner garment with short sleeves which she wears indoors)*

GORGO *(referring to the style of the overfold)*
Praxinoa, that full gathering suits you really well. Do tell me what you gave for the material.

PRAXINOA
Don't speak of it, Gorgo; it was more than eight golden sovereigns, and I can tell you I put my very soul into making it up.

GORGO
Well, all I can say is, it's *most* successful.

PRAXINOA
It's very good of you to say so. *(to Eunoa)* Come, put on my cloak and hat for me, and mind you do it properly *(Eunoa puts her cloak about her head and shoulders and pins the straw sun hat to it)*. *(taking up the child)* No; I'm not going to take *you*, Baby. Horse-bogey bites little boys. *(the child cries)* You may cry as much as you like; I'm not going to have you lamed for life. *(to Gorgo, giving the child to the nurse)* Come along. Take Baby and amuse him, Phrygia, and call the dog indoors and lock the front door.

(in the street) Heavens, what a crowd! How we're to get through this awful crush and how long it's going to take us, I can't imagine. Talk of an antheap! *(apostrophising)* I *must* say, you've done us many a good turn, my good Ptolemy, since your father went to heaven. We have no villains sneaking up to murder us in the streets nowadays in the good old Egyptian style. They don't play those awful games now — the thorough-paced rogues, every one of them the same, all queer!

that gave meaning to each detail, we see the genius of the two architects, Paeonios of Ephesus and Daphnis of Miletus.

Outside of Asia Minor, the most striking artistic expression of the new architectural conception was found in Doric Rhodes, the vital crossroads for the trading ships passing through the Aegean. At Lindos, on the western coast of the island, there was an ancient sanctuary on the acropolis dedicated to the goddess Lindia, later to become identified with Athena; originally this sanctuary consisted only of a sacred wood where the people worshiped a pole as a symbol of the divinity. This was succeeded later on by two archaic temples, and in the fourth century a new edifice, with facades decorated with Doric columns, was built. Facing the sea, it stood on the top of the steep hill that in the Hellenistic age was organized almost as an enormous stage setting for the sacred site: a monumental staircase, set upon the archaic steps cut out of the rock, linked the lower terraces with the upper one where the temple stood. The staircase was wedged in between two wings of the L-shaped portico, which transformed the harsh terrain with their architectural rhythms (Figure 99).

The Doric colonnade that ran along the entire breadth of the hill unified the front of the porticoes and the stairway; this was then echoed by the columns of the eastern front of the propylaeum on the upper terrace. This propylaeum, with its two jutting lateral elements, was connected to the stairway, continuing its ascending rhythm, while toward the west it defined the level space of the temple, which thus became a porticoed plaza. The continuous ambivalence of the architectural bodies that resolved into one another, the mixing of the natural setting with the formal values — these created the expressive wealth of this complex, which adopted the stark Doric style without conceding anything to exuberant Asian decorativeness.

The Antithesis of Public and Private Life

The Didyma temple and the Lindos sanctuary reveal a special sensitivity to the concept that architecture did not have to be a rational form superimposed on a natural setting but could be conceived and executed in relation to this setting. This bespeaks a profound difference in the conception of the world between fifth-century classicism and the Hellenistic spirit. With the creation of large factories, already begun in the fifth century, the Agora and the *polis* had become insufficient social structures for the new economic situation; the increase of products required the creation of larger markets. The new commercial class replaced the landed aristocracy, and its interests surpassed by far the narrow confines of the city-state. The corresponding dimensions to the new economic realities was the Macedonian empire and the kingdoms into which it eventually was divided during the struggles among Alexander's successors. The new productive capacity increased man's dominion over nature. The antagonism between nature and man, rational and irrational at the same time, was no longer being felt with the sense of drama that Plato had imparted to it. Already in Aristotle the position granted to the natural sciences, to the observation of nature, to *empeiria* ("empiricism") was considerable. The irrational and the natural were vital dimensions for the Greek in the Hellenistic age.

On the other hand, in the vast kingdoms of the post-Alexandrian period, participation in political life was restricted to a limited circle of the king's court while other individuals devoted themselves solely to their work and private lives. Thus the division between public and private, which had been maturing since the crisis at the end of the fifth century, was aggravated. This became especially clear among the ruling class. Pericles had asserted his power by having the Parthenon erected, and thus he identified his greatness with that of Athens. Alexander's successors viewed their kingdoms as an enhancement of their own personal glory, and built palatial residences and luxurious ships (such as the one belonging to Ptolemy IV of Egypt), filled with works of art of all kinds. The influence of the image of the Eastern potentate certainly contributed

101. Priene: The Temple of Athena Polias as it has been set up in modern times. As we view the rough, craggy landscape today, it is hard to imagine that the city was laid out on a severely geometric plan.

102. Delos: In the foreground are columns of the agora of the Italians; in the background, left, are visible two of the Naxian lions; in the background, right, are the columns of the Establishment of the Poseidoniastes, erected by the cult-worshipers from the Syrian city of Berytus.

THE END OF GREECE'S FREEDOM WITH THE FALL OF CORINTH (146 B.C.)

This year likewise saw the ruin of Corinth. The head men of the Greeks had been deported to Italy by Aemilius Paulus, whereupon their countrymen at first through embassies kept requesting the return of the men, and when their prayers were not granted some of the exiles in despair of ever effecting a return to their homes committed suicide. The Greeks took this situation with a very bad grace and made it a matter of public lamentation, besides evincing anger at any persons dwelling among them that favored the Roman cause; yet they displayed no open symptoms of hostility until they got back the remnants of those hostages. Then those that had been wronged and those that had obtained a hold upon the good of others fell into strife and began a real warfare. The quarrel began by the action of the Achaeans in bringing charges against the Lacedaemonians as being responsible for what had happened to them. The mediators whom the Romans despatched to them they would not heed. They rather set their faces toward war, acting under the supervision of Critolaus. Metellus was consequently afraid that they might lay hands on Macedonia, — they had already appeared in Thessaly — and so he went to meet them and routed them.

At the fall of Critolaus, the Greek world was split asunder. Some of them had embraced peace and laid down their weapons, whereas others had committed their interests to the care of Diaeus and were still involved in factional turmoil. On learning this the people of Rome sent Mummius against them. He got rid of Metellus and gave his personal attention to the war. Part of his army sustained a slight reverse through an ambuscade and Diaeus pursued the fugitives up to their own camp, but Mummius made a sortie, routed him, and followed to the Achaean entrenchments. Diaeus now gathered a larger force and undertook to give battle to them, but, as the Romans would make no hostile demonstration, he conceived a contempt for them and advanced to a depressed piece of ground lying between the camps. Mummius seeing this secretly sent horsemen to assail them on the flank. After these had attacked and thrown the enemy into confusion, he brought up the phalanx in front and caused considerable slaughter. As a consequence Diaeus in despair killed himself, and of the survivors of the battle the Corinthians were scattered over the country, while the rest fled to their homes. Hence the Corinthians within the wall believing that all their citizens had been lost abandoned the city, and it was empty of men when Mummius took it. After that he won over without trouble both that nation and the rest of the Greeks. He now took possession of their arms, all the offerings that were consecrated in their temples, the statues, paintings, and whatever other kind of ornament they had; and as soon as he could send his father and some other men to arrange terms for the vanquished he caused the walls of some of the cities to be taken down and declared them all to be free and independent except the Corinthians. The dwellers in Corinth he sold, and confiscated their land and demolished their walls and all their houses besides, out of fear that some states might again unite with them, since they constituted the greatest state. To prevent any of them from remaining hidden and any of the other Greeks from being sold as Corinthians he assembled everybody present before he had disclosed his determination, and after having his soldiers surround them in such a way as not to attract notice he proclaimed the enslavement of the Corinthians and the liberation of the remainder. Then he instructed them all to take hold of any Corinthians standing beside them. In this way he arrived at an accurate distinction.

Thus was Corinth overthrown. The rest of the Greek world suffered temporarily from murders and levies of money, but afterward came to enjoy such immunity and prosperity that it used to be said: "If they had not been taken captive as early as they were, they could not have been preserved."

ZONARAS:
Epitome of Dio Cassius (9:31)

to the formation of this new concept of the sovereign, but the change was undoubtedly sustained by economic and political causes within Hellenistic society.

As the individual's interests came to be centered on his private life, the dwelling, and the city as an architectural dimension in which the house was set, assumed a new importance. Toward the middle of the fourth century, because the Maeander River in Asia Minor had turned into a swamp, Priene was reconstructed far from the sea, on the barren slopes of Mount Mycal. The city, surmounted by an almost inaccessible acropolis, was set on four terraces with great differences in their levels. Proceeding east to west, this difference was less marked, as this was the direction for the busiest streets; proceeding north to south, the terraces often had to be approached by long stairways. Despite this, a strictly rectangular plan, with streets and blocks of set dimensions, was imposed on this apparently refractory environment. But it did not succeed in overwhelming the environment; on the contrary, the city's design ended by highlighting its scenographic aspects. The principal artery was the one that, from the western gate, led to the agora, skirting along its northern side. The agora, surrounded by long porticoes, was completed about 150–130 B.C. In the center, besides numerous semicircular seats, was the altar of Hermes. Connected to the agora was the sanctuary of Zeus (Figure 100), including a small tetrastyle Ionic temple.

On the uppermost terrace, at the foot of the acropolis, stood a sanctuary of Demeter; on the terrace below the theater and the Temple of Athena Polias (Figure 101) dominated the city. The latter was built by

Priene: Plan of the city
1 *Temple of Demeter*
2 *Temple of Athena*
3 *Theater*
4 *Upper gymnasium*
5 *Agora*
6 *Sanctuary of Egyptian divinities*
7 *Temple of Aesclepius*
8 *Sacred Portico*
9 *Stadium*
10 *Lower gymnasium*
11 *Maeander River plain*
12 *Hilly outpost*

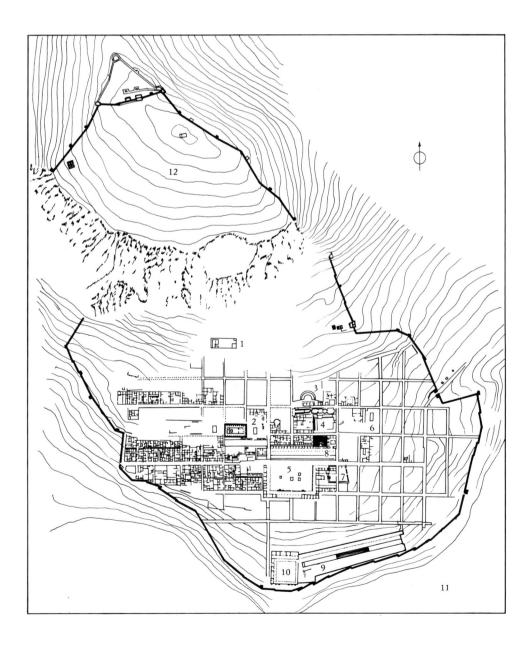

Pytheas, the architect of the Mausoleum of Halicarnassus, between 350 and 330 B.C., for the most part with funds offered by Alexander the Great during one of his sojourns at Priene. Hexastyle, with only eleven columns on the long sides, the temple was planned on the basis of rigorous mathematical relationships; yet the main facade, because of the greater depth of its pronaos, took on a particular prominence, thus breaking up the symmetry.

After regaining its independence, Delos — which from far back in the archaic world had been the center of Greek tribal exchanges — was transformed into an important commercial port of call; its function as a large wheat market was particularly facilitated by the island's proximity to Egypt. The first symptom of the new prosperity of Delos was the construction of the theater, with a seating capacity of five thousand, dated to the end of the fourth or the beginning of the third century B.C. The island was by then populated with traders coming from every part of the Mediterranean — Italians, Egyptians, Near Easterners — and adopted a truly cosmopolitan character. Its greatest moment of splendor was in the second century B.C.: the great hypostyle hall, the Exchange, with its interior forty-eight columns, was built then. Each ethnic community of traders had its own warehouses and offices in the Exchange. In addition to the agora of the Delians near the sanctuary of Apollo, there now grew up the agora of the Italians and the Establishment of the Poseidoniastes (Figure 102). This imposing construction — built about 110 B.C. in a location that actually intersected the old sacred way of the lions — belonged to the association of traders, warehousemen, and sailors from the Syrian city of Berytus. These people gathered together not only because of their common business interests but also because they all worshiped Baal (the ancient Phoenician god of storms, mountains, and rain), assimilated by the Greek Poseidon; thus, this edifice united commercial and social functions with a sacred character. It was set up on two sides of a large Doric peristyle: on the western side, near the entranceway, was the sanctuary with three chambers; the middle one was dedicated to Poseidon–Baal; and two others were dedicated to the goddess Roma and to Aphrodite–Astarte. It was during this period, too, that the sanctuaries of various Near Eastern, Egyptian, Syrian, and Samothracian gods sprang up on the slopes of Mount Cynthus, where some of the most ancient sacred sites of the island had long been situated.

At Delos, the plan of the town was not homogeneous; the most ancient quarter, around the theater, with some blocks from the first half of the third century, was irregular, perhaps because the small area did not yet have an urban character. From the second half of the third century, when the area of the northern quarter was occupied for the first time, the constructions were based on town-planning, even though the plan was not perfectly rectangular. The houses were set around a large courtyard, often surrounded by columns. The most important room, the sitting room, was almost always to the north and opened on to the peristyle; in order to guarantee the greatest amount of light for this room, the corresponding side of the peristyle was often raised. The floors were decorated with splendid figured mosaics, while the walls had refined paintings. The house of the Athenian couple Dioscurides and Cleopatra did not correspond to the usual scheme; in fact, the living room opened onto the south side of the peristyle (Figure 103). Facing this were the statues of the couple erected, so the inscription tells us, in 137 B.C. The precious expression of Asian Hellenism is seen particularly in the rendering of the drapery; the mantles that entirely cover the figures, although marked by many folds, still allow us to see the folds of the chiton underneath, which molds the figures' bodies. They are animated by a rolling rhythm, marked by the contrast between the torso and the lower half of the body.

The private residence at Delos mirrored a moment of economic expansion and prosperity, not only because of its distinctive luxury but also because it was being used to house only one well-to-do family. From the Greek world this residence was adopted in the Italian world, and some of the best preserved examples are those found at Pompeii. At Rome this type of house became the model of the luxurious residence of the republican period and up to the middle of the first century A.D. As we can see,

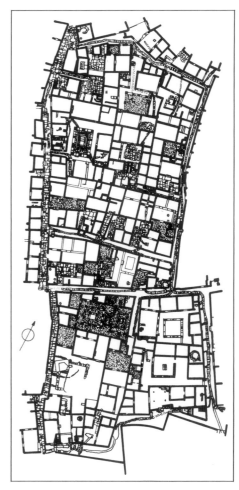

Delos: Plan of the residential quarter

Athens: Plan of Temple and sanctuary of Olympian Zeus
1 Hadrian's Arch
2 Roman baths
3 Basilica
4 Propylon

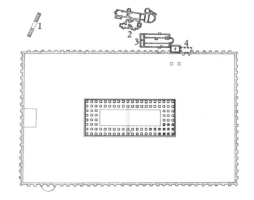

103

103. Delos: The house of the Athenian couple, Dioscurides and Cleopatra (second century B.C.), with the statues of the two proprietors).

Following page:
104. Athens: The Temple of Olympian Zeus. The group of surviving columns, which occupies the southeastern corner of the temple, dates from the age of Hadrian. These columns are some 57 feet high. Immediately behind the temple is the Helicon hill (on the other side of which nestles the Olympic stadium) while in the distant background is Mount Hymettus, where the blue-gray marble known as Kara was cut.

through Hellenism the confines of the Greek world expanded until they included the entire Mediterranean.

Thus, when Antiochus IV Epiphanes (175–164 B.C) decided to resume the construction of the Temple of Olympian Zeus in Athens, interrupted more than three centuries earlier by the expulsion of the Pisistratidae, he entrusted the project to Cossutio, an Italian architect. The Hellenistic temple followed the plan of the ancient Temple of Hera of Rhoicos at Samos. The colossal Ionic temples of the archaic age, characterized by the density of innumerable columns and by exuberant decorative effects, now met with the favor of the new Hellenistic taste. The Temple of Olympian Zeus (Figure 104), where the decorative elements seem to be emphasized by the substitution of Corinthian columns for the original Ionic columns, thus became connected with the Hellenistic reconstructions of the great temples at Ephesus, Didyma and Sardis.

Yet the edifice, not far from the Acropolis (where it was exposed to an immediate comparison with Pericles' monuments) must have seemed to be, exactly because of its immensity, extraneous to the natural landscape and the Athenian setting. Thus, after the death of the Syrian king, Antiochus, the temple remained unfinished once again. Sulla, during the sacking of the city in 86 B.C., took back some of the columns to be used in the Temple of Capitoline Jupiter in Rome. Here, in this minor footnote to history, we may catch various glimmers of the fading Greek world — the Acropolis, Pericles, Olympian Zeus, a great temple — and realize that the torch had passed to Rome.

APPENDICES
GREEK MONUMENTS THROUGH THE AGES

Recovery of the Ancient Greek World

In 1453 the Turks captured Constantinople; in 1458 the Turks occupied the Acropolis of Athens. These two dates mark a most definitive, and bitter, break in the history of the Greek nation. Yet long before such events produced the irremediable political break, the eclipse of Pericles' world had occurred. The monuments on the Acropolis had fallen into almost total oblivion before the Turks arrived, and Western Europeans had all but lost sight of the ancient Greek world. Medieval art, including Byzantine art, had moved along substantially different routes from those of ancient Greece and Rome. Classicism — defined for the moment as the search for solid volume accompanied by compositional clarity — had ceased to appeal to the inheritors of the Greek and Roman worlds.

Ironically, just as the Greeks' last links with their political past were being broken, that classical heritage was being revived elsewhere. The Renaissance attitude toward classical Greece was actually far more complex than is sometimes presented. The encounter was certainly intense and profound in the fields of literature and philosophy. It is accepted, for instance, that Plato and Aristotle, more or less filtered through Augustine and Thomas Aquinas, provided the spiritual-intellectual sustenance of the Middle Ages that, in turn, produced the Renaissance. In the artistic world, too, interest in antiquity was lively; connoisseurs began to form collections, while the artists sketched the ancient remains. Yet most of the available material was that found in Italy — Roman and Etruscan or Greek imports. But Renaissance individuals evidently felt no urgent need to verify and rediscover the essential artistic world that corresponded to the Hellenic philosophical works. They were content in their profound conviction that their contemporary experience was, because of deep "spiritual" affinities, a sort of continual interior rediscovery of antiquity.

In fact, although the remains of ancient Athens were virtually unknown to Europeans, the Acropolis was visited between 1434 and 1448 by an Italian merchant, Ciriaco dei Pizzicolli of Ancona, who produced three volumes of commentary and drawings on the subject. In 1437 Ciriaco went to Florence to see Donatello and Ghiberti; his sketches of Greek relief carvings were included in the collection of archaeological drawings compiled by Giuliano da Sangallo. This visit of Ciriaco did not appear to have had any appreciable effect on the conceptions of the Florentine artists. However, the relief carving that Ciriaco had copied in Santa Sofia in Constantinople, for example, had considerable influence because its circular plan was one of many concepts being discussed by architects of the time.

The work of Vitruvius, the first-century B.C. Roman architect, did have considerable importance; his *De architectura* was rediscovered and republished before the end of the fifteenth century. Yet the work of Vitruvius was reinterpreted, especially by Leon Battista Alberti, as if he had been a contemporary of Plato, so that Vitruvius' precepts (dictated by a technical empiricism) were subordinated to a broader philosophic vision no trace of which is to be found in the original Latin text. Operations of this kind could succeed to the degree that the claim of the perfection of the ancients always bears within itself the negation of history: such a claim implies a classical ideal set outside of time.

The idea that the Renaissance had of ancient Greece was therefore somewhat arbitrary, but the vitality of the Renaissance experience at least rejected a classicism that was merely a philological imitation of the ancient world. The artistic culture of the Renaissance was, if anything, more closely linked with ancient Rome, but the assimilation of Hellenic thought was reflected in a profound harmony of taste. It should be enough to mention the intrinsic relationship that Albert noted between architectural structure and decoration, employed to define the "personality" of the monument, to render its meaning and deepest motives explicit. The modern scholar Chastel writes: "The revolution had consisted of the integral study of the edifice as a coherent development of geometric forms, without subordinating the originality of the conception to the solution of concrete problems. The importance attached to the 'idea' as applied to the theoretical 'model' led to the break with Gothic techniques." The Renaissance encounter with ancient Greece was thus a profound stimulus to European civilization in that it developed into a spontaneous convergence of conceptions.

Ever since the Renaissance, then, the idea of the preeminence of Greek art has periodically gained hold in European culture; indeed, it is the underlying premise of the on-going conflict known as "the quarrel between the ancients and the moderns." For example, the Carracci in Bologna became supporters of the vague ideal of classicism. So, too, in the works of Giovanni Pietro Bellori, archaeologist and art critic on the Roman scene in the last decades of the seventeenth century, there was announced the poetics of the "beautiful ideal," entering into controversy with Caravaggio's naturalism and mannerism. It longed for the return to classical clarity and moderation, harking back to the last phase of Plato's thought, where art was considered a participant in the Ideal.

But the real rediscovery of Greece was the offspring of the eighteenth-century Enlightenment, and was born in the climate of reaction to Baroque art. Enlightened rationalism rejected the complex and extravagant forms of the seventeenth century. Indeed, the Enlightenment's encounter with Greek art seemed inevitable, since it was searching for the rigorous definition of architectural surfaces and the preeminence of rationality over expressive elements. And if any one Enlightenment individual can be credited with the rediscovery of Greek art, it was Johann Joachim Wincklemann. Born in Saxony on December 9, 1717, Wincklemann went on to study both theology and medicine before focusing his attention on the ancient world. In 1755 he gained a certain amount of fame with the publication of his essay, "Thoughts on the Imitation of Greek Works of Painting and Sculpture," in which Wincklemann articulated the superiority of Greek art because of its striving toward ideal beauty. In November of that year, he went off to Rome and there published in 1763 (although with the date of 1764) his basic study, *History of Ancient Art*. Aside from its insights into classic art, this work marked the passage in modern Europe from the empirical and episodical approach to ancient monuments over to the systematic reconstruction of classical art.

Even so, Wincklemann's work could not help but reflect the limits imposed by his cultural formation. In particular, the concept that Greek art could represent a moment of abstract perfection ended up cutting the intrinsic link that connected the artistic productions of the Greeks to all the other components of their social-economic formation. This failure conflicted sharply with the need for true historical reconstruction, which Wincklemann yet felt so strongly that he dedicated the second part of his work to it. Again, though, the evolutionary criteria he imposed to distinguish the origin, growth, and then decadence of ancient art led to still graver consequences, namely the incapacity to understand and evaluate critically those artistic manifestations that deviated from the canons of ideal beauty. This classification, moreover, was determined arbitrarily on the basis of the ancient materials then known, and these were, for the most part, Roman copies of Greek works. And the choice of the works to be copied, the taste that had animated the copyists, was the secondhand classicism prevalent in Imperial Rome.

Wincklemann first had the opportunity to acquaint himself with these works by collaborating with his patron, Alessandro Cardinal Albani, who was gathering in his Villa Albani, then under construction, his celebrated collection of ancient sculptures. Then from 1763 on, Wincklemann served as Prefect of Antiquities at Rome. Meanwhile, Greece itself remained largely unknown and unexplored, although there had existed in England since 1732 the Amateurs' Society, which would later play an important part in revealing the Greek world to Europeans. Wincklemann himself was to die in 1768 before he could ever actually visit Greece, so his ideas to the end were dependent on Greek literature and Roman copies. But Wincklemann's ideas had a great impact on Europe. He aroused, among others, the enthusiasm of Goethe, who dedicated an essay to him in 1805. The author of *Faust* could see the reflection of his personal search for classical serenity, perhaps more longed for than realized. Long before that, of course, Wincklemann had inspired the appeal to Hellenic perfection that was expressed in Gotthold Ephraim Lessing's *Laocoon*, published in 1766. And in the meantime, the researches and studies in Italy and Greece began to affect the appreciation of ancient art.

The few Greek originals found in Rome, such as the Laocoon statue, in their exuberance were far from the classicism of the Roman copies and were often of only modest quality. But all this heterogeneous material was included in the abstract category of classical. This was defined as "calm grandeur and noble simplicity," concepts that were inevitably inadequate for any description of at least five centuries of artistic production. "Each time there was a major discovery of original works of ancient art," the modern scholar Bianchi Bandinelli has observed, "the archaeological world was forced to change its convictions: first it was faced with the Elgin marbles and the Bassae frieze, then it confronted the sculptures from Olympia and the altar at Pergamum. And each time these cardinal works of ancient art met with more doubtful amazement than admiration and understanding, because they did not fall into the concept of 'classical art' that the scholars had formulated."

But by the time this phenomenon was underway, the process of reevaluation of Greek art was at least underway, an ongoing process that continues to this day. Meantime there remained the other problem: the actual recovery of the remains. Here we have space only to focus on one example, and we naturally choose the Acropolis at Athens. During the

Byzantine period — before the coming of the Turks, that is — the Parthenon and the Erechtheum had been transformed into Christian churches. With the Turkish occupation, the Acropolis became a fortress, and this made access more difficult to foreigners. The limestone hill, inhabited exclusively by Turks, was covered by houses, and a house was even installed in the Erechtheum; the Propylaea became the palace of the Turkish military commander; the Parthenon housed a mosque. When in 1674 the French Ambassador, the Marquis de Nointel, obtained permission to visit the Acropolis, the little Temple of Athena Nike was more or less intact, but within a few years that was demolished to make room for a new bastion.

During the Venetian siege in 1687, led by Francesco Morosini, cannon were turned on the Parthenon and the gunpowder stored there exploded. The Acropolis burned for two days and there was the danger of another powder magazine in the Erechtheum also exploding. The southern side of the Parthenon was smashed to bits during this episode and its central metopes disappeared; fortunately, however, they had been carefully sketched by the artist who accompanied the Marquis de Nointel in 1674. The Venetians then occupied the rock and remained until April 6, 1688; before abandoning the hill, Morosini decided to bring back with him the horses of the chariot that formed the central group of the west pediment. (The sculptures of the east pediment, representing the birth of Athena, had evidently already been destroyed, perhaps when the Parthenon had been changed into a church in Byzantine times.) But in the course of Morosini's attempt to take down the west pediment sculptures, they fell and shattered; typically, no one bothered to collect the fragments, but perhaps this was just as well because the Venetians had already used various ancient fragments to repair walls.

When the Venetians withdrew, the Turks once again took over the Acropolis, but the remains were left pretty much as they had been. A few European travelers visited the Acropolis in the decades that followed, but the important turning point came with the Athenian sojourn of two Britons, James Stuart and Nicholas Revett, in 1751; Revett returned from August 31, 1765 to June 11, 1766. These two scholars carried out a quite careful study of the remains, making precise drawings. The results appeared in their monumental work, *Antiquities of Athens;* the second of the two volumes, which appeared in 1788, one year after Stuart's death, was dedicated to the Acropolis. By means of these valuable drawings, Europeans could finally acquire adequate knowledge of the architecture of the fifth century B.C.

For all this, the troubles of the Acropolis monuments were not over. In 1800, Sir Thomas Bruce, the seventh Earl of Elgin, who had been the English ambassador to the Turkish Sultan, arrived in Athens. He was accompanied by a group of artists and artisans, headed by the Neapolitan painter Lusieri. The expedition was not able to go up the Acropolis until the following July, when a special authorization arrived from the Sultan, giving permission to the group to make drawings, copies, and casts, and to take specimens from the antique monuments. Before Lord Elgin and his party were finished, they removed the following: twelve statues from the Parthenon pediments, fifteen metopes from the south side, fifty-six slabs from the cella frieze, a Caryatid from the Erechtheum, most of the frieze and metopes from the Athena Nike balustrade, as well as numerous architectural elements taken from other monuments on the Acropolis.

This spoliation made a great impression on certain contemporaries, above all on Lord Byron, the great English Romantic poet, who unlike Lord Elgin, nourished a strong faith in Greece's forthcoming independence (for which he would eventually sacrifice his life). On the crude pillar that Elgin had substituted for the lovely Caryatid on the Erechtheum, it was said, Byron wrote a ferocious epigram: *"Quod non fecerunt Goti, fecerunt Scoti"* (an allusion to the seventeenth-century Romans' epigram about the spoliations by the Barberini family: "What the barbarians did not do, the Barberini did."). The best that can be said of Lord Elgin is that he was sincerely worried about saving the precious sculptures, especially after what had occurred during the Venetian siege. What he had not anticipated was that this example would prove fatal; the monuments, until then respected by the Turks, were turned into a mine of ornamental elements. Dodwell narrates that when he visited the Acropolis in 1805 and complained to the Turkish commandant about what was happening, the Turk replied angrily: "What right have you to complain? Where are the marbles that your countrymen have taken away from the temples?"

The ensuing story of the marbles taken away by Lord Elgin was certainly adventurous, and not only because of the shipwreck of one of the loads, later recovered. Faced with Phidias' sculpture, the academic world was disappointed, and it was only because such men as the great Italian sculptor, Antonio Canova, interceded that the English Parliament in 1816 finally decided to buy the marbles for about £35,000 — only two-thirds of what they had cost Elgin. The fate of these sculptures was thus exemplary, for it showed to what extent the academy and classicism had, ironically, precluded the possibility of understanding the real classical world, all in the name of an abstract classicism set outside time and history.

Canova was asked to "restore" the marbles of Phidias, but he had the good sense to refuse. Such modesty was not equaled by Thorwaldsen, the neo-classic Danish sculptor who had been given the task of restoring the Aegina sculptures, found in 1811. The next year the sculptures from Bassae were discovered, and in 1829 the sculptures from the Temple of Zeus at Olympia were recovered. The rediscovery of Greek antiquity, born with the Enlightenment, now fed on several sources: the philological spirit, the renewed love for history, the new Romantic aesthetic. And when, on the first of April 1833, the Turks left Athens under the triumphant banner of the Greek Revolution, the Acropolis was once again in the hands of Greeks. The clean-up of the Acropolis began in 1835, and with this began the revival of Greek monuments in the modern world, another story in itself.

Chronological Chart

DATES (B.C.)	CRETE	GREECE	ANATOLIA
2000	MIDDLE MINOAN PERIOD First palaces at Knossos, Phaestos, Mallia	Decline of Helladic culture First appearance of Greek-speaking Achaeans (?)	Hittites and Luwians active Troy frequently rebuilt on same site
1900	Crete emerges as commercial power throughout eastern Mediterranean	MIDDLE HELLADIC Horse and spoke-wheeled chariot introduced by Achaeans	
1800	Linear A script in use	No known writing	Hittites emerge as dominant people in Anatolia
1700	Earthquake damages palaces; Minoans quickly reconstruct; beginning of "golden age" of Minoan culture, society, and economy	Achaean warrior class consolidates power over indigenous population Growth of palace-centers; Mycenae emerges as power	
1600		LATE HELLADIC Grave circles A and B (shaft graves) used during this century by royalty at Mycenae	Troy VI has close relations with Helladic culture
1500	Linear B, recording Greek, indicates Mycenaeans control Crete LATE MINOAN	Mycenaeans convert to *tholos* tombs	Hittites among first to use iron
1400	Major Minoan palaces destroyed, evidently by earthquake related to Thera eruption	Mycenaeans emerge as major Mediterranean power Lion Gate at Mycenae Mycenaeans fortify palaces	Suppiluliumas I, king of Hittites, at height of power
1300	Minoans remain on major sites but decline of Minoan civilization	Iron comes into use	Troy VI destroyed c. 1260: Destruction of Troy VIIa (in Homer's Trojan War?)
1200	End of distinctive Minoan culture	Mycenaean centers (Mycenae, Tiryns, Pylos) destroyed Mycenaean culture declining	Phrygians dominate Anatolia
1100	SUB-MINOAN Minoans move inland and up into mountain retreats	Mycenae completely destroyed	
1000	Dorians move into Crete Proto-Geometric style in pottery	Dorians move down across Greece Writing, various arts and crafts lost in Greek "dark age," although pottery still made	Ionians and other Greeks emigrate to western shores of Asia Minor
900	Increased contacts with east (e.g. Cyprus)	City-states emerge at Athens, Thebes, Corinth, Sparta	
800	Geometric style in pottery Emergence of Greek-style city-states	776: First Olympiad Homeric epics written down Greeks found colonies in Italy & Sicily	Emergence of Ionian civilization (by immigrants and influences) which stimulates Attic civilization
700	Orientalizing style Daedalic style	Orientalizing style	

DATES (B.C.)	HISTORIC EVENTS
683	Archons of Athens elected annually
621	Draco writes law code for Athens
c.594	Solon granted powers to reform Athens
584	Fall of Cypselidae, rulers of Corinth
560–527	Pisistratus, tyrant of Athens (intermittently)
521–486	Darius I, King of Persia
510	Expulsion of Hippias from Athens: end of tyranny
507	Cleisthenes introduces democratic constitution
499	Revolt of Ionian cities against Persians
490	Battle of Marathon
485–478	Gelon, tyrant of Syracuse
485–465	Xerxes, King of Persia
480	Battles of Salamis and Himera
479	Battle of Plataea
478–467	Hieron I, tyrant of Syracuse
477	Creation of the League of Delos
474	Battle of Cumae (Italy): Greeks defeat Etruscans
461	Pericles emerges as popular leader
453	Treasury of Delian League taken to Athens
448	Peace of Callias between Athens and Persia
431	Beginning of the Peloponnesian War
429	Death of Pericles; Cleon becomes popular leader
427–424	First Athenian expedition to Sicily
422	Cleon falls at Amphipolis
421	Peace of Nicias signed by Athens and Sparta
415–413	Second Athenian expedition to Sicily
413–404	Second phase of the Peloponnesian War
411–410	First oligarchical coup in Athens
405–367	Dionysius I, tyrant of Syracuse
404	Second oligarchical coup: The Thirty Tyrants
399	Socrates tried and condemned to death
371	Battle of Leuctra; Liberation of Messenia
338	Philip II of Macedon assures his conquest of Greece at battle of Chaeronea
323	Death of Alexander the Great

GREECE	ITALY & SICILY
Temple of Artemis at Corfu (590)	
Temple of Hera at Olympia (590)	
Pediments of blue-bearded figures and apotheosis of Herakles on Acropolis (570)	
Temple of Apollo at Delphi (545–505)	Paestum: Treasury at Sele (c. 560)
Temple of Apollo at Corinth (540)	Selinunte: Temple C (550–530)
	Selinunte: Temple D (535)
Temple of Athena on Acropolis (c. 530)	Paestum: Basilica (535)
	Selinunte: Temple F (525)
	Paestum: Temple of Ceres (510)
Athenian Treasury at Delphi (507? 490?)	
	Paestum: Temple of Sele (c. 500)
Temple of Aphaea at Aegina (495–480)	
	Syracuse: Temple of Athena (480)
	Himera: Temple (480)
	Selinunte: Temples E, A, O (480–460)
Temple of Zeus at Olympia (468–460)	
	Agrigento: Temple of Hera (460)
	Paestum: Temple of Poseidon (450)
The Parthenon (447–432)	
Propylaea on Acropolis (437–432)	
Erectheum (435–)	
Temple of Apollo at Bassae (430–420)	Agrigento: Temple of Concord (430)
Temple of Athena Nike on Acropolis (c. 425)	Segesta: Temple (425–415)
Balustrade of Winged Victories (410?)	
Temple of Athena Polias at Priene (350–330)	
Temple of Zeus at Nemea (340)	
Monument of Lysikrates (334)	

Recommended Reading

Ever since the ancient Greeks began writing about themselves, there has been no end to the books about the ancient Greek world: the problem, indeed, is to find those suited to a reader's particular needs. This list, then, is a representative selection of books that complement various aspects of the ancient Greek world as viewed in this volume. The books have been chosen on the basis of their accessibility in terms of price, recent printings, and attempt to communicate with the general public. As for the ancient Greeks, they still provide the best accounts, and fortunately all—Homer, Hesiod, Herodotus, Thucydides, Aeschylus, Sophocles, Euripides, Aristophanes, Plato, Pausanias — are widely available in paperback editions.

Arias, Paolo Enrico: *A History of 1000 Years of Greek Vase Painting* (Abrams, 1963; Thames & Hudson, 1963)

Bieber, M.: *History of the Greek and Roman Theater* (Princeton University Press, 1961)

Boardman, John; Doerig, José; Fuchs, Werner: *Greek Art & Architecture* (Abrams, 1967; Thames & Hudson, 1967)

Burn, Andrew: *Greek City States: From Their Rise to the Roman Conquest* (McGraw-Hill, 1969)

Carpenter, Rhys: *Architects of the Parthenon* (Penguin, 1970)

Cottrell, Leonard: *The Bull of Minos* (Grosset & Dunlap, 1962; Evans Bros., 1962)

Demargne, Pierre: *The Birth of Greek Art* (Golden Press, 1969)

Dinsmoor, W.B.: *The Architecture of Ancient Greece* (Argonaut)

Dunbabin, T.J.: *Western Greeks: The History of Sicily & South Italy from the Foundation of the Greek Colonies to 488 B.C.* (Oxford University Press, 1948)

Finley, M.I.: *Early Greece: The Bronze and Archaic Ages* (Norton, 1970; Chatto, 1968)

Flaceliere, Robert: *Daily Life in Greece at the Time of Pericles* (Macmillan, 1965; Weidenfeld & Nicolson, 1965)

Folsom, Robert S.: *A Handbook of Greek Pottery: A Guide for Amateurs* (New York Graphic Society, 1968)

Graves, Robert: *The Greek Myths* (Penguin, 1957)

Grene, David; Lattimore, Richmond (editors): *The Complete Greek Tragedies* (University of Chicago Press, 1960)

Guido, Margaret: *Sicily: An Archaeological Guide* (Praeger, 1967; Faber, 1967)

Hadas, Moses: *Ancilla to Classical Reading* (Columbia University Press, 1954)

Hafner, German: *The Art of Rome, Etruria, & Magna Graecia* (Abrams, 1967)

Hamilton, Edith: *Mythology* (various editions)

Hammond, Nicholas G.L.: *A History of Greece to 322 B.C.* (Oxford University Press, 1959)

Hanfmann, George: *Classical Sculpture* (N.Y. Graphic Society, 1967)

Hawkes, Jacquetta: *Dawn of the Gods* (Random House, 1968; Chatto, 1968)

Hogarth, David: *Ionia and the East* (Haskell, 1969)

Hutchinson, R.W.: *Prehistoric Crete* (Penguin, 1962)

Jenkins, Romilly: *Dedalica: A Study of Dorian Plastic Art in the 7th Century B.C.* (McGrath, 1971)

Lawrence, A.W.: *Greek Architecture* (Penguin, 1967)

MacKendrick, Paul: *The Greek Stones Speak* (Mentor)

Marinatos, Spyridon: *Crete and Mycenae* (Abrams, 1960; Thames & Hudson, 1960)

Martin, Roland: *Living Architecture: Greek* (Grosset & Dunlap, 1967; Macdonald, 1967)

Matz, Friedrich: *Crete and Early Greece* (Crown, 1962; Methuen, 1963)

Nilsson, Martin P.: *History of Greek Religion* (Norton, 1964; Oxford University Press, 1949)

Richter, Gisela: *Sculpture and Sculptors of the Greeks* (Yale University Press, 1970)

Rose, H.J.: *Gods and Heroes of the Greeks* (Meridian, 1958; Methuen, 1957)

Rouse, W.H.D.: *Gods, Heroes, and Men of Ancient Greece* (Signet, 1957)

Scully, Vincent J. Jr.: *The Earth, the Temple, and the Gods* (Praeger, 1969)

Starr, Chester: *The Ancient Greeks* (Oxford University Press, 1971)

Thomson, George: *Aeschylus and Athens* (Grosset & Dunlap, 1969)

Vermeule, Emily: *Greece in the Bronze Age* (University of Chicago Press, 1964)

Willetts, R.F.: *Everyday Life in Ancient Crete* (Putnam's, 1969; Batsford, 1969)

Woodhead, Arthur: *The Greeks in the West* (Praeger, 1962; Thames & Hudson, 1962)

Zimmern, Alfred: *The Greek Commonwealth: Politics and Economics in Fifth-Century Athens* (Oxford University Press, 1961)

Recommended Viewing

Nothing makes the world of the ancient Greeks seem as real as a visit to the actual sites, a pilgrimage that more and more people make each year. The next best thing is a visit to a museum with a collection of Greek antiquities, and there are many such major collections.

The British Museum, London
Fitzwilliam Museum, Cambridge
Laing Art Gallery and Museum, Newcastle upon Tyne
The Metropolitan Museum of Art in New York City, New York, U.S.A.
The Museum of Fine Arts in Boston, Massachusetts, U.S.A.
The Victoria and Albert Museum, London

There are also many other collections of Greek antiquities throughout North America, some highly specialized some more general, and all open—within certain restrictions—to the general public. The list that follows should allow people everywhere in North America to start an acquaintance with the remains of this great civilization.

Alabama: Birmingham Museum of Art
California: Los Angeles County Museum of Art
    Malibu: J. Paul Getty Museum
    San Francisco: M. H. DeYoung Memorial Museum
    Santa Barbara Museum of Art
    Palo Alto: Stanford University Museum
Colorado: Denver Art Museum
Connecticut: *Hartford: Wadsworth Atheneum
    New Haven: Yale University Art Gallery
Hawaii: Honolulu Academy or Arts
Illinois: *Chicago Art Institute
    Chicago: Field Museum of Natural History
    Urbana: University of Illinois, Classical and European Culture Museum
Indiana: Bloomington: Indiana University Museum of Art
Kansas: Kansas City: University of Kansas, Wilcox Museum
    Lawrence: University of Kansas, Museum of Art
Louisiana: New Orleans: Isaac Delgado Museum of Art
Maine: Brunswick: Bowdoin College Museum of Art
Maryland: Baltimore: *The Walters Art Gallery
    Johns Hopkins University, Archaeological Museum
Massachusetts: Cambridge: Harvard University, Fogg Art Museum
    *Worcester Art Museum
Michigan: Ann Arbor: University of Michigan, Kelsey Museum of Archaeology
    Detroit Art Institute
Minnesota: Minneapolis Art Institute
Missouri: Columbia: University of Missouri, Museum of Art and Archaeology
    Kansas City: Nelson Gallery of Art and Atkins Museum of Fine Arts
    *St. Louis Art Museum
Nebraska: Omaha: Joslyn Memorial Art Museum.
New Jersey: Newark: The Newark Museum
    Princeton: Princeton University, The Art Museum
New York: Buffalo: Albright-Knox Art Gallery
    New York City: The Brooklyn Museum
Ohio: Akron Art Institute
    Cincinnati Art Museum
    *Cleveland Museum of Art
    Dayton Art Institute
    *Toledo Museum of Art
Oregon: Portland Art Museum
Pennsylvania: *Philadelphia: University of Pennsylvania. University Museum
Rhode Island: *Providence: Rhode Island School of Design
Texas: Houston: Museum of Fine Arts of Houston
Virginia: *Richmond: Virginia Museum of Fine Arts
Washington: Seattle Art Museum
Washington, D.C.: Dumbarton Oaks Research Library and Collection
CANADA: *Ontario: Toronto: Royal Ontario Museum
    Quebec: Montreal Museum of Fine Arts

* = above average collection

Glossary

Acroterion: Carved or molded figure or decorative element placed over roof beam ends, especially at outer angle of pediment cornice.

Adyton: A chamber usually situated at the back of the cella and with limited access; it was "the holy of holies," the most sacred part of the temple into which only priests were allowed to enter.

Amphiprostyle: A temple with the same rows of columns, or porticoes, at the two ends.

Architrave: The stone lintel (originally a wooden beam) that extends from the top of one column to another or lies along the wall of an edifice. It becomes the lowest element of the entablature; when it rests along the tops of columns it can also be called the epistyle.

Astragal: A small rounded convex molding.

Capital: The topmost section of a column; depending on its design, it becomes one of the major elements that distinguishes the three main orders of Greek architecture: the simple molded capital is Doric; the scroll-shaped, or volute, is Ionic; and the capital carved as stylized acanthus leaves is Corinthian.

Caryatid: A sculptured female figure, usually draped, used as a column or pilaster to support an entablature or roof. The name is said to be derived from Caryae, a city in the Peloponnesos, famed for its priestesses at a temple of Artemis.

Cella: A Latin word adopted in architectural writing to indicate either (1) the entire interior portion of a temple (that is, excluding the peristyle) or (2) the chamber within the interior between the pronaos and opisthodomos. In this volume, the Greek words are used instead: sekos for the entire interior, naos for the main chamber.

Cornice: The uppermost element of the entablature on which the roof beams rest.

Dipteral: A temple having two rows of columns along each of its sides.

Distyle: Generally called "distyle in antis" in reference to a temple with two columns in front between the ends of the lateral walls.

Dromos: A road or passageway, usually narrow, relatively short, and often walled, that leads to a Mycenaean tomb.

Echinus: Convex molding, circular in shape, that sits atop a column and forms part of the Doric capital.

Entablature: The upper section of a temple or monumental structure that rests atop the columns; in the classical orders, it includes the architrave, the frieze, and the cornice.

Entasis: The slightly convex curve or swelling built into a column about two-thirds the way up to avoid the optical illusion that the column was concave (because of the mass of the upper structure it supported).

Epistyle: *See* ARCHITRAVE

Frieze: The section of the entablature between the architrave and the cornice. The Doric frieze was divided into metopes and triglyphs; the Ionic frieze was a continuous band, often carved in relief.

Geison: A Greek term for the cornice.

Hexastyle: An edifice with six columns across the ends.

Hypostyle: A hall filled with columns or pillars that hold up the ceiling; it was more typical of Egyptian architecture than of Greek.

In antis: A temple with no peristyle but with lateral walls that end in the front with two pilasters between which are two columns.

Intercolumniation: The distance measured between the centers of the vertical axes of two columns; also used simply to indicate the clear space between two columns.

Megaron: The architectural form associated with a Mycenaean palace or home, derived from structures in Asia Minor and the Near East and in some ways anticipating the basic plan of later Greek temples. Usually preceded by an open court, the megaron was an elongated rectangular form that had an open porch with columns, a vestibule-chamber, and the main room, often with a hearth.

Metope: That part of the Doric frieze that had originally been an open space between the ends of the roof beams; this space was filled with a slab, first of painted terra-cotta, and later of stone that was often sculptured in relief.

Naos: The chamber between the pronaos and the opisthodomos, where the idol and a table for offerings were often kept.

Naiskos: A small temple, or chapel, of a simple design.

Opisthodomos: An open area behind the naos and corresponding to the pronaos at the front end of the cella. There was usually no direct access to it from the naos; it had to be approached from outside. Sometimes it was used to hold offerings or treasures.

Pediment: The triangular section at the two ends of the roof of a temple or monumental building; it includes the sloping cornice and the tympanum, and in classical buildings was often filled with sculptures, either free-standing or in full-relief.

Peribolos: The sacred enclosure or wall that surrounded a temple area.

Peripteral: A temple composed on all four sides by a continuous row of columns.

Peristyle: The rows of columns and the covered colonnade that run along the sides of a temple; the term is also used to refer to an inner court lined with a colonnade.

Pilaster: A semidetached column or pillar at the end or along the side of a wall.

Pronaos: The vestibule chamber of the cella that leads into the naos.

Propylaeum: An entrance gate, usually monumental in conception and either set in the wall or set apart as an independent structure.

Propylon: A simplified version of a propylaeum.

Prostyle: A temple with a free-standing row of columns only on its front.

Pseudodipteral: A temple in which the peristyle is separated by about twice the normal distance from the cella because an inner row of columns has been eliminated.

Sekos: The part of the temple enclosed by walls, and as such, equivalent to the cella (in its first meaning).

Sima: The gutter of a building; it could be molded or treated as a decorative form.

Stylobate: Literally "base of the columns," the term indicates the uppermost level or step, which served as a foundation stone for the columns.

Tetrastyle: A four-columned portico.

Treasury: A small edifice dedicated by a city in a sanctuary or at a special site; the city's offerings, memorials, trophies, etc., would then be placed in this building.

Tholos: A round edifice. In Mycenaean culture, it refers to a stone-walled round tomb. In the classic age, it is usually a temple (also known as a monoptery) or some memorial; often it had a circular peristyle.

Triglyph: The slightly projecting slab in a Doric frieze, usually with vertical channels (called glyphs).

Tympanum: The triangular wall within the pediment and framed by the cornice; it served as the background for any pediment sculptures.

INDEX

(Numbers in italics refer to pages of illustration captions)

190

The various architectural drawings and site plans have been done by Giuliano and Giovanni Battista Minelli, who utilized the following works, with the kind permission of the publishers:

Enciclopedia dell'Arte Antica, Classica e Orientale (Treccani, Rome). *Bulletin de Correspondance Hellenique* (Boccard, Paris, 1969). **DU** — *Kulturelle Monatschrift* (1959). *Neue Deutsche Ausgrabungen im Mittelmeergebiet und im Vorderen Orient* (Gebr. Mann Verlag, Berlin, 1959). *I Templi Greci*, H. Berve-G. Gruben (Sansoni Editore, Florence, 1962). *Arte Egea*, P. Demargne (Feltrinelli, Milan, 1964). *The Architecture of Ancient Greece*, W.B. Dinsmoor (Batsford Ltd., London, 1950). *Aegina I*, A. Furtwaengler (Munich, 1906). *A History of Greece*, N.G.L. Hammond (Clarendon Press, Oxford, 1959). *Athenatempel*, F. Krauss (Walter de Gruyter, Berlin, 1959). *A Handbook to the Palace of Minos — Knossos*, J.D.S. Pendlebury (Max Parrish, London, 1958). *The Erechtheum*, Stevens-Caskey-Paton-Fowler (Harvard Univ. Press, Cambridge, 1927). *Mnesicle Architetto*, C. Tiberi (Officina Edizioni, Rome, 1964).